# SUPPORTING
# TEACHING
# & LEARNING
## IN SCHOOLS

Louise Burnham

Brenda Baker

www.pearsonschoolsandfe.co.uk

✓ Free online support
✓ Useful weblinks
✓ 24 hour online ordering

0845 630 44 44

Heinemann

Part of Pearson

D0183958

Heinemann is an imprint of Pearson Education Limited, Edinburgh Gate, Harlow, Essex, CM20 2JE.

www.pearsonschoolsandfecolleges.co.uk
Heinemann is a registered trademark of Pearson Education Limited
Text © Louise Burnham, Brenda Baker 2010

Edited by Juliet Mozley
Designed by AM design
Typeset by Phoenix Photosetting, Chatham, Kent
Original illustrations © Pearson Education Ltd 2010
Illustrated by Phoenix Photosetting/Gemma Correll
Cover design by Wooden Ark
Picture research by Susanna Prescott
Cover photo Front: © Masterfile UK Ltd; Back: Patrick Rowe
Printed in Spain by Grafos S.A.

First published 2010

14 13 12 11
10 9 8 7 6 5 4 3

**British Library Cataloguing in Publication Data**
A catalogue record for this book is available from the British Library.

ISBN 978-0-435032-03-6

**Websites**
The websites used in this book were correct and up to date at the time of publication. Pearson Education Limited is not responsible for the content of any external Internet sites. It is essential for tutors to preview each website before using it in class so as to ensure that the URL is still accurate, relevant and appropriate. We suggest that tutors bookmark useful websites and consider enabling learners to access them through the school/college intranet.

# Contents

# Acknowledgements

Louise Burnham would like to thank the following individuals for their help and advice during the writing of this book:

Sue Robertson and Unicorn Primary School in Beckenham for allowing me to reproduce excerpts from school policies; Val Hughes and Sandhurst Junior School in Catford for a copy of their feedback form; Graham Jameson and Edmund Waller School in New Cross for their example of a staffing structure; Richard Rieser and Disability Equality in Education for their medical and social model of disability; Linda Mellor and Elizabeth Evans for their thorough proofreading; Virginia Carter, Juliet Mozley and Céline Clavel for all of their support during this project; and as always, Tom, Lucy and Richard for putting up with my unsociable working hours!

The publisher would like to thank the following organisations for permission to reproduce material: retributive and restorative justice table, Transforming Conflict, an organisation which supports schools wanting to develop a whole-school approach based on the principles of restorative justice, p.39; BSI, Kitemark logo, p.124; the British Toy & Hobby Association, Lion Mark logo, p.124; the Food Standard Agency, Eatwell plate, p.216 © Crown copyright, click-use licence number C2010000590; Disability Discrimination in Education Course Book: Training for Inclusion and Disability Equality, p.239 © Crown copyright, click-use licence number C2010000590.

A special thank you to Madley Brook and Springfield schools, Witney, St Barnabus School, Oxford and Faringdon Community College.

The publisher would like to thank the following for their kind permission to reproduce photographs:

Alamy Images: Janine Wiedel Photolibrary p.110(br), Stockbroker/MBI p.230(t); Education Photos: John Walmsley p.4(c), p.65(br); Getty Images: Peter Cade/Iconica p.51, Photostock Israel/Flickr p.225(t); iStockphoto: Chris Schmidt/Track 5 p.19(br); Pearson Education Ltd: Ian Wedgewood p.6(tr), p.31(b), p.68(b), p.76(cr), p.93, p.150(br), p.153(t), p.166(c), Jules Selmes p.15, p.35, p.84(tr), p.109, p.128(b), p.135(c), p.157, p.185(t), p.191, p.197(tl), p.203, p.205(br), p.210(t), p.233, p.244(c), p.257(br), p.275(br), p.286, p.291, Lord & Leverett p.38(tr), Studio 8 p.71, p.91, p.101(tr), p.117(tr), p.261, p.270(tr); Retna Pictures Ltd: John Powell p.264(c); Shutterstock: Boudikka p.31(b);Thinkstock: Bananastock p.177, p.293; Digital Vision p.1, p.121, p.249, p.279; Katy McDonnell/Digital Vision p.141; Katy McDonnell/Photodisc p.215.

All other images © Pearson Education

Every effort has been made to trace the copyright holders and we apologise in advance for any unintentional omissions. We would be pleased to insert the appropriate acknowledgement in any subsequent edition of this publication.

# Introduction

Welcome to this handbook for the *Level 2 Certificate for Supporting Teaching and Learning in Schools*. If you are using this book you will be setting out to be or already working in school as a teaching assistant. This handbook has been written for assistants in both primary and secondary schools.

You may find yourself referred to under the general title of 'teaching assistant' within your school, but you may also be called a classroom assistant, school assistant, individual support assistant, special needs assistant or learning support assistant. These different job titles have come into effect due to the different types of work which assistants are required to do within the classroom. In recent years, the role of the teaching assistant has developed and become professionalised so that qualifications now exist at different levels. These reflect the diverse job roles which are now present in schools for learning support staff.

This book contains everything you need to complete your Level 2 Certificate in Supporting Teaching and Learning in Schools. It also contains the units you need if you are studying for the Level 2 Certificate in Supporting the Wider Curriculum in Schools.

As you work towards this qualification, you will be developing your skills and expertise in a number of areas, and you will need to think about how the theory fits in with your experiences in the classroom. As you gain experience and expertise in your work with children and young people, you may also find it a useful reference, particularly for specific issues such as working with bilingual children.

The Level 2 Certificate is made up of a number of different units of assessment, which sit within the QCF (Qualifications and Credit Framework). When you complete a unit successfully you will gain a certain number of credits.

The credit value of each unit indicates the size of the unit and approximately how long it will take to achieve. Credit is based on how long an average learner would take to complete a unit, and 1 credit is roughly equal to 10 hours of learning, including time spent in the following ways:

- classes or group sessions
- tutorials
- practical work
- assessments.

It also includes any time you spend that is not supervised, for example doing homework, independent research or work experience.

## Units of assessment

The units that make up these qualifications have been developed by the Sector Skills Councils responsible for setting and monitoring standards for specific occupational groups. In the case of Supporting Teaching and Learning, this is the Training and Development Agency, known as TDA. You will see that the unit reference numbers (see table on page vii) carry the prefix TDA, which shows that TDA is the Sector Skills Council who developed or owns the units. There are other Sector Skills Councils or awarding organisations that work closely with TDA, and you may come across these acronyms linked to other units that you study:

● SfCD – Skills for Care and Development

● CWDC – Children's Workforce Development Council

● ASDAN – Award Scheme Development and Accreditation Network.

## The Level 2 Certificate overview

Although the units in the new qualification are not exactly the same as the National Occupational standards that made up NVQs, the areas they cover are similar. Each unit has several learning outcomes and each of these is broken down into a number of assessment criteria. All the learning outcomes of the unit have to be assessed in order for you to complete the unit.

The Certificate in Supporting Teaching and Learning in Schools at Level 2 is made up of three groups of units:

● Mandatory units

● Optional Group A units

● Optional Group B units.

Everyone taking this qualification needs to complete all nine units in the Mandatory group (24 credits), and then choose additional units from both Optional Group A (3 credits) and Optional Group B (3 credits) to make the full credit total of 30.

## List of units in this book

| Unit Reference No. | Unit title | Credit value |
|---|---|---|
| | **Mandatory units** | |
| TDA 2.1 | Child and young person development | 2 |
| TDA 2.2 | Safeguarding the welfare of children and young people | 3 |
| TDA 2.3 | Communication and professional relationships with children, young people and adults | 2 |
| TDA 2.4 | Equality, diversity and inclusion in work with children and young people | 2 |
| TDA 2.6 | Help improve own and team practice in schools | 3 |
| TDA 2.7 | Maintain and support relationships with children and young people | 3 |
| TDA 2.8 | Support children and young people's health and safety | 3 |
| TDA 2.9 | Support children and young people's positive behaviour | 2 |
| TDA 2.10 | Support learning activities | 4 |
| | **Option A units** | |
| TDA 2.5 | Schools as organisations | 3 |
| | **Option B units** | |
| TDA 2.11 | Contribute to supporting bilingual learners | 2 |
| TDA 2.12 | Prepare and maintain learning environments | 3 |
| TDA 2.13 | Provide displays in schools | 3 |
| TDA 2.14 | Support children and young people at meal or snack times | 3 |
| TDA 2.15 | Support children and young people with disabilities and special educational needs | 4 |
| TDA 2.16 | Support children and young people's play and leisure | 3 |
| TDA 2.17 | Support children and young people's travel outside of the setting | 3 |
| TDA 2.18 | Support extra-curricular activities | 3 |
| TDA 2.19 | Support the use of information and communication technology for teaching and learning | 2 |

## Assessing your skills and knowledge

Your awarding organisation, such as Edexcel, CACHE or City & Guilds, will allow you to be assessed using a range of different methods, based on the learning outcomes and assessment criteria in the unit. Your assessor or tutor will provide you with help and support throughout the assessment process. Some common assessment methods are described below but others may be used as well:

● knowledge, understanding and skills (competence) that you demonstrate through your practice in a work setting and that are observed directly by your assessor

● evidence from an expert witness who may be an experienced practitioner who has worked alongside you, or others with suitable backgrounds who can vouch for your practice

● questions (oral and written) and professional discussion, usually with your assessor, which allows you to talk about what you know

● assignments and projects of different types

● assessment of your work products such as plans, displays, observations, materials you have made to support children

● recognised prior learning.

Sometimes your awarding organisation will insist on a specific method such as a test or an assignment. Again your tutor or assessor will provide you with help and support to decide the best approach.

## Units that must be assessed in the workplace

In this qualification, TDA require that the following assessment criteria MUST be assessed in an appropriate setting, for example a primary school or secondary school:

| TDA 2.6 | Assessment criteria 1.1, 1.2, 1.3, 4.1, 4.2, 4.3, 4.4, 4.5 and 4.7 |
| --- | --- |
| **TDA 2.8** | Assessment criteria 2.1, 2.2, 2.3 and 3.2 |
| **TDA 2.9** | Assessment criteria 2.2, 2.3, 2.4 and 3.1 |
| **TDA 2.10** | Assessment criteria 1.3, 1.4, 1.5, 2.1, 2.2, 2.3, 3.1, 3.3, 3.3, 4.1, 4.2, 4.3, 5.2, 5.3 and 5.4 |
| **TDA 2.12** | Assessment criteria 1.2, 1.3, 1.4, 1.5, 2.1, 2.2, 2.3, 2.4, 3.2, 3.3, 3.4 and 3.5 |
| **TDA 2.13** | Assessment criteria 2.1, 2.2, 2.3, 2.4, 3.1, 3.2, 3.3, 3.4, 4.2, 4.3, 4.4, 4.5, 5.1, 5.2 and 5.3 |
| **TDA 2.14** | Assessment criteria 4.2, 4.3, 5.2 and 5.3 |
| **TDA 2.15** | Assessment criteria 3.1, 3.2, 3.3, 3.4, 4.1, 4.2, 4.3 and 4.4 |
| **TDA 2.16** | Assessment criteria 2.2, 2.3, 2.4, 2.5 and 3.4 |
| **TDA 2.17** | Assessment criteria 2.1, 2.2, 2.3, 2.4, 3.1, 3.2, 3.3, 3.4 and 3.5 |
| **TDA 2.18** | Assessment criteria 1.2, 1.3, 1.4, 2.1, 2.2, 2.3, 2.4, 2.5, 2.6, 3.1, 3.2, 3.3 and 3.4 |
| **TDA 2.19** | Assessment criteria 2.3, 2.4, 3.1, 3.2, 3.3 and 3.4 |

# How to use this book

All the chapters in this book are matched closely to the specifications of each unit in the syllabus and follow the unit learning outcomes and assessment criteria — making it easy for you to work through the criteria and be sure you are covering everything you need to know.

## Key features of the book

An activity that brings learning to life and suggests how to introduce new ideas, activities or practice into your school or setting

A real-life scenario exploring major issues to broaden your understanding of key topics; demonstrates how theory relates to everyday practice and poses reflective questions

An activity that helps you to create or gather evidence for your portfolio

An activity that encourages you to reflect on your own performance

A short task to enhance your understanding of a piece of information (for example Internet research or a practical idea you could introduce in your school)

A short activity linked thematically to the unit, specifically designed to develop your professional skills

Highlights where content in the unit enables you to apply Functional Skills in the broad areas of English, ICT and Maths (matched to the latest (2009) FS Standards at Level 1). The tips and explanations given show how Functional Skills can be contextualized to work in early years and will be of particular benefit to learners on Apprenticeship programmes

 Several activities based on video footage showing other Teaching Assistants in everyday situations

 Simple definitions of some of the more complex terms or pieces of jargon used in the book

 Highlights where text gives evidence for Assessment Criteria or where related information can be found in other units

Getting ready for assessment An activity to help you generate evidence for assessment of the unit

Check your knowledge At the end of each unit, questions to help you consolidate your understanding and ensure you are ready to move on to the next unit

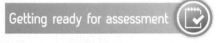 A checklist of key points to help you remember the main underpinning knowledge in a unit

# TDA 2.1 Child & young person development

This unit requires you to have knowledge of the areas of development of children and young people in different age ranges. In particular, you will need to be competent in understanding the needs of the children and young people with whom you are working, particularly during transitions.

## By the end of this unit you will:

1. know the main stages of child and young person development
2. understand the kinds of influences that affect children and young people's development
3. understand the potential effects of transitions on children and young people's development.

# Know the main stages of child and young person development

## The expected pattern of children and young people's development from birth to 19 years, including physical, communication and intellectual, and social, emotional and behavioural development

For this unit you will need to be able to describe the expected pattern of development of children and young people from birth through to 19 years. Although you may be looking at and discussing different aspects of child development separately, it is important to remember that development is a **holistic** process, and that each child is unique and will develop in their own way and at different rates.

Milestones of development are given as a broad average for when children may be expected to reach a particular stage. You may notice that in particular classes or year groups, some pupils stand out because they have reached particular milestones in advance of or later than others. Sometimes if children's growth patterns are very different from their peers, this may have an effect on their behaviour. For example, children in the last two years of primary school may start to become taller and develop some of the first signs of puberty. Girls in particular can become much taller than boys and this can put pressure on them to behave differently. There may need to be additional provision made in this instance, for example, when getting changed for PE. There may also be pupils who are very tall or very small for their age, and this can sometimes affect how they are treated by their peers. You should also

**Communication and intellectual**
- developing creative and imaginative skills
- using skills in different ways
- using language to explain reasoning
- problem solving
- decision making

**Social, emotional and behavioural**
- taking turns
- co-operating with others
- developing social skills
- developing self-esteem and self-expression
- learning about the feelings of others

**Areas of development**

**Physical**
- fine motor skills (writing, threading, painting and drawing)
- gross motor skills (running, jumping, hopping, skipping, balance)
- general coordination
- hand-eye coordination

*You will need to be aware of different areas of development.*

remember that many of the skills and areas of development overlap with one another. For example, playing football may be considered a physical skill, but a child cannot learn to play without having social, communication and cognitive skills as well. The patterns of development on the next few pages should therefore be seen as a guide to give you an overall idea of the different stages.

**Physical development**

This is an important area of children's overall development and one which can often be assumed will take place automatically as they grow and mature. Although children do develop many skills naturally as they get older, it is imperative that they have the opportunity to develop them in a variety of ways, and they will need support in order to do this. They will need to develop:

● gross motor skills, using larger muscles such as those in arms and legs — for example, throwing, walking and running

● fine motor skills, using smaller muscles such as those in the fingers — for example, a pencil or a knife and fork, or doing up their clothes.

### 0–3 years

This is a period of fast physical development. When they are first born, babies have very little control over their bodies. Their movements are dependent on a series of reflexes (for example, sucking, grasping) which they need in order to survive. They will, however, in their first year gradually start to learn to have more control over their bodies so that by 12 months, most babies will have developed a degree of mobility such as crawling or rolling.

In their second year, babies will continue to grow and develop quickly and it is at this stage that most children will start to walk. Their ability to control their movements means that they are able to start to use their hands for pointing, holding small objects and starting to dress and feed themselves. They will also be able to play with a ball and will enjoy climbing, for example, on stairs or furniture.

In their third year, children will start to have more control over pencils and crayons and will enjoy looking at and turning pages in books. They should be able to use cups and feed themselves. They will be starting to walk and run with more confidence, and will be exploring using toys such as tricycles.

### 3–7 years

At this stage, children will be able to carry out more coordinated movements and will be growing in confidence as a result. They will be refining the skills developed so far and will have more control over fine motor skills such as cutting, writing and drawing. They will also become more confident in activities such as running, hopping, kicking a ball and using larger equipment.

## 7–12 years

Children will continue to grow and develop and will now be refining many of their skills. They may start to have hobbies and interests which mean that they are more practised in some areas, for example, sport or dance. They may also be able to make very controlled finer movements such as those required for playing an instrument or sewing. Girls in particular will start to show some of the early signs of puberty from the age of 10 or 11. In boys, puberty usually starts later, when there will be another period of rapid physical growth.

## 12–16 years

During **adolescence**, young people will be growing stronger. Boys will be starting to go through **puberty** and many girls will have completed the process and have regular periods. As a result, between these ages there can be a great variety in height and strength. At the end of this stage, most boys will be taller than most girls, although this is an average.

> ### Key term
>
> **Adolescence** – the name given to the interval between childhood and adulthood
>
> **Puberty** – the stage of physical development at which children and young people's bodies reach sexual maturation. It can begin as early as eight in girls and arounds two years later in boys. It can go on past the age of 20

> ### CASE STUDY: Physical development
>
> Imogen is supporting Kia, who is in Year 8. Kia has a physical impairment which means that she has reduced mobility and is unable to keep up with her peers when carrying out physical tasks, although she is able to participate to a limited extent and tries hard. Imogen has noticed that some of the other pupils have started to be unkind to Kia and say things behind her back, although Kia does not seem to have noticed.
>
> - What could Imogen do to help Kia?
> - Should she inform anyone else in the school, and if so, who?

*How much variety do you notice in pupils' strength and skills at sport?*

## 16–19 years

This is the stage at which young people are adults, but although many girls may have reached physical maturity, boys will continue to grow and change until their mid-20s.

## Communication and intellectual development

It is widely acknowledged that communication and intellectual development are closely related due to the importance of language and its link to learning. Children's intellectual development will also depend to a wide extent on their own experiences and the opportunities they are given from the earliest stages. It is also important to understand that children will learn in a variety of ways and that some will find particular tasks more difficult than others due to their own strengths and abilities. There have been a number of theories of development and many of them will influence the way in which we approach our work with children. Many psychologists will have different ideas about how children learn — some feel that a child's ability is innate and others that it depends on the opportunities that they are given. This is often called the 'nature versus nurture' debate. We should bear these theories in mind when thinking about stages of learning.

## 0–3 years

From the earliest stages, adults will usually try to communicate with babies even though they are not yet able to understand what is being said. This is because it is important for babies to be stimulated and have an interest shown in them. In cases where babies are neglected and do not spend time with adults, they will find it very difficult to learn the skills of effective communication later. At this age, babies will be listening to language from those around them and will enjoy songs and games. Most will start to try to speak at around 12 months, although pronunciation will not be clear and words will usually be used in isolation. Between 1 and 2 years they will start to put words together, and their vocabulary will start to increase fairly rapidly so that by 2 years most children will have about 200 words. Between 2 and 3 years, children will start to use negatives and plurals in their speech and although their vocabulary will increase rapidly, they will still make errors in grammar when speaking, for example, 'I drawed it.'

## 3–7 years

As children become more social and have wider experiences, they will start to use an increasing number of familiar phrases and expressions. They will also ask large numbers of questions and will be able to talk about things in the past and future tenses with greater confidence. This will be a period of development in which children are becoming skilled at aspects of number and writing, as well as continuing to learn about their world. They will still be looking for adult approval and will be starting to learn to read.

## 7–12 years

By this stage, most children will be fluent speakers of a language, and will be developing and refining their skills at reading and writing. Their language skills will enable them to think about and discuss their ideas and learning in more abstract terms. They will be developing their own thoughts and preferences, and will be able to transfer information and think in a more abstract way.

## 12–18 years

Young people will usually now have a clear idea about their favourite subjects and activities and will usually be motivated in these areas. They will be selecting and taking GCSEs and A levels which they are able to

*Have you noticed pupils looking for adult approval?*

achieve. They may lack confidence or avoid situations in which they have to do less popular subjects, to the extent that they may truant. It is often very important to teenagers that they feel good about themselves and that they belong.

### 16–19 years

By the time they come to leave school, young people will be thinking about career and university choices based on the qualifications they have selected. They will be able to focus on their areas of strength and look forward to continuing to develop these as they move on.

## DVD activity

### Video clip 1 — Child development

1. Watch the short clip on child development which includes a brief narrative.
2. Write a case study on a child you support and include:
   - age, sex, health, social background and position in family
   - friendships — do they have lots of friends, or one or two close friendships?
   - attitude to learning — are they eager to learn?
   - physical development — are they big or small for their age? Does this affect their relationships or their confidence?
   - whether they have any areas of special educational need.
3. Think about the different areas of development and whether the child is making expected progress for their age. How have the child's experiences and background in these areas influenced their behaviour and learning?

You may need to carry out a few observations on the child or note down some of their interactions as they occur. Include these work products as evidence. Remember to speak to the class teacher and check your school's procedures before selecting your child. You should also check with the child's parent or carer, and change the child's name for the purpose of the study.

Billy is in Year 5 and is in care. He has been very settled in school but recently has started to demonstrate some disruptive behaviour in the class in which you are based. The class teacher is newly qualified and is finding it difficult to cope with his behaviour, and while you feel you get on well with Billy and have tried talking to him, he seems to be getting worse.

- What else could you do in this situation?
- Why is it important to act as soon as possible?

**BEST PRACTICE CHECKLIST:** Supporting social, emotional and behavioural development

- Make sure you are approachable and give children and young people your time.
- Set fair but firm boundaries and explain the reasons for these.
- Ensure children and young people feel valued and are given praise and encouragement.
- Give children the chance to develop their independence.
- Be sensitive to their needs.
- Encourage them to think about the needs of others.
- Act as a good role model.

## Social, emotional and behavioural development

This area of development is about how children and young people feel about themselves and relate to others. They need to learn how to have the confidence to become independent of adults as they grow older and start to make their way in the world. They also need to learn acceptable norms for behaviour and be able to develop their independence. They will need to have a safe and secure environment in order to feel confident and develop to the best of their ability.

### 0–3 years

Very young children will be starting to find out about their own identities. They will need to form a strong attachment, the earliest of which will be with parents and carers. In nurseries, children are usually given a key worker who will be their main contact. At this stage of development, children may start to have tantrums through frustration and will want and need to start doing things for themselves.

### 3–7 years

Children will still be developing their identities and will be starting to play with their peers and socialise using imaginative play. This will help them to develop their concept of different roles in their lives. It is important that they are able to learn to understand the importance of boundaries and why they are necessary. They will also respond well to being given responsibility, for example, class helpers, and will need adult approval.

### 7–12 years

Children's friendships will become more settled and they will have groups of friends. They will need to have the chance to solve problems and carry out activities which require more independence. They will continue to need praise and encouragement, and will be increasingly aware of what others may think of them.

### 12–16 years

At this stage, the self-esteem of children and young people can be very vulnerable. Their bodies will be taking on the outer signs of adulthood, but they will still need guidance in many different ways. They will want to be independent of adults and spend more time with friends of their own age, but may continue to display childish behaviour. They can find that they are under the pressures of growing up and of increasing expectations; they may be unsure how to behave in different situations.

### 16–19 years

Children enter adulthood but will still sometimes need advice and guidance from other adults. They will lack experience and individuals will vary in emotional maturity and the way in which they interact with others.

## Functional skills

### ICT: Using ICT

You could select the age of children who you work with and then take some pictures of resources in your setting that are there to support each stage of development for the age of the child who you work with. You could present your findings to your assessor, which would help to show your understanding of the different milestones.

## Portfolio activity

In order to gather evidence for this assessment criterion, you may have to use a range of methods to show that you know and understand the stages of development for each age group. You can do this in a variety of ways, including those suggested below.

- Write a reflective account, making sure that you include all ages and all areas of development.
- Have a professional discussion with your assessor to show that you know and understand the milestones of each particular age and stage.
- Your assessment centre may prefer to provide an assignment to cover the learning outcomes.

## How different aspects of development can affect one another

Although development is often divided into different 'headings', it is important to remember that these areas are interconnected and link with one another. For example, developing physically and refining physical skills also affects pupils' ability to become independent, socialise and grow in confidence. When planning or thinking about activities to carry out with pupils, you should try to think not only in 'subjects' but also in terms of the broader picture. Many activities will stimulate interest and encourage pupils to develop skills in different areas. For example, an activity such as cooking, or food technology for older pupils, will develop a range of skills.

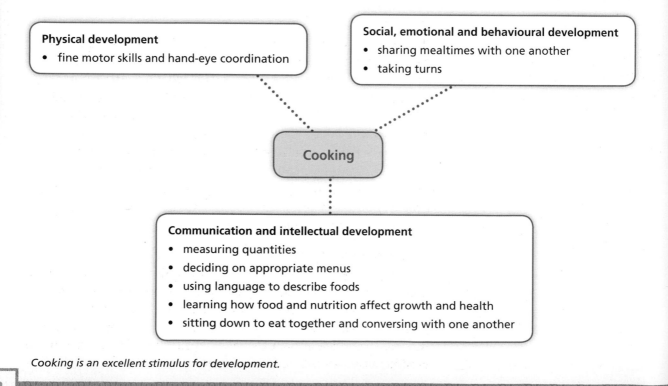

**Physical development**
- fine motor skills and hand-eye coordination

**Social, emotional and behavioural development**
- sharing mealtimes with one another
- taking turns

**Cooking**

**Communication and intellectual development**
- measuring quantities
- deciding on appropriate menus
- using language to describe foods
- learning how food and nutrition affect growth and health
- sitting down to eat together and conversing with one another

*Cooking is an excellent stimulus for development.*

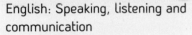
# Understand the kinds of influences that affect children and young people's development

Pupils' development is influenced by a wide range of factors, such as:

● their background

● their health

● the environment in which they are growing up.

These will all have an impact on the different areas of development. You need to have an awareness of some of these factors so that you know how pupils may be affected.

## The kinds of influences that affect children and young people's development, including background, health and environment

### Pupils' background and family environment
Pupils will come from a range of different family environments, cultures and circumstances. Many families will go through significant changes in the time the child is at school and you should remember that the school may not be aware of them. These may include family break-up or the introduction of a new partner, bereavement, illness, moving house or changing country. Any one of these may affect children's emotional and/or intellectual development; you may notice a change in pupil behaviour and ability to learn as a result (see also 'Transitions' on page 11 of this unit).

### Pupils' health
If pupils suffer from poor health or a physical disability or impairment, this may restrict their developmental opportunities. For example, a child who has a medical condition or impairment may be less able to participate in some activities than other children. This may initially affect physical development, but may also restrict social activities, for example, on the playground. The child's emotional development may also be impacted depending on their awareness of their needs and the extent to which they are affected. It is important that adults in school are aware of how pupils may be affected by these kinds of conditions and circumstances, so that we can support them by ensuring that they are included as far as possible.

### Poverty and deprivation
Poverty and deprivation are likely to have a significant effect on pupil development. Statistics show that children who come from deprived backgrounds are less likely to thrive and achieve well in school, as parents will find it more difficult to manage their needs, which will in turn impact on all areas of their development. This will all affect the way in which pupils are able to respond in different situations.

### Personal choices

The personal choices of children will affect their development as they grow older, as they decide on friendship groups, extra-curricular activities, academic involvement and so on. They may need advice and support from adults to enable them to make the choices which are right for them.

### Looked after/care status

If a child is looked after or in care, this may affect their development in different ways. However, they will usually be monitored closely and there will be regular meetings with the school to ensure that they are making expected levels of progress. Where there are any issues, these will then be addressed straight away.

### Education

In some cases children may come to school without any previous education, for example, if they are from another country where formal education may begin later. Alternatively they may come from a home schooling environment or a different method of schooling, so the way in which they have been taught may be different. They may need to have some additional support until they become settled.

The different circumstances, or environment, to which pupils are exposed during their childhood and teens will also affect their development. Many families go through significant changes or transitions, such as:

- illness
- moving house
- family break-up
- changing country.

These circumstances will all have an impact on the way pupils are able to respond in different situations.

## The importance of recognising and responding to concerns about children and young people's development

If you have concerns about pupils' development in any area, you should always share them with others. In the case of primary pupils, refer to the class teacher in the first instance, followed by the SENCO (Special Educational Needs Coordinator). In secondary schools you may wish to go straight to the latter. Even if concerns have already been noted by others in your school, it is still worth raising them, as your observations will also be taken into consideration. You should give dates and examples of the reasons for your concerns, if possible, so that they can be backed up. It is also important to remember that if a school has concerns about a pupil, their parents must always be informed.

---

**CASE STUDY:** Referring concerns

David is a classroom assistant in a large Year 6 class of 33 pupils. The class has just come up from Year 5 and he has noticed that one of the girls in his literacy intervention group finds it very difficult to understand comprehension questions, to the extent that she is confusing word order and therefore the meaning of what she is being asked to do. When he tells the teacher about it she replies, 'Oh, don't worry, that's just Ciara, she's always been scatty.'

- What should David do if he continues to be concerned?
- How else can he support Ciara?

---

**Portfolio activity**

Make a note of whom you would speak or refer to if you had concerns about a pupil with whom you are working. Does your school have a particular procedure for doing this?

# Understand the potential effects of transitions on children and young people's development

## Transitions experienced by most children and young people

Whatever age group you are supporting, at some stage you will be working with children or young people who are going through a **transition** phase. The term 'transition' is applied to different situations in which children and young people pass through a period of change. As well

# Primary/Secondary School Transitions Policy

### Statement of Intent
At Western View Secondary School we recognise that the transition from primary school to secondary is an important step in a child's school life and it is our intention to make this a positive experience for every child.

### Aims
We endeavour to provide our children with a smooth transition from Year 6 (primary school) to Year 7 (secondary school). We ensure that the pace and quality of learning is sensitively maintained through the transition period so that children can continue to make good progress and develop the skills they will need to succeed in Key Stage 3.

### Procedures
Transition to secondary school may be a stressful time for some children. We have built excellent relationships with local primary schools. The school also has procedures which will minimise difficulties or concerns and help children to settle into the new school environment as quickly as possible by:

- holding open days each October for Year 6 pupils and their parents.
- liaising with Year 6 primary teachers to discuss the strengths of individual children and any difficulties or specific needs they may have
- Year 7 teachers visiting primary schools in the spring term to speak to groups of pupils and answer any questions they may have
- the school holding one information evening and one information morning in May for parents with opportunities to speak to teachers and visit classrooms and specialist areas
- inviting Year 6 pupils in June to spend a day at the secondary school and take part in 'taster' sessions.

### Additional support
We understand that some pupils may take longer to find their way around, feel part of their new school and come to terms with the new curriculum and learning and teaching methods. We aim to support pupils by:

- providing a buddy system – an older child is paired with each Year 7 child to give advice and support
- assigning a teaching assistant to each Year 7 classroom for each lesson during the first term, to provide support for the curriculum and pastoral support
- having a senior teacher with specific responsibility for transition who is available to answer children's or parents' concerns.

*A transitions policy.*

as the more obvious school-based transitions such as starting school, changing classes or key stages, or passing on to secondary school, children will pass through other periods of transition which may be long or short term. These may include changes in personal circumstances or experiences, passing through puberty, or simply a change in timetable or their activity in the classroom. Transitions include those that are common to all children and young people, such as moving school and puberty, and those that are particular only to some, such as bereavement.

When it comes to times of change and transition, you should give children every opportunity to talk about what is going to happen so that they are prepared for it. In some cases, such as bereavement, this may not be possible. However, where they are given some warning or opportunity to ask questions about events, some of the negative or harmful effects on their development can be reduced.

## Transitions that only some children and young people may experience

In some cases, transitions will happen which children and young people are not prepared for, and these can be difficult to manage if you do not have policies and procedures in place for dealing with them. Parents should always inform schools when the unexpected happens, but it can sometimes be overlooked. Therefore, if you notice a pupil who is behaving uncharacteristically, you should always ensure that you inform other staff members. The kinds of transitions which are likely to happen at some stage include the following:

- **Bereavement** — even if it has been expected, the death of a close friend or family member may be very traumatic for a child or young person. Your school should have procedures in place ready for this eventuality and be able to support all staff in helping pupils deal with bereavement.

- **Parental separation** — it is likely that at some stage you will be supporting a pupil whose parents are separating. This will affect pupils in different ways and you will need to be sensitive if speaking to parents.

- **Parental change of partner** — this can have a very big impact on children and young people, depending on the amount of contact they have with the absent parent and the way in which a new partner is introduced. Again, you may need to be sensitive if speaking to parents.

- **New sibling** — very young children will find this the most difficult to cope with, as they may be vying for parental attention for the first time. However, older children too may be affected by the arrival of a new sibling.

- **Moving house** — if the pupil is remaining in the same area or at the same school, it is likely that this will be an exciting event, although it may be a little unsettling. However, if the pupil is moving away from

---

**CASE STUDY:** Managing transitions

Milly has worked in her current job as a support assistant for two years. She is working with a Year 1 class and has known them since Reception. She has noticed that one of the children, Josh, has recently become very quiet and withdrawn. Another teaching assistant tells her that she thinks that Josh's dad has recently moved out and that another man has moved in with his mum.

- What should Milly do?
- Why is it important for her to be sensitive in this situation?
- What should she remember about confidentiality?

the school, or has just arrived from some distance away, it is likely that they will need some additional support in order to settle.

● **Change of carer** — pupils who are in care or who have had a number of different homes may find it difficult to manage a change of carer. However, your school should have support and advice from social services and should work closely together to ensure that these transitions go smoothly.

● **Illness or injury** — pupils may be affected by illness or injury and so need to come to terms with a change in circumstances, whether these are their own or of a loved one.

## How transitions may affect children and young people's behaviour and development

It is important for children to have positive relationships during periods of transition, as they will need to feel secure in other areas of their lives. They may need to talk to someone about how they are feeling and you should make sure that there are opportunities for them to do this. If you have advance notice that a child or group of children will be going through a period of change, this will give you an opportunity to plan how you will support them. Transitions may affect children and young people's behaviour and development in different ways. They may:

● become quiet and withdrawn
● be very anxious
● start to demonstrate uncharacteristic behaviour
● become attention seeking.

If they do not receive support, their social and emotional development may also be affected, as transition can potentially be traumatic for children

---

**CASE STUDY:** Supporting transitions

You are working in the lower school in a large secondary. Chayma has recently started at secondary school and has come straight from her home country, so has not been at school in the UK before. Although your school has transitions activities in place and is doing some work with pupils on their new school, you can see that Chayma is finding her new environment difficult.

• Whom might you speak to about this?
• Is there anything else you could do to help?

---

**BEST PRACTICE CHECKLIST:** Supporting transitions

• Keep an eye out for any uncharacteristic behaviour.
• Encourage pupils to use any school-based support — for example, a 'Listening ear' group, or to go to an adult who they trust if they are worried or upset.
• Work to ensure positive relationships during periods of transition.
• Be sensitive to pupils' needs and think about how the transition may be affecting them.
• Ensure pupils have opportunities to talk about and discuss what is happening, and to ask any questions.
• Give pupils the opportunity to visit new classes or schools.
• Liaise with pupils who are already in the year group in order to build relationships and facilitate questions from the children who are moving on.

## Functional skills

### English: Writing

Writing this case study is a good opportunity to practise your English skills. The amount of detail you include in your case study is important and as a result of this, your writing must be organised. It is important that you plan your work carefully before you start.

## Getting ready for assessment

In order to gather evidence for this unit, you will need to show that you know and understand different stages of child development. Choose a pupil with whom you work and write a case study about them, considering each area of their development and any additional needs. Write about how their development may have been influenced, and in particular how they have been affected by transitions. You will need to change their name and seek permission from parents in order to carry out the study.

## Check your knowledge

1. What are the different areas of child development?

2. Give two examples of ways in which different areas of development can affect one another.

3. What kinds of influences are there on children and young people's social and emotional development?

4. How are communication and intellectual development related to one another?

5. Why is it important to recognise and respond as soon as possible to concerns about children and young people's development?

6. Which kinds of transitions do you think have the most potential to affect children and young people?

7. Why is it important to have procedures in place before rather than to react to different situations as they arise?

8. What can you do to support pupils most effectively during these periods?

### References and further reading

- Donaldson, Margaret (1986) *Children's Minds*, HarperCollins
- Lindon, Jennie (2005) *Understanding Child Development: Linking Theory and Practice*, Hodder Arnold
- Meggitt, Carolyn (2005) *Child Development – An Illustrated Guide*, Heinemann
- Pound, Linda (2005) *How Children Learn: From Montessori to Vygotsky – Educational Approaches and Theories Made Easy*, Step Forward Publishing
- Tassoni, Penny (2003) *Supporting Special Needs – Understanding Inclusion in the Early Years*, Heinemann

# TDA 2.2 Safeguarding the welfare of children & young people

Legislation, guidelines and policies place a duty on all those working in schools to ensure the health, safety and security of children in their care. You need to have the necessary knowledge and confidence to take the correct action if children are taken ill or have an accident. You will learn how to recognise the characteristics and types of abuse and how to respond to concerns when children may be at risk.

## By the end of this unit you will:

1. know about the legislation, guidelines, policies and procedures for safeguarding the welfare of children and young people including e-safety

2. know what to do when children or young people are ill or injured, including emergency procedures

3. know how to respond to evidence or concerns that a child or young person has been abused, harmed or bullied.

# Know about the legislation, guidelines, policies and procedures for safeguarding the welfare of children and young people including e-safety

The concept of **safeguarding**, which works to protect children, has only been developed in the last 50 years. The need for improved legislation has been highlighted by high-profile cases, such as the death of Maria Colwell in 1973 and, more recently, Victoria Climbié in 2000. These cases shocked the nation and showed weaknesses in procedures.

## The United Nations Convention on the Rights of the Child (1989)

This treaty sets out the rights and freedoms of all children in a set of 54 articles. Included in those rights are those which ensure that children are safe and looked after. Article 19 states children's rights to be 'protected from all forms of physical or mental violence, injury or abuse, neglect or negligent treatment, maltreatment or exploitation including sexual abuse' by those looking after them. Those countries which signed up to the Treaty, including the UK in 1991, are legally bound to implement legislation which supports each of the articles.

# Identify the current legislation, guidelines, policies and procedures for safeguarding the welfare of children and young people including e-safety

## Children Act 1989

This Act identifies the responsibilities of parents and professionals who must work to ensure the safety of the child. This Act includes two important sections which focus specifically on child protection.

Section 47 states that the local authority has a duty to investigate when 'they have reasonable cause to suspect that a child who lives, or is found, in their area is suffering, or likely to suffer, **significant harm**'.

Section 17 states that services must be put into place by local authorities to 'safeguard and promote the welfare of children within their area who are **in need**'.

## Education Act 2002

This sets out the responsibilities of local education authorities (LEAs), governing bodies, head teachers and all those working in schools to ensure that children are safe and free from harm.

## Children Act 2004

This provides the legal framework for Every Child Matters. It includes the requirement for:

- services to work more closely, forming an integrated service

## Key terms

**Safeguarding** – this term has replaced the term child protection. It includes promoting children's safety and welfare as well as protecting children when abuse happens

**Significant harm** – the seriousness or impact of harm through a single action or over a period of time

**In need** – children who are unlikely to maintain, or be given the opportunity to maintain, a reasonable standard of health or development, or whose health could be impaired without the support of local authority services. It also includes children with disabilities

### Reflect ?

Following the death of Victoria Climbié in February 2000, an inquiry was set up into what had gone wrong. Lord Laming, who led the inquiry, reported that there was a failure in the system. He said that the services responsible for the protection of children had not been working together. His recommendations were included in the Children Act 2004. Identify the different services which may work closely with schools to safeguard children.

- a 'common' assessment framework to help the early identification of need

- a shared database of information which is relevant to the safety and welfare of children

- earlier support for parents who are experiencing problems.

## Policies which safeguard

Schools must develop a range of policies which ensure the safety, security and well-being of their pupils. These will set out the responsibilities of staff and the procedures that they must follow. Policies may be separate or incorporated into one health and safety policy, but they must include sections which cover the following issues of:

- safeguarding and protecting, and procedures for reporting

- e-safety

- bullying, including cyber-bullying (see page 28).

The Department for Education (DfE) provides guidance for local authorities including schools. Schools use this guidance to develop their own policy and procedures which must be followed. Two of these are listed below.

### Working Together to Safeguard Children (2010)

This is guidance which sets out the duties of organisations and how they must work together to safeguard children and young people.

### What to do if you're worried a child is being abused (2006)

This is guidance to help those working with children safeguard and promote their welfare. It also looks at the actions which all adults working with children should take if they are concerned.

### Portfolio activity

Read through the summary of the guidance document 'What to do if you're worried a child is being abused'. You can download this from the Department for Education at www.education.gov.uk, from www.teachernet.gov.uk or from the Department of Health (www.dh.gov.uk)

### Functional skills

**English: Reading**
This is a detailed document that contains a lot of information. Reading the document will help to develop your reading skills. To demonstrate your understanding of the document you could:

- summarise the role of all child care practitioners

- produce a checklist for practitioners on what to consider when information sharing.

# Describe the roles of different agencies involved in safeguarding the welfare of children and young people

All adults within the school have a responsibility to safeguard the welfare of children. There must also be a named member of staff with particular responsibilities for safeguarding children and for e-safety.

Schools have a responsibility to:

- develop children's awareness and their knowledge of what is acceptable and not acceptable behaviour, including when using the Internet

- know, support and protect children who are identified as being at greater risk — that is, on the '**at risk register**'

- provide opportunities for professional training of all staff relating to safeguarding

- put into place policies and security systems for e-learning activities, for example, provide training for children and use filtering software

- observe for signs that abuse may be happening, changes in children's behaviour or failure to thrive, and refer any concerns

- monitor, keep records and share appropriate information with other agencies.

The safety and welfare of children depends upon agencies working together. For example, when assessing the needs of individual children there may be a meeting between the child and family, health services, social services and the school. The diagram below includes agencies which work in partnership to safeguard children.

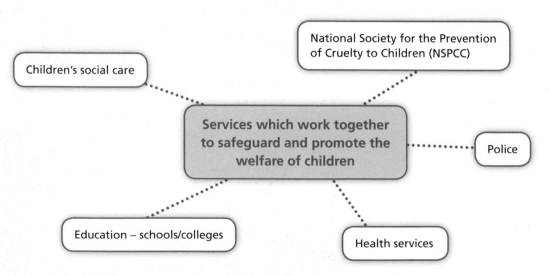

*How do services work together to support children in need?*

## Children's social care

Children's social care has a key role to safeguard and promote the welfare of children who are in need. To do this, they must work in partnership with parents and other agencies. When concern has been raised about a child, and they are thought to be at risk, children's social care has particular responsibilities to decide on the course of action to take. If it is found that the child may be at risk of harm or abuse social workers will:

● carry out an initial assessment of children who are thought to be at risk to find out about: for example, the child's needs, the ability of parents to meet the child's needs, family and environmental factors

● meet and conduct interviews with the child and family members

● liaise with and gather relevant information about the child and their circumstances from other agencies

● take the lead during the **Child Protection Conference**

● take action when a child is thought to be in immediate danger.

## Police

The police work closely with children's social care to protect children from harm. The police have particular role to play. All forces have a Child Abuse Investigation Unit (CAIU). Their role and responsibilities include:

● making a decision on whether a crime had been committed and if so, to begin a criminal investigation

● gathering evidence from children's social care, other agencies and others thought to be involved

● taking emergency action if children are in immediate danger — this may involve removing the child or removing the perpetrator

● attending court to give evidence when a crime has been committed.

*What are the benefits for children when agencies work closely together?*

## Health professionals

Health professionals, in particular GPs and doctors in emergency departments, may examine children with injuries which they suspect may be non-accidental. They have a duty to alert children's social care when abuse is suspected. Health professionals may also:

● carry out a medical examination or observations of a child thought to be at risk of abuse or who has suffered abuse

● contribute to children's social care reports

● give evidence in court if a crime has been committed.

## The National Society for the Prevention of Cruelty to Children (NSPCC)

The NSPCC is a third-sector (charitable) organisation. Its role, as its name suggests, is to work to protect children from harm. The NSPCC is the only third-sector organisation (charity) which has the **statutory** power, alongside the police and children's social services, to take action when children are at risk of abuse. The NSPCC also:

● provides services to support families and children

● provides a helpline for people to call who are worried about a child

● provides a helpline for children in distress or danger

● raises awareness of abuse, for example, through advertising and training materials

● works to influence the law and social policy to protect children better

● shares expertise with other professionals.

## E-safety

The UK Council for Child Internet Safety (UKCCIS) was launched in 2008 in response to concerns about Internet safety. Its role is to safeguard children in relation to this issue. The Council has produced a strategy to increase awareness of Internet safety, set out measures to protect children from unsuitable sites and establish codes of practice.

## The Local Safeguarding Children Board (LSCB)

The LSCB has particular roles and responsibilities to oversee the work of other agencies. The Board is made up from experts from the range of children's services. Serious cases of abuse are always reviewed by the LSCB. You can find out about your LSCB through your own local authority.

### Key term

Statutory – power given in law

### Skills builder

Charities such as Barnardo's and Kidscape also work to safeguard children. Find out about what they do and the materials they produce to inform and support people who work with children, parents and children and young people. This task will help you to develop your research skills.

### Functional skills

**ICT: Finding and selecting information**

The Internet is a good starting point to find out information about these charities. Try using a range of different search engines to find the information you require.

# Know what to do when children or young people are ill or injured, including emergency procedures

## Identify the signs and symptoms of common childhood illnesses

As a teaching or learning support assistant, you will often work closely with individual children. You are therefore likely to notice when they are unwell and may be incubating an illness. This can take place over a period of days. You may notice that a child:

- looks pale
- appears more tired or lethargic
- is quiet or irritable
- has dark rings around eyes
- has lost their appetite
- looks flushed or has a rash.

It is important that you can recognise the signs and symptoms, but it is not your role to diagnose or jump to conclusions. If children display signs of common illnesses, the school will inform their parents so that they can take the child home. Older children and young people will be able to describe how they feel. If you work with a younger age group, or children with communication difficulties, they may be unable to tell you their symptoms.

| Illness | Signs and symptoms | When children are able to return to school |
|---------|-------------------|-------------------------------------------|
| Flu | Headaches, weakness, fever, cough, sore throat, aching muscles and joints | When recovered |
| Tonsillitis | Very sore throat, difficulty swallowing, fever, pain in ears and neck | No specific advice – children return when well |
| Diarrhoea/ vomiting | Diarrhoea, stomach pains/vomiting, dehydration | Two days after last episode of diarrhoea or vomiting |
| Chickenpox | Itchy rash with blister-like appearance, fever | Five days after onset of rash |
| Mumps | Painful and swollen jaw, pain when swallowing, fever | Five days after onset of swollen glands |
| Rubella (German measles) | Runny nose, temperature, red-pink rash, sore throat, headache | Six days after onset of rash |
| Measles | Fever, runny nose, cough, blotchy red-brown spots, greyish-white spots in the mouth | Four days after onset of rash |
| Glandular fever | Fatigue, sore throat, swollen glands, fever | No specific advice – children return when well |
| Impetigo | Red sores around mouth and nose developing into yellow-brown crusts | When lesions are crusted or healed |
| Ringworm | Skin ringworm – ring-like red rash with raised rim; scalp ringworm – scaly patches on scalp which may feel inflamed and tender | May return to school when treatment has started |

Table 1: Signs and symptoms of common illnesses in children.

The length of time children must stay away from school will vary between the type of illness and between children. Advice given to schools on how soon children can return is included on the table and is taken from Health Protection Agency guidance (2009). Some childhood illnesses such as measles and mumps must be notified to the local authority.

If meningitis is suspected immediate medical help should be sought. Meningitis can be difficult to spot in the early stages but can very quickly become life-threatening. Children with meningitis may be displaying any of the following signs:

- fever
- severe headache
- neck stiffness
- vomiting

- joint or muscle pain
- dislike of bright lights
- seizures/convulsions
- a rash.

## Describe the actions to take when children or young people are ill or injured

All schools must have at least one qualified first aider. It is essential that you know who the named first aiders in the school are and how they can be contacted. Schools will have systems in place for summoning urgent medical help to the classroom or school grounds. There may be intercom systems or a 'red card' or 'orange card' system alert, depending on the urgency of support needed.

### Dealing with minor injury

It is inevitable that all children will at some time suffer minor cuts, bruises and abrasions. These can be dealt with within the school and do not require children to be sent home. These can be washed with clean water, but lotions or creams should never be applied.

### Reporting and recording

If a child has been feeling ill during the day, or has had a minor injury, the school needs to send a report to the parents or carer. Reporting to parents is particularly important when a child has suffered a head bump. Even where there are no obvious symptoms, the parents must be aware of what has happened and the symptoms they should look for.

Information on incidents and accidents must be recorded in the school incident or accident report book. If you have observed an incident or accident you will have to provide details on what occurred and the action you took. You should make notes as soon after the event as possible. A manager or member of staff with the authority to do so will complete and sign the reports. Serious accidents have to be reported to the **Health and Safety Executive** by law.

## Identify circumstances when children and young people might require urgent medical attention

When working in a school, you are likely to be in a situation where you have to make a decision about calling for urgent medical attention. It is important therefore to recognise the signs and circumstances when you must summon immediate help.

An emergency situation which requires urgent medical attention includes:

- severe bleeding
- unconsciousness
- choking
- breathing difficulties
- head injuries
- epileptic seizure
- suspected fractures
- when it is suspected that children have taken drugs or abused substances
- disorientation.

### Accidents

When an accident occurs you must always call for immediate help, even if you are a first aider yourself. You must find out what has happened so that accurate information can be given when dialling 999. Other children can become very distressed when they witness an accident, so you should try to remain calm.

Immediate action should be taken as follows.

- Reassure the child.
- Do not move the child unless it is absolutely necessary.
- If children are unconscious they should be put into the recovery position.
- Do not give the child any food or drink.
- Keep the child warm, for example, by placing a coat over them.
- Ensure other children in the area are not at risk of being hurt.

You do not have to achieve a first aid qualification to achieve your Level 2 Certificate in Supporting Teaching and Learning in Schools, but it is beneficial for all those working with children. Schools may offer training in basic first aid.

### Asthma

One of the most common conditions in the schools is asthma. In some schools there may be as many as one in four children with this condition. Asthma affects the airways of the lungs. The symptoms are wheezing and coughing. Most children with asthma manage the illness well and carry an inhaler with them. You should know where these are kept and how to support children when using it. When children have an asthmatic attack which is not helped by the inhaler, it is essential to seek medical help.

## Epilepsy

Children with epilepsy may rarely have attacks, but it is important that you are aware of what to do when this happens. A first aider should always be called. A child who has an attack must be kept safe from harm. As they recover from the seizure, they will need to be reassured. Urgent medical help must be sought if a child:

- does not recover immediately
- has more than one seizure
- has not been diagnosed as an epileptic.

## Anaphylaxis

Many children have allergic reactions, which cause sneezing, wheezing, itchy eyes or swelling. In rare cases children may have severe allergic reactions which can be life-threatening and need immediate treatment. Common triggers for children with anaphylaxis are foods such as eggs, nuts and seafood. Stings from insects can also cause anaphylaxis. Children in anaphylactic shock have difficulty breathing and suffer swelling (which may be in the throat) which is life-threatening. Children who have been diagnosed may have an auto-injection kit of adrenaline (sometimes called an EpiPen®) available at the school. Immediate medical help must be sought in the event of a reaction, even if adrenaline has been given.

## Sickle cell disease

This gets its name from the sickle-shaped red blood cells which are present in children with the disease. These clump together causing severe pain. This is known as an 'aplastic crisis'. The school may have medication to give immediately and you should reassure the child and keep them warm. When children suffer a crisis, you should always seek medical help.

## Diabetes

Diabetes happens when the body does not produce insulin. Some children may need to inject themselves with an insulin pen during the school day, so may need a quiet area to do this. Sometimes, following activity or when children have not eaten enough carbohydrates, their blood glucose levels can fall. You need to be aware of the signs of this which include hunger, pallor, feeling shaky and irritable, a fast pulse, glazed eyes, tingling lips, drowsiness, trembling and nausea. This state is called hypoglycaemia (often referred to as a 'hypo'). When this happens the child requires something sugary such as sweets, glucose tablets or a sugary (not low-cal) drink. This is followed by carbohydrates such as biscuits or a cereal bar. Children can usually return to their school work. Immediate medical help will be required if a child continues to show signs of a hypo or they become unconscious.

### Knowledge into action

Find out about any health conditions of children who you support. Seek advice on ways that you can support them to manage their illness and how to recognise when immediate medical attention is required.

## Link

Further information on the importance of diet to prevent illness and life-threatening incidents is included in TDA 2.14 Support children and young people at meal or snack times.

## Functional skills

### English: Reading
By using the policies from your school to answer these questions in the Portfolio activity, you are developing your reading skills.

## Functional skills

### Mathematics: Representing
Once you have completed the task above, you could look at the figure of children with health conditions and have a go at converting it into a fraction, decimal and percentage. What percentage of children in your school have a health condition?

## Portfolio activity

Refer to the school policies to describe what actions you, and others in the school, should take in each of the following scenarios.

1. Grace is 5 years old. Her mother reported that she complained of stomach pains but wanted to come to school. Although she usually eats well, you notice that she did not eat her dinner. During the afternoon, Grace vomits as she is leaving the classroom.

2. Daniel is 9 years old. You are aware that he has diabetes. Shortly after playtime you notice that Daniel looks very pale. The other children in the group are working on their 3D models, but Daniel is sitting quietly by himself in the reading area. You ask him if he is OK but he looks glazed and does not appear to have heard you.

3. As you walk across the playground, you notice a group of boys around a boy on the floor. You see that it is 12-year-old Nikhil. He is moving but appears very dazed. The other boys tell you that he had banged his head on a post when playing football which had knocked him out for a few moments.

## Describe the actions to take in response to emergency situations including fires, security incidents and missing children or young people

If you are working in a school, you should already be aware of the policies and procedures for emergency situations. You may have taken part in an evacuation practice.

### Fire and other emergencies
Buildings need to be evacuated quickly in the event of a fire, gas leak or bomb scare. There will be clear procedures on how to do this in your school. These procedures must be displayed in each area of the school, giving information on:

● how to raise the alarm in the event of a fire, gas leak or bomb scare

● what to do if you hear the fire alarm

● the route you should take – including a plan of the route from each room or area in the school

● the nearest assembly point – for example, in a playground.

Registers should be available so staff can make a check that all children are safely out of the building.

Information should also be given on what *not* to do, such as:

● not collecting or allowing children to collect personal belongings or put on coats

● not re-entering the building until you have been informed that it is safe to do so.

As a teaching or learning support assistant, you may work in different areas of the school, so it is important that you know the different routes from each area that you work in. You should be given regular opportunities to practise evacuating groups of children from the building safely. This will give you more confidence in escorting the children safely and calmly.

## Security

Security should be in place which minimises the risks to children. You must know what these are and ensure that you follow the procedures at all times. These procedures will include:

● signing-in procedures/visitor badges

● security locks on doors

● procedures for collection of younger pupils

● registration.

All visitors to the school should be identified by badges. If you are unsure about someone you see, always report your concern to someone higher up.

## When children are missing

Security procedures should minimise the risks of children going missing from school, so it is essential that you follow school guidelines. You may be asked to accompany children on school visits and to supervise a group. Staff should make regular checks that all children are present. Some schools require children to wear fluorescent jackets or caps of the same colour, so they can be easily spotted.

If children are missing, staff must take action immediately by:

● reporting to the teacher responsible

● ensuring that other children are present and safe — checking the register

● checking all areas of the school or grounds

● informing the child's parents

● informing the police.

# Know how to respond to evidence or concerns that a child or young person has been abused, harmed or bullied

## What is abuse?

Abuse is when something happens to the child which is in breach of their rights and which affects their health and development. Abuse also happens when someone fails to do something to protect a child's rights, health and development. Abuse can happen to any child whatever their background or situation. Abuse always has an impact on the child's well-being. Children with a disability are more vulnerable to abuse.

Abuse is a sensitive subject. When studying the issues surrounding abuse you may feel anxious, both personally and about your role and responsibilities in the school. There are many agencies, including children's charities and social services, that you can contact if you need to discuss your feelings as you work through this section (see the end of this unit).

## Identify the characteristics of different types of child abuse

Abuse can take many forms. Within the child protection system there are four main categories used:

- physical abuse
- emotional abuse
- sexual abuse
- neglect.

Children may often suffer more than one type of abuse. A child who is being sexually abused, for example, may also be threatened and made to feel worthless.

| Form of abuse | Description |
|---|---|
| Physical abuse | Physical abuse happens when a child is physically hurt or injured. Hitting, kicking, beating with objects, burning, scolding, suffocating, throwing and shaking are all forms of physical abuse. |
| Sexual abuse | Sexual abuse happens when a child is forced or persuaded into sexual activities or situations by others. This may be:<br>• physical contact – including touching or acts of penetration<br>• non-physical contact – involving children in looking at pornographic materials or sexual acts. |
| Emotional abuse | Emotional abuse happens when the child suffers persistent ill-treatment which affects their emotional development. It may involve making the child feel frightened, unloved, worthless or in danger. Sometimes expectations of the child are inappropriate for their age. Emotional abuse may happen alone, but often takes place with other types of abuse. |
| Neglect | Neglect happens when there is a persistent failure to provide for a child's health, development and psychological needs. This can include providing inadequate food, shelter, clothing or medical care, or not providing for their educational or emotional needs. |

*Table 2: Types of abuse.*

## Bullying

Bullying is also recognised as a type of abuse. Bullying is always distressing for the victim and can have serious consequences. Bullying should always be taken seriously. Emotional bullying is the most commonly reported by children and young people and is often more difficult to spot. Bullying can take place both inside and outside the school.

Bullying happens when an individual or a group shows hostility towards an individual and this can be:

● emotional, such as name-calling, 'sending to Coventry' (not talking to someone), taking or hiding personal items, humiliating, spreading rumours or teasing

● physical, such as pushing, kicking, hitting, pinching or threatening to use physical force

● racist, such as racial taunts or gestures

● sexual, such as inappropriate physical contact, sexual comments and innuendo, or homophobic taunts.

## Cyber-bullying

In recent years, a new form of bullying known as 'cyber-bullying' has become increasingly common. One in five children were cyber-bullied in 2008. Cyber-bullying may be emotional, racist or sexual forms of abuse. It happens through emails, text messages or telephone calls. Information about someone may also be shared by putting it on to social networking sites. This can include the sharing of private photographs.

Children and young people who use this method of bullying often feel disassociated from their actions, but the consequences can be just as serious for the child. This type of bullying can be particularly distressing as children are unable to get away from it. It even invades their home.

### Functional skills

**ICT: Developing, presenting and communicating information**
You could design a poster about cyber-bullying suitable for the age of the children who you work with. You could display your poster in your IT area.

## Self-harm

Self-harm is when children deliberately hurt themselves. They usually do this secretly and it can involve cutting, burning, pulling out hair or banging their head. Self-harm often happens as a result of other types of abuse. If you notice signs of self-harm or children tell you that they are harming themselves, you must take the same action as if they are being harmed by another person.

| Type of abuse | Physical signs | Behavioural signs |
|---|---|---|
| Physical | • Unexplained burns or scalds, bruises, fractures<br>• Bruises/abrasions around mouth<br>• Grasp marks<br>• Bruises to both eyes<br>• Bite marks<br>• Bruises to the soft part of face<br>• Marks showing the outline of an implement such as a stick or belt buckle | • Withdrawn behaviour<br>• Aggressive behaviour<br>• Reluctance to change for PE<br>• Fear of parents being approached for an explanation<br>• Flinching when approached or touched<br>• Depression<br>• Running away from home |
| Sexual | • Bruises or scratches<br>• Difficulty in walking or sitting<br>• Sleep problems<br>• Stomach problems<br>• Frequent headaches<br>• Vaginal bleeding or discharge<br>• 'Love bites' | • Self-harming behaviour<br>• Eating disorders<br>• Displaying inappropriate sexual behaviour<br>• Behaviour/knowledge inappropriate for age<br>• Using sexually implicit language<br>• Withdrawn or confused<br>• Secrecy, e.g., wiping 'history' from the Internet or closing a web page when adult present |
| Emotional | • Delay in physical and/or emotional development<br>• Speech disorders | • Poor concentration<br>• Self-harming behaviour<br>• Overreaction to problems or mistakes<br>• Difficulty in making friends<br>• Attention seeking or aggressive<br>• Low self-esteem<br>• Rocking/thumb sucking/hair twisting<br>• Abuse of drugs, solvents or alcohol<br>• Truancy<br>• Self-harming behaviour |
| Neglect | • Hunger<br>• Poor personal hygiene<br>• Under or overweight<br>• Tiredness or lethargy<br>• Inappropriate or inadequate clothing<br>• Untreated health problems<br>• Developmental delay<br>• Frequent illness | • Difficulty in making friends<br>• Lateness/poor school attendance<br>• Stealing (for example, food from other pupils) |

*Table 3: Signs and indicators of abuse.*

The signs included in Table 3 are indicators that abuse *may* be happening and do not always mean that abuse *is* happening. Some children may have clothes which are not washed as frequently as they might be, but it does not mean that they are being neglected. Young children frequently fall and bruise their knees. Mongolian blue spots look like bruises on the lower back of children with darker skin, but are actually birthmarks. This does not mean that you should ignore signs. You must always report concerns.

# Describe the risks and possible consequences for children and young people using the Internet, mobile phones and other technologies

When we think of the types of abuse it is easier to imagine how this may happen in the 'real world'. There are now significant risks of sexual and emotional abuse for children in the 'virtual' world. The virtual world is expanding into different types of technology. Children can now access the Internet through their mobile phones and online games.

It is impossible and unreasonable to suggest that children and young people should not use the Internet. The Internet plays an important role in children's lives and helps to support their education. Research shows that almost all children have access to the Internet either at home or in school. The majority of children say they cannot live without the Internet. Communicating through chat rooms and blogging are usually part of their everyday lives. It is important therefore that that children and young people know the risks and are able to protect themselves.

## Risks when using the Internet

There are risks of sexual or emotional abuse when using the Internet. Research shows that the most common risks for children are:

- giving out personal information about themselves

- accessing inappropriate information — often accidentally when innocent words are entered into a search engine.

*Children's Online Risks and Safety (National Foundation for Educational Research (NFER), 2009)*

## Consequences of sharing personal information

Children increasingly use social networking sites and online diaries. These have a minimum age but children of 9 years or younger have been known to use them. Children often place information about themselves online, which makes it easy for them to be identified. Some include addresses, phone numbers and sometimes even photographs. This makes them easy targets for adults who wish to exploit them by:

- talking to and building 'friendships' with children online with the intention of meeting the child — this is called grooming

- encouraging children to engage in conversations which are sexual in nature

- taking and/or distributing photographs using the Internet.

## Risks of accessing inappropriate information

There is a high risk that children may access inappropriate or even pornographic materials when innocently searching for information on the Internet. Schools must have filtering systems in place which prevent access to unsuitable sites. Children and young people must always be supervised when using computers in schools to minimise these risks.

## Over to you!

In 2007 Dr Tanya Byron was asked by the government to review the use of the Internet by children and young people. She realised that it is important to involve young people. This helps them to understand the risks and know how to keep themselves safe. Find out about her recommendations.

However vigilant staff and parents may be, the risks and consequences are increasing. It is essential that children are aware of the risks, and of ways to protect themselves. They should also know how to report concerns. All schools must now have a policy which ensures that children are protected and are taught how to use the Internet safely.

## Describe actions to take in response to evidence or concerns that a child or young person has been abused, harmed (including self-harm) or bullied, or may be at risk of harm, abuse or bullying

Children spend almost half their waking hours in school, so it is not surprising that schools have a particular responsibility to look for signs that abuse may be happening. An NSPCC study in 2002 reported that one in six children had experienced serious maltreatment by parents. It is likely that among the children you support that there will be children who have experienced some form of abuse.

As a teaching assistant or learning support assistant, you will build special relationships with children. You may regularly work with children in small groups or on a one-to-one basis. You are likely to be the person who the child feels more comfortable to talk to when the rest of the class are not around. It is important that you know how to recognise when abuse may be happening and what action you should take.

*Do you know what action to take if you recognise abuse is happening to a child?*

## Key term

**Disclose** – share information, often of a personal nature

While you must avoid jumping to conclusions you must always be observant. You may notice physical signs or changes in a child's behaviour, or the child may hint or **disclose** to you that they are being abused or bullied. You must also think about how you would respond if a child were to hint or disclose this to you.

Always:

● report concerns about possible signs or changes in behaviour to the designated person or your manager

● take what children say seriously – it will take a lot of courage to tell you and children will rarely lie about abuse

● reassure children that they are not to blame if they tell you they have been abused

● tell children that you will have to tell someone who can help them

● write down what you have observed or what has been said – but keep the information secure.

Never:

● promise to keep information a secret

● investigate further or ask questions

● appear shocked

● make promises to children.

Remember:

● it is not your responsibility to draw conclusions – only report what you have noticed or have been told

● you have a statutory duty to report concerns under the Education Act 2002

● you can receive support from your tutor, the designated child protection officer or your local children's social services or NSPCC.

## CASE STUDY: Responding to concerns

Chris works as a teaching assistant in a local primary school. As a group of Year 5 children were getting changed for PE, Chris noticed bruising in lines across the back of a boy called Marc. He asked Marc how he had hurt himself but he said, 'It's nothing' and quickly put on his top. As Marc left the room he approached Chris and said, 'Please don't say anything to Mum, or Uncle Paul will be cross with me.'

• Why does Chris need to take action about this?

• Describe the action that Chris should take.

# Describe the actions to take in response to concerns that a colleague may be failing to comply with safeguarding procedures or harming, abusing or bullying a child or young person

All organisations which work with children have a responsibility to recruit staff who are suitable to work with children. When you first applied to work with children, you would have been asked to complete a form to disclose any convictions that you may have. Even with these checks in place abuse can, and has, happened within schools. This is called institutional abuse.

All staff have a duty to comply with policy and procedures. Failure to comply may put children at risk of harm or abuse, so concerns should always be reported to the designated person for safeguarding or the head teacher.

If you have concerns that a colleague is abusing a child, your actions should be exactly the same as if the abuser is a parent, family member or stranger. These actions were described in the previous section. You must act immediately to protect children by informing the head teacher. If the allegation is against the head teacher, you should report concerns to the designated person for child protection or directly to the local education authority.

These are difficult situations but your first priority must always be to the child. It is important that you do not discuss what has happened with others, although you may need to seek support for yourself.

## Describe the principles and boundaries of confidentiality and when to share information

Confidentiality is essential in schools. The same rules of confidentiality apply whether you are employed by the school or you are working as a volunteer. You may have been told sensitive information about a child because it helps you to carry out your role, for example, about their health or particular needs. This is sensitive information and should never be a topic for discussion in the staffroom or with other parents.

As a teaching or learning support assistant, you may find that parents approach you to tell you personal or sensitive information. You must let them know that you would need to share it with your manager or supervisor. Information can be passed on without permission when a child is at risk of abuse or harm. However, the information should only be passed to specific people who 'need to know'. They can then take action and provide support to protect the child. If you are in doubt, you should always ask for advice.

### Information sharing

In some circumstances, when a child may be at risk of significant harm, information can be shared without consent with professionals who need to know. Failure to share information has been highlighted in a number of serious child abuse cases. Sharing information ensures that problems are identified early and action is taken when children are thought to be at risk of abuse. There will be systems within your school on ways that this is done. You should always ask for advice before sharing information.

### Functional skills

**ICT: Using ICT**
Computers are often used to keep a record of any information about children. It is important to remember that if you have a confidential file on your computer, you should have it password protected.

## Getting ready for assessment

To achieve this unit, you need to know about the framework of legislation, policies and procedures which work to safeguard the welfare of children. You need to know what action to take if children are ill or injured, including how to follow emergency procedures in your school. You will explore types of child abuse and signs to look for and know what you should do if you are concerned about a child's welfare.

- Write a brief summary of relevant legislation.

- Obtain policies and procedures from the school which relate to safeguarding, bullying and e-safety.

- Discuss the procedures for responding to illness and accidents with the person in the school responsible for health and safety.

- Find out about the organisations which work closely with your school and ways that information is shared with them.

- Research common childhood illnesses.

- Take the opportunity to attend training sessions for first aid or enrol on a first aid qualification.

- Discuss the procedures for responding to concerns about abuse or bullying with the designated, or named, person responsible for safeguarding.

## Check your knowledge

1. Name two pieces of legislation which help to safeguard children.

2. What is the term for abuse through text messaging or emails?

3. Which charity plays a leading role in the safeguarding of children?

4. What are the signs that a child with diabetes is experiencing a 'hypo'?

5. Why should head bumps always be reported to parents even if there are no obvious effects?

6. Look at the following statements and answer true or false. Give reasons for your answer.

   a) Children who are disabled are more likely to be abused.

   b) Abuse does not happen in schools as checks are always carried out when staff are appointed.

   c) Statistics show that cyber-bullying is carried out by boys and girls equally.

   d) Bullying may have long-term effects.

   e) You should pass on concerns about a child even if they ask you to keep it a secret.

### References and further reading

- Working together to safeguard children – DfE publication (www.education.gov.uk)
- What to do if you're worried a child is being abused – DfE publication (www.education.gov.uk) or Department of Health (www.dh.gov.uk)

### Websites

**www.dcsf.gov.uk/ukccis** – UK Council for Child Internet Safety
**www.everychildmatters.gov.uk** – Every Child Matters
**www.hpa.org.uk** – Health Protection Agency
**www.nhs.uk** – information on children's health
**www.nspcc.org.uk** – National Society for the Prevention of Cruelty to Children, a third-sector organisation working to safeguard children
**www.teachernet.gov.uk** – information and resources for teachers

# TDA 2.3 Communication & professional relationships with children, young people & adults

A crucial part of your role will be effective communication and professional relationships with children, young people and adults. You will have contact with a range of teachers and possibly other professionals, as well as parents and pupils. You will need to demonstrate that you have good relationships in your interactions with all pupils and adults and that you are an effective role model.

## By the end of this unit you will:

1. know how to interact with and respond to children and young people

2. know how to interact with and respond to adults

3. know how to communicate with children, young people and adults

4. know about current legislation, policies and procedures covering confidentiality and sharing information, including data protection.

# Know how to interact with and respond to children and young people

## How to establish respectful, professional relationships with children and young people

In order to build relationships with children and young people, you will need to adapt your behaviour and communication accordingly. As well as demonstrating effective communication skills, you will need to show that you are approachable and able to work in an environment of mutual support.

Children of all ages, cultures and abilities need to feel secure and valued, and your interactions with them should demonstrate this. It is important to get these relationships right from the start. In other words, you need to establish ground rules and mutual respect at the beginning, and discuss with pupils the factors that will be important when working together. You should remember that this is crucial — start by talking about how you are going to work together and what each person wants to get out of it. In this way you will develop a mutually respectful relationship.

You will also need to have an awareness of the kinds of issues which are important to pupils, and take time to talk these through with them when necessary. Through positively communicating with and being involved with pupils, you will show them that they are part of the school community. However, this is not the same as giving all pupils attention whenever they demand it!

*Make sure you establish ground rules for your relationships with pupils.*

### Link

For more on this topic, see TDA 2.7 Maintain and support relationships with children and young people.

## Functional skills

**English: Speaking, listening and communication**

Classroom management is a very important part of your role in school. This case study could provide an opportunity for you to discuss your classroom management techniques and share good practice with your peers.

## Link

For more on how to communicate appropriately with children and young people, see TDA 2.9 Support children and young people's positive behaviour. For stages of communication development, see TDA 2.1 Child and young person development, and also page 42 of this unit.

**CASE STUDY:** Establishing respectful professional relationships

Georgia has just started working with a group of Year 8 pupils. She has been given a list of names but does not know the group. She does not know anything about the pupils before starting the group except that they need additional literacy support. Georgia starts the first session by welcoming the group and then goes straight into the first activity. About halfway through the session, some of the group start to talk among themselves and are not participating.

- Why do you think this might have happened?
- How might you have approached your first meeting with the group?
- Is there anything Georgia can do to encourage the pupils to participate and rescue the situation?

## How to behave appropriately for a child or young person's stage of development

You should ensure that when you are communicating with children and young people you take into account their stage of development. Children of different needs and ages will require varying levels of attention and support according to their needs and the amount of time they can concentrate. As you become more experienced in your work with children, you will be able to recognise the features which you may meet with different age groups. If you work with a pupil who has additional needs, you will need to ensure that you have advice from other professionals who have assessed their stage of development and those areas on which they need to focus.

### Pupils in Foundation Stage and Key Stage 1

These pupils are still very young and are developing their communication and language skills. If you are speaking to them, you should ensure that you get down to their level so that you are not towering over them, as this can be very intimidating for them. You may still need to remind them about the importance of listening to others and taking turns to speak. They will also need you to be very clear and check their understanding after you have spoken to them, by asking them to repeat back to you. If you work with children of this age, you will know that they tire quickly and are unable to concentrate for long periods. They may also find it difficult to manage times of change or excitement, so you will need to be prepared for this if you are making changes from the normal school day.

### Pupils in Key Stage 2

When they go into Key Stage 2, many pupils will be starting to mature in the way in which they communicate. They will be more used to the formalities of conversation and will be less self-centred. They may be more considerate and invite others to speak first. However, you will still need to remind some pupils about waiting for their turn when speaking and this may start to be part of their personality, although it may still be due to immaturity.

*How do you think a pupil would feel if you were standing towering over them rather than at their level?*

## Pupils in Key Stages 3 and 4

Pupils of this age will be used to formal and informal language. They will know and understand how we communicate with one another and will be used to the increasing number of technologies which they can use to stay in touch with one another. It is likely that they will often communicate themselves through texts and emails. Teenagers will often become more self-conscious about speaking in front of others and can become embarrassed easily. You may need to give them more time to do this in groups to regain their confidence if this happens and to encourage them to speak out.

In addition, it is likely that children who speak English as an additional language will take longer to develop their vocabulary and as a result their patterns of speech may differ. Learning more than one language should not mean that they are hindered, but it needs to be handled in a sensitive way so that children's identities are valued. Your school should support the development of children's home languages through the involvement of families, the inclusion of different cultures and the celebration of pupils' individuality.

## How to deal with disagreements between children and young people

You will probably have to deal regularly with disagreements between pupils and their peers. This quite often takes place at breaks and lunchtimes, but may also occur during learning time. When managing arguments, you will need to make sure that you go back to the beginning and find out exactly what has happened and hear from all sides. It is important for pupils to feel that they have been heard and to put their point of view across. You will need to establish whether one of them was in the wrong and decide if apologies are required or if any further steps are needed, such as referral to another member of staff.

Children and young people also need to be able to understand how their own feelings might affect their behaviour and you may need to talk to them about this. For example, saying to a child, 'I know you are upset because you could not do cooking today' will help them to make the link between emotion and behaviour. In this way they will be more able to understand how to think about others.

One effective way of encouraging children to understand and respect others' feelings is through discussion and activities such as 'Circle Time'. Although this may not always be practical with very young children, as they are often required to sit for a long time and wait for their turn before speaking, older children will benefit from talking through issues as they occur. A whole-class forum is often a good way of doing this.

Strategies such as the Restorative Justice programme are also popular in schools. These are taken from the criminal justice system and have worked well as a method of resolving behaviour issues and learning from what happens. The table below, taken from the Transforming Conflict website, an organisation which promotes restorative justice, shows how you can encourage and support pupils as they learn to understand how the impact of what they do affects others.

| Retributive justice | Restorative justice |
| --- | --- |
| Negative behaviour is 'breaking the rules' | Negative behaviour is adversely affecting others |
| Focus on blame/guilt/who was the culprit | Focus on problem solving and expressing needs and feelings |
| Adversarial relationships | Dialogue and negotiation |
| Imposition of pain/unpleasantness to punish and deter | Restitution leading to reconciliation |
| Attention to rules | Attention to relationships |
| Conflict represented as impersonal and abstract | Conflict identified as interpersonal with value for learning |
| One social injury replaced by another | Focus on repair of social injury |
| School community as spectators | School community involved in facilitation |
| People affected by behaviour are not necessarily involved | Encouragement of all concerned to be involved |
| Accountability defined in terms of punishment | Accountability defined as understanding the impact of the action and putting things right |

Table 1: Retributive and restorative justice (source: www.transformingconflict.org – Restorative Justice in School.).

## How own behaviour could promote effective interactions or impact negatively on interactions with children and young people

The way in which you behave towards others will always have an impact on the children and young people with whom you work. This is because they will always take their lead from the adults around them and will be quick to point out anything which you tell them to do but do not do yourself. You should also remember to consider how you approach other people and how you respond to them. If your own interactions with others are effective, this will promote the same positive outcome in your communication with children and young people. This is also important for adults because parents and other adults who come into the school are also more likely to give beneficial support if communication is strong and effective and this, in turn, benefits pupils. It is also important for pupils that we model effective communication skills. This means checking what we are saying sometimes in moments of stress or excitement, so that they can understand what our expectations are. If we ask pupils to behave in a particular way and then forget to do it ourselves, they will find it harder to understand the boundaries of what is acceptable.

# Know how to interact with and respond to adults

## How to establish respectful, professional relationships with adults

When working with other adults, whether this is within or outside the school environment, you will need to be able to work in an environment of mutual support and openness. In school surroundings you will not be able to work independently of others, nor would it be practicable to do so. Although you will need to maintain your professionalism in a school environment, you should also be able to support other adults in a practical and also a sensitive way.

Your relationships with adults may be with:

● other members of your school team

● parents

● other professionals who come into school to support pupils.

Depending on the relationship you have with colleagues, parents or other professionals and the context in which you are speaking to them, the way in which you behave and interact will be affected.

The support you will be required to give other adults will be on several levels (which you can remember with the acronym PIPE).

● **Practical:** You may be working with others who are unfamiliar with the classroom or school surroundings and who need to have help or advice with finding or using equipment and resources.

● **Informative:** You may need to give support to those who do not have information about a particular situation. Alternatively, you may be asked to prepare and write reports about specific pupils.

● **Professional:** You may be in a position to support or help others with issues such as planning, or you may be asked whether others can observe your work with pupils or discuss your work with them.

● **Emotional:** It is important to support others through day-to-day events and retain a sense of humour.

---

**CASE STUDY:** How own behaviour impacts on pupils

Kim is a teaching assistant in a junior school. She works in Years 3 and 4 during different times in the week. Jackie, who is hearing impaired, is in the Year 3 class, although she does not need individual support as she manages her own hearing aids. Kim always takes time to check that Jackie is OK, even if this is just by raising her eyebrows and smiling at the start of a learning activity. She has a good relationship with Jackie.

● Why is it important that Kim or another adult ensures that Jackie is OK, even if she is usually able to work on tasks without support?

● How do you think this will impact on other children in the class?

---

**Functional skills**

**English: Writing**
Using the information on PIPE, you could write a diary account of a time when you have offered each of these levels of support to adults in your setting. Try to keep your diary account accurate and think carefully about your spelling, punctuation and grammar.

## BEST PRACTICE CHECKLIST: Establishing and maintaining professional relationships

- Remain professional in the school environment and when communicating with other practitioners in contact with the school.
- Treat others with respect.
- Notice the efforts and achievements of others.
- Give practical support where needed.
- Avoid speaking about others in a negative way such as gossiping.

The principles of relationship building with children and adults in any context are that if others are comfortable in our company, they will be more likely to communicate effectively. Where people do not get along or are suspicious of one another, the tendency is that they will avoid one another wherever possible and so reduce the opportunities to develop relationships. Positive relationships are not something which should be left to chance and it is important to consider the ways in which we can develop them.

## The importance of adult relationships as role models for children and young people

In your role as a professional adult working with children and young people, you will need to remember that you should be an effective role model for pupils. This means that you will have to show them how to relate to and communicate with others at all times through your own interactions and relationships with other adults and pupils. It is also important for pupils to see all adults behaving appropriately and professionally in school.

We build relationships with others in school on a daily basis in a number of ways. Children and young people will always respond to positive communication and relationships from adults. They are more likely to want to be in school and to learn if they have good relationships and are supported by adults who get along with one another. Occasionally the school ethos may not be in line with the beliefs or ideas held by parents, and this may cause disagreement or conflict. However, this should be seen as an opportunity for adults to discuss and agree on what is best for the pupil.

## CASE STUDY: The importance of adult relationships as role models

Hanif and the class teacher in Year 2 with whom he works do not get along well together. This is not because they have had any disagreements, but each of them has preconceived ideas about the other and they manage to avoid spending any time together when the children are not in class. This has been noticed by other members of the staff team. They have been working together for just under a term when the Christmas production means that they have to spend some time discussing and planning together. They have started to do it in lesson time and Hanif has stayed behind after school to have a meeting with the teacher.

- Do you think that it matters that Hanif and the teacher are not particularly keen to spend time together?
- Why might this have an impact on the pupils?
- Is there anything that you might do differently in Hanif's position?

# Know how to communicate with children, young people and adults

Communication may be:

- verbal
- non-verbal
- informal
- formal.

## How communication with children and young people differs across different age ranges and stages of development

### Age and maturity

Children of different ages will require varying levels of attention. Younger children may need more reassurance, particularly when first starting school. They may also need to have more physical contact as a result. As children become more mature, they may need more help with talking through issues and reflecting on their thoughts. You will need to adapt your vocabulary and repeat what you have said when speaking to younger pupils to check their understanding.

### Communication difficulties

You should take care and act sensitively with children who have communication difficulties, as they will need to take their time and feel unpressured when they are speaking. Some children or young people may not have many opportunities to speak, or may be anxious or nervous. You should adapt the way in which you communicate according to their individual needs. If they have a speech disorder, such as a stammer, or conditions which make it difficult for them, you should allow them to take their time. Try not to fill in words for them or guess what they are going to say, as this will add to their distress.

You may need additional training, for example, in British Sign Language, to be able to communicate effectively or know the most effective strategies to use. In some cases where pupils have special educational needs, you may need to have additional equipment in order to communicate with one another.

## The main differences between communicating with adults and communicating with children and young people

There are many similarities between communicating with adults and with children:

- always maintaining eye contact and interest
- responding to what they are saying
- treating them with courtesy and respect.

**Link**

See also page 37.

**Over to you!**

Think about the different stages of development as outlined in TDA 2.1 Child and young person development. How might children and young people's communication needs be different at the start and the end of formal education?

However, when communicating with children and young people, we also need to think about how we maintain the relationship of carer to child and what this means in a school context. However well you get on with children and young people, you need to remember that they need to see you in this way and that your relationships with them will always need to be formal when in school.

When communicating with children and young people, we need to be very clear and unambiguous in what we say. They need us to communicate clearly what is expected of them, so that they learn to communicate well themselves. We should try not to use complicated language or long lists of instructions, which make what we are saying more difficult to grasp. Sometimes we forget the importance of making sure that children understand what we mean and might ask them, 'What did I just ask you to do?' when they did not even understand the question or request.

As adults, we need to show children and young people how to get along with one another and communicate effectively. We should also model the kind of behaviour we expect from them. If we are able to show them that we value and respect others, they are much more likely to learn to do the same. Children copy adult behaviour from an early age, whether this is positive or negative, as part of the learning process and because they will always seek adult approval.

Showing respect for others is crucial whether you are communicating with adults or children. You need to acknowledge what others are saying and thank them for their contributions, even if you do not agree with their opinions or ideas.

*Do you always show good manners and respect to others when communicating with them?*

# Examples of communication difficulties that may exist

There may be a number of different reasons that communication difficulties have arisen; they may occur between individuals or groups of people. When working with pupils or in teams with other adults, you may find that areas of difficulty arise from time to time. These may be due to an area of special need or because individuals have different attitudes or beliefs from others in the group.

## Poor communication

Often areas of conflict occur when communication has not been effective. This may be because information has not been passed on or because of a misunderstanding. The best way to resolve areas of poor communication is to discuss them to establish the cause and then find a way forward together. The important thing is not to ignore the problem or talk about it to everyone except the individual or group of people concerned.

## Opposing expectations

Sometimes people do not have the same ideas about the purpose of an activity or meeting, or come with a different idea in mind. You should always clarify exactly what you are there to do and why.

## Cultural differences

It may be that adults and pupils within the school have different cultures and expectations, and therefore communicate in different ways. For example, in some cultures eye contact is not encouraged, which may mean that people do not pick up on as many non-verbal cues.

## Different values and ideas

Different personalities may have very different methods of dealing with different situations. For example, although the school may request that pupils do things in a particular way, parental views may be very different.

## External factors

You may be working with an adult or pupil who has a number of home pressures or other issues which may be affecting the way in which they communicate. As we get to know people, we can identify if they are behaving uncharacteristically and ask if there is anything wrong or whether we can help. When working with external professionals, it is likely that they are under time or other pressures of which you are not aware.

## Individuals with special needs

You will need to show care and sensitivity towards pupils and adults who have communication difficulties (see above), as they may need to take their time and not feel under pressure when they are speaking or signing. People with specific needs may not have many opportunities to speak or may be anxious or nervous, and you will need to adapt the way in which you communicate to their individual needs.

### Lack of confidence

Sometimes adults or children and young people will act in an aggressive way if they are not sure about what they are doing or if they lack confidence. This may come across in a personal way to others, but is more to do with how they perceive themselves and their own abilities. You need to be sensitive to this and to offer them encouragement and support.

### Portfolio activity

Think about ways in which you may need to adapt the way you communicate for different people in school. Make a list of whether they are adults or children and the different things which you need to take into account.

## BEST PRACTICE CHECKLIST:
### Communicating with others

- Make sure you are friendly and approachable – smile!
- Speak clearly and give eye contact to the person with whom you are speaking.
- Ensure you use the correct form of address when speaking to others.
- Use an appropriate method of communication for the other person.
- Use positive body language and gestures.
- Be sympathetic to the needs of others.
- Remember to act as a good role model for pupils.
- Acknowledge the help and support of others as much as you can.
- Do not interrupt or anticipate what others are going to say.

## How to adapt communication to meet different communication needs

You may need to adapt your method of communication in order to meet the needs of the person with whom you are speaking. This will depend on:

- the age and experience of the person with whom you are speaking
- the context of the conversation
- the communication needs of the individual.

As well as thinking about the communication needs of children and young people, it is important that we are sensitive to the needs of other adults, particularly if they have communication difficulties. It is possible that you will adapt the way you communicate with them without realising that you are doing it. We often change the way we react to others depending on the way in which they react to us. For example, if you are speaking to a parent or carer who is hearing impaired, you might make sure that you are facing them and giving eye contact so that they can lip-read. However, if you have contact with adults who have other communication difficulties, you may need to reflect and make sure you adapt your means of communication.

Often, schools will send out or gather information in a particular way – for example, through letters or emails. Depending on their individual needs, the recipients may not be able to access this method of communication easily, and this will not always be apparent. You may need to observe sensitivity, for example, if you need to ask a parent or carer why they have not responded to a note that was sent home.

If you need to communicate with other adults who speak English as an additional language, you may need to have a translator and meet together if information you are communicating to one another is difficult to convey.

### Functional skills

**ICT: Developing, presenting and communicating information**
It is important that the children communicate effectively with others as well as the staff. You could design some posters to be displayed around school that highlight the key points from the checklist above. Remember the age of the children who will be reading the posters.

## DVD activity

**Video clip 2 – Communicating with other adults**

In order to achieve your qualification, you will need to show that you are able to develop and maintain positive relationships both with adults and pupils in the school environment. In this clip, the teaching assistant, Wendy, is seen communicating with parents and teachers in different situations. Some of these are more relaxed than others.

1. What kinds of issues does Wendy have to deal with in this clip?

2. Explain why it can sometimes be difficult to exchange information quickly and efficiently in a school situation. Name some situations which you may have found more challenging to deal with. How have you resolved them?

3. Do you think that Wendy has to show consideration for the needs of the individual or adapt her method of communication when speaking to these parents and teachers? How does she demonstrate positive relationships with them?

4. After you have watched the clip, write a brief outline to show how, as part of your role, you have communicated different kinds of information to adults in your school while following school policy. You can also ask a parent or staff member to write a witness testimony for your portfolio stating how you have shown positive relationships with others over time, giving examples and stating any areas of difficulty which you have overcome.

## How to deal with disagreements between the practitioner and children and young people or other adults

It is likely that at some point in your work you will have disagreements with others. In many cases, disagreements are down to lack of or miscommunication with others – however, they should be managed very carefully so that bad feeling does not persist afterwards. As adults we can sometimes misread or perceive information wrongly and may think that someone has communicated something to us when they have not. We will sometimes blame others for saying things that could be ambiguous or for having a different point of view from ourselves.

Where there are areas of conflict with other adults, you will need to show sensitivity and try to resolve the situation as soon as possible. The longer a problem is allowed to go on, the more difficult it will be to put right. If you need another adult to act as a mediator, you will need to speak to your line manager and explain what has happened. It is impossible to work effectively if you are working in an atmosphere of tension or bad feeling, and it is unlikely that the situation will resolve itself without specific action.

You should not be drawn into a disagreement with a child or young person and you will need to manage this carefully and seek advice if necessary. If a pupil has been defiant or is arguing with you, you should tell them that you are not going to discuss anything with them until you have both taken time out.

**Link**

See also TDA 2.9 Support children and young people's positive behaviour.

## BEST PRACTICE CHECKLIST:
### Coping with and avoiding disagreements

- Ensure you use the correct title or form of address when speaking to other adults.
- Do not make assumptions about others.
- Be as supportive to others as you can.
- Be polite at all times.
- Discuss any areas of disagreement as soon as you can, with a mediator present if appropriate.
- Provide or obtain any vital information promptly.
- Be sympathetic to the needs and situations of others.
- Seek advice from another adult if you cannot reach an agreement.
- Acknowledge the help and support of others as much as you can.

### CASE STUDY: Dealing with disagreements

Duncan is working in Key Stage 3 as a language support assistant. He is based mainly in French classes, but is also asked to work in some Spanish lessons as and when extra support is needed. Although he does not mind this flexibility and enjoys having a varied timetable, he has had some problems this week because his line manager is out of school on a trip and he has not been given the correct timetable. The following week Duncan goes to see his line manager and has some trouble disguising his annoyance.

- Do you think that Duncan should approach this meeting in the way he has?
- What would be the best way of starting his conversation with his line manager?

# Know about current legislation, policies and procedures covering confidentiality and sharing information, including data protection

## Relevant legal requirements and procedures covering confidentiality, data protection and the disclosure of information

Adults who work with children and young people in any setting need to have some idea about current legislation as it will affect their practice. There is an increased awareness of how important it is to recognise the uniqueness of each child and have respect for their human rights. Legislation is an area which is constantly under review and you will need to keep up to date through reading relevant publications.

### Every Child Matters (England 2003) based on Children Act 2004

This Green Paper stresses the importance of more integrated services and sharing of information between professionals. It came into being after the tragic case of Victoria Climbié, when there was no communication between health and social workers.

### Data Protection Act 1998

In schools we ask parents and carers for a variety of information so that we are able to care for children as effectively as we can while they are with us. However, we can only ask for information which is directly relevant, for example, health or medical information, records from previous schools, or records for children who have special educational needs. This is **confidential information** and must only be used for the

### Key term

**Confidential information** — information that should only be shared with people who have a right to have it, for example, the teacher, your line manager or an external agency

purpose for which it was gathered. If the information needs to be passed on to others for any reason, parental consent will need to be given. This usually involves parents signing a consent form.

Under the Data Protection Act 1998, any organisation which holds information on individuals needs to be registered with the Information Commissioner's Office (ICO). This is designed to ensure that confidential information cannot be passed on to others without the individual's consent. There are eight principles of practice which govern the use of personal information. They state that information must:

- be processed fairly and lawfully
- be used only for the purpose for which it was gathered
- be adequate, relevant and not excessive
- be accurate and kept up to date where necessary
- be kept for no longer than necessary
- be processed in line with the individual's rights
- be kept secure
- not be transferred to other countries without adequate protection.

You will need to be aware of a range of information in your role as a teaching assistant, from issues around the school to the individual needs of the children and young people with whom you work. You should know how and when to share any information you have access to. If you are at all concerned or unclear about whom you can speak to, your first point of contact should be your line manager, or in the case of pupils with SEN, the SENCO. Many teaching assistants working in primary schools are also parents of children at the same school, and other parents may

*What damage could gossip cause?*

sometimes put pressure on them to disclose or reveal information. You should not pass on any information about the school or pupils before being certain that this is the correct thing to do. By passing on information without using the correct channels, you will be abusing your position of professional trust and this can be very damaging.

You should also be very careful if taking photographs for displays or if filming children for any purpose; again, parental permission will need to be given for this. You should not take pictures of children for your portfolio.

You should not pass on information to:

- other children in the school
- other parents
- other professionals unless parents have been consulted
- visitors.

## The importance of reassuring children, young people and adults of the confidentiality of shared information and the limits of this

When you are gathering information, whatever this is, you may sometimes be in a position where you need to reassure others about the fact that it is confidential. If you attend meetings or need to be told about confidential items you should make sure that you let others know your obligations. In most cases, parental consent would need to be given before any information about children can be shared with other professionals. However, if there are any issues to indicate that the pupil is at risk from the parents or if there is a legal obligation placed on the school to disclose information, this can be done (see below).

There may also be cases where information on pupils needs to be accessible to all staff, for example, where pupils have specific medical conditions such as asthma or epilepsy. In this case there should be an agreed system within the school for making sure that all staff are aware of these pupils. Some schools may display photographs of them in staff rooms or dining areas, for example, and remove the photographs if the premises are used by others during the evening.

## The kinds of situations when confidentiality protocols must be breached

If you find yourself in a position where someone confides in you, it is important to remember that there are some situations in which you will need to tell others. This is particularly true in cases of suspected child abuse or when a child or young person is at risk. You should at all times tell the individual that you will not be able to maintain confidentiality if they disclose something to you which you cannot keep to yourself for these reasons.

**CASE STUDY:** Breaching confidentiality protocols

Said is working in Year 4 and has good relationships with other adults and children in the school. He is working outside the class one day when Darren, who is in the class, asks if he can speak to him. Darren is clearly upset and says that he really needs to talk to someone in private about something that has happened to him.

- What should Said do first?
- What should Said say to Darren?

## Getting ready for assessment

For this unit you will need to show that you have good relationships with the adults and pupils with whom you work. As well as demonstrating this to your assessor through the interactions you have with them, you can gather evidence for this unit through witness testimonies from adults (on headed paper from their organisation or your school), which verify how you do this. Alternatively, and if it is possible, you should ask the adults with whom you work to speak to your assessor. You may be able to cover a considerable amount of information for your portfolio in this way.

If you have been involved in a situation where communication has broken down, you can tell your assessor about it during a professional discussion and ask them to record what has been said and whether you acted appropriately. The actual incident and individuals involved do not need to be named, so you can avoid writing any sensitive information in your portfolio.

## Check your knowledge

1. Name three ways in which you can interact effectively with children and young people.

2. Why is it important to take into account children and young people's age and stage of development when communicating with them?

3. How might a learning mentor be of support to pupils when managing communication and relationships?

4. Describe how you might deal with a disagreement between two children on the playground.

5. Who are the different adults with whom you might come into contact in school?

6. Explain what is meant by a role model and why it is important.

7. What do you need to remember regarding confidentiality when working with children and young people?

### Websites

**www.mandbf.org.uk** – Mentoring and Befriending Foundation, formerly the National Mentoring Network

# TDA 2.4 Equality, diversity & inclusion in work with children & young people

This unit focuses on the importance of promoting equality and diversity in all aspects of work with children and young people. You will explore how prejudice and discrimination impact on individuals and groups in a school setting and ways that you can support policies and procedures to break down barriers.

## By the end of this unit you will:

1. understand the importance of promoting equality and diversity in work with children and young people
2. understand the impact of prejudice and discrimination on children and young people
3. understand inclusion and inclusive practices in work with children and young people.

# Understand the importance of promoting equality and diversity in work with children and young people

## Identify the current legislation and codes of practice relevant to the promotion of equality and valuing of diversity

Each school must produce a range of policies which formally sets out the guidelines and procedures for ensuring equality. These must take account of the rights of all individuals and groups within the school. When considering the way policies work to ensure equality and inclusion, we often just think of the teaching and learning that is happening in the classroom. Policies must also pay regard to the values and practice which are part of all aspects of school life. Before exploring the policies in your own school, it is helpful to gain an understanding of relevant legislation and its purpose. You do not need detailed knowledge of each one, but it is important to understand the legal duties of the school. This will help you to understand your own role and responsibility to adhere to legislation and policy.

The rights of all children and young people are stated in the United Nation's Convention on the Rights of the Child (1989). The UK government ratified the treaty in 1991 and must ensure that the rights of children in the UK are protected through law. These rights are extensive and include the right to education and the right for children to have their views respected. Table 1 lists relevant legislation, which forms a basis for government **statutory** codes of practice and frameworks and school policies and procedures relating to equal opportunity and inclusive practice.

## Key terms

**Statutory** – required by law

**Special educational needs (SEN)** – children who have learning difficulties or disabilities that make it harder for them to learn or access education than most children of the same age

| Legislation | Purpose |
|---|---|
| Disability Discrimination Act 1995 | Protects the rights of all those with disabilities. It also places a duty on schools (and other organisations) to eliminate barriers to ensure that individuals can gain equal access to services |
| Disability Discrimination Act 2005 | Places a duty for schools to produce a Disability Equality Scheme (DES) and an Access Plan. Schools must encourage participation in all aspects of school life and eliminate harassment and unlawful discrimination |
| **Special Educational Needs** and Disability Act 2001 | Makes it unlawful for educational providers to discriminate against pupils with a special educational need or a disability |
| Race Relations (Amendment) Act 2000 | Outlines the duty of organisations to promote good relationships between people from different races. |
| Human Rights Act 1998 | Sets out rights of all individuals and allows them to take action against authorities when their rights have been affected |
| Children Act 1989 | Sets out the duty of local authorities (including schools) to provide services according to the needs of children and to ensure their safety and welfare |

| Legislation | Purpose |
|---|---|
| Children Act 2004 | Sets out the duty to provide effective and accessible services for all children and underpins the five Every Child Matters outcomes |
| Education Act 1996 | Sets out the school's responsibilities towards children with special educational needs. The Act also requires schools to provide additional resources, equipment and/or additional support to meet their needs |
| Equality Act 2010 | Sets out the legal responsibilities of public bodies, including schools, to provide equality of opportunity for all citizens. This brings together nine equality laws |

Table 1: Legislation relating to the rights of children and young people.

### Functional skills

**ICT: Finding and selecting information**
You could use the Internet to search for further information on any of the above legislation. When doing this, it is important that you consider the relevance of the information that you find.

To support schools in their duty to implement this legislation there are a number of statutory frameworks, codes of practice and guidelines, some of which are listed as follows.

### The Special Educational Needs Code of Practice 2001

This outlines the statutory guidance for policy and the procedures and responsibilities towards children with special educational needs. It includes the levels of support which should be provided to children, depending upon their individual need.

### Code of Practice on the duty to promote race equality (2002)

This is a statutory code which supports public authorities (including schools) to meet their duty set out in the Race Relations (amendment) Act. It requires all schools to produce a written race equality policy which includes information on practical ways in which schools will work to promote race equality. School policies must demonstrate that they are working towards the following outcomes of:

### Link

You will find more detailed information about legislation, policy and strategies for supporting children with special educational needs or disabilities in TDA 2.15 Support children and young people with disabilities and special educational needs.

- reducing the gap of educational achievement between different ethnic groups
- improving relationships between different racial groups
- improving the behaviour of pupils
- promoting greater involvement of parents and the community
- ensuring that staff working in the school reflect cultural diversity of society
- an admissions policy which does not discriminate.

The policy must also include the strategies that will be used to monitor the difference that policy makes to individuals and the school.

## Removing barriers to achievement: the government's strategy for SEN (2004)

This provides a framework for schools to remove barriers and raise achievement of children with special educational needs and disabilities.

The document sets out the government's vision for the education of children with special educational needs (SEN) and/or disabilities. The principles included are the need for:

● early intervention

● the removal of barriers

● raising achievement

● the delivery of improvements through partnerships across services.

## Disability Equality Scheme and Access Plan

The Disability Discrimination Act 2005 builds on the 1995 Act by requiring all schools to produce a Disability Equality Scheme (DES). The DES must set out ways that schools promote equality of opportunity and promote positive attitudes towards pupils, staff and others with disabilities. In addition there must also be an action plan. This plan must identify how discriminatory barriers are removed. For example:

● an improvement to the physical environment, such as ramps, lifts, room layout, lighting

● providing information in different ways for children with a disability, such as audio, pictorial, larger print.

## School policies

Many schools have a mission statement which sets out the commitment of the school toward inclusion and equality of opportunity. You may have read this on your school's website or in correspondence. There must also be written policies, designed to reflect the rights and responsibilities of those within the school environment. Policies should also provide guidance for staff and visitors to the school on ways to ensure inclusive practice.

There may be a number of separate policies or they may be combined. Policies must include ways that schools work in relation to:

● race/cultural diversity

● equality of opportunity/inclusive practice

● safeguarding/bullying

● gifted and talented pupils

● special educational needs

● disability and access.

Policies are developed in response to legislation, codes of practice and statutory frameworks. The different ways in which schools promote the rights and equality of opportunity for children and young people must be included in the policies. There is now a greater focus on the outcomes — that is, the difference that legislation has made to individuals and groups within the school. Schools must monitor the strengths and any weaknesses in policy. During school inspections, Ofsted also make judgements about the school's inclusiveness.

Legislation is frequently amended in response to outcomes, so it is important that you are familiar with up-to-date policies and procedures within your own setting. The development of legislation, policies and practice should be seen as a cycle.

## Portfolio activity

Obtain copies of policies in your own school and identify the ways in which they meet the requirements of the legislation, frameworks and codes of practice identified in this unit.

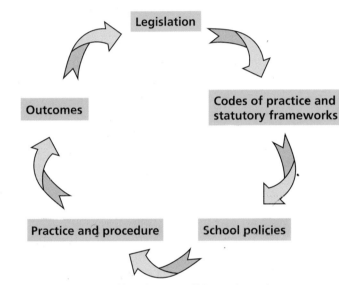

*The cycle of development of legislation, policies and practice.*

# Describe the importance of supporting the rights of all children and young people to participation and equality of access

All pupils have the right to a broad and balanced curriculum. This must also be supported by high-quality teaching and learning experiences. Schools have a duty to ensure that all pupils have equal access to the curriculum irrespective of their background, race, culture, gender, additional need or disability. The references to the curriculum within this chapter include the curriculum in its widest sense. That is, not only the learning happening in the classroom, but everything which happens in the life of the school. To understand the importance of supporting the rights of children and young people, it is helpful to look in more detail at the intended outcomes of legislation, codes of practice and policies. Policies on inclusion and equality of opportunity can only be successful if they help to raise achievement and to promote self-identity and good relationships through the **participation** of all children and young people.

## Key term

**Participation** – asking children and young people what works, what does not work and what could work better, and involving them in the design, delivery and evaluation of services, on an ongoing basis

## Raising achievement

Promoting equality of access to the curriculum will maximise the personal achievement of children and young people. For a number of years, studies have shown that some groups of children do not meet their expected levels of attainment. The groups which have raised particular concern are children from black and minority ethnic groups or children who are vulnerable because of their economic or physical circumstances. This is sometimes referred to as the 'attainment gap'.

Equal opportunity does not mean treating pupils the same, but ensuring that the curriculum meets the individual needs of all pupils. This involves understanding the barriers which exist. Intervention strategies, such as additional support, can then be put into place at an early stage before children fall too far behind. High expectations, of all children, are fundamental to raising achievement.

## Improving participation

Participation involves everyone within the school. There should be opportunities to talk to children and their parents about all aspects of the school and the curriculum. This could include the development and the review of school policies. Participation can be achieved formally through student councils and parents' meetings. It may also take place in the classroom when children and young people can be asked about how they learn best, what works for them and what could be improved.

### Functional skills

**English: Speaking, listening and communication**
This case study provides an excellent opportunity for discussion. Listen carefully to the views of others so that you can respond appropriately. You may have experience of something similar that takes place in your setting; this is a good opportunity to share your views and good practice with others.

### CASE STUDY: Participation

Meadow Hill is a secondary school. One of the teachers was aware that a number of children were complaining that they had nowhere to go at lunchtime. They told her that they would like an area where they could chat to their friends, play games or do homework. The teacher approached the Head, on their behalf, and an area that could be used was identified. It was then decided to set up a working group which represented the diversity of young people within the school.

The group met regularly with the Deputy Head to decide on how the area should be used and the resources and equipment that would be needed. Care was taken with the layout to ensure that there would be easy access and suitable equipment and resources for pupils with disabilities or who had learning needs. At last the area was opened and is now used regularly by all the pupils. It includes an area for children to socialise and also quieter spaces with resources and computer facilities for study.

- What were the advantages of involving children in the design of this area?
- Why is it important to involve a diverse group of children?
- Suggest one way of gaining the views of all children in the school.

### Developing a sense of identity

Schools must recognise and support all pupils' access to everything that is happening in the school. This will promote a sense of belonging and self-esteem. When children and young people are able to participate fully, they feel valued for who they are and the contribution that they make. This can be achieved by acknowledging and reflecting diversity within the school in the methods of teaching and the resources and materials used.

Children and young people must also have the opportunity to become independent learners. When they are able to make choices, and have control of their own learning, children are more likely to be motivated and achieve their full potential. This gives children a feeling of self-worth and well-being. Consider how you would feel about yourself if you had no choice about how to go about a task or if you had to rely on others to help you to carry out simple activities. Think about the children and young people that you work with. Do they have opportunities to:

- discuss and share their own ideas and beliefs?
- take part in after-school activities, join clubs and social events?
- choose ways to study and to present their work?

**Portfolio activity**

Identify a pupil with whom you work closely who has a special educational need or disability. Identify two strategies that you could use to help them to develop their independence and identity.

**Functional skills**

ICT: Developing, presenting and communicating information
When you have completed the task above, you could use PowerPoint® to produce a short presentation to share with your group that shows how you have helped the pupil to develop their independence and identity.

### Improving relationships between individuals and groups

Policies which promote equality and inclusion give out a positive message and encourage an atmosphere of mutual respect. Children must have their rights protected, but should also learn about their responsibilities to others. Respect can be promoted informally through your everyday contact with groups of children and young people. Your own attitudes and actions will provide a model for children, so it is important that you demonstrate consideration and fairness in all your interactions.

Your role may also include more formal pastoral support or helping to deliver curriculum programmes such as Personal, Social, Health and Economic education (PSHE) and Citizenship. These programmes have a particular focus on rights and responsibilities. They prepare children and young people for living and working in a diverse society.

## Describe the importance and benefits of valuing and promoting cultural diversity in work with children and young people

**Culture** can have many different meanings and the way the term is used has changed over time. Culture can cut across nationality and religions. It is what gives groups of people in our society their identity. It also refers to the way groups live, for example, shared customs, thoughts, arts, language and social activity. Recognising and promoting the cultural diversity of individuals and groups within the school will enrich learning and promote the knowledge and understanding of all pupils.

You may work with children whose home language is not English, particularly if you are bilingual yourself. It is important that schools celebrate the bilingual or multilingual skills of pupils. Schools will have a policy in place which states how to ensure inclusive practice, including the additional support for pupils who need to improve their English.

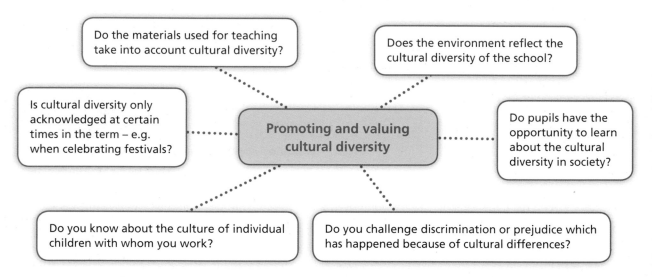

*How well do you manage to promote and value cultural diversity?*

It is important that you understand the cultural diversity of the pupils within the school and particularly those you are supporting. You will then be able to help pupils to make sense of their learning by making connections to their own lives. Your role may include providing pastoral support to individual children. Understanding and taking account of their background and culture is essential for you to build effective relationships and provide support.

The diverse cultures in society should be recognised and reflected throughout the curriculum. For example, incorporating music, foods, stories and drama from a range of cultures will contribute to a rich curriculum. This will demonstrate that you are not only valuing the culture of groups but also supporting all pupils to explore and understand cultures which are different from their own.

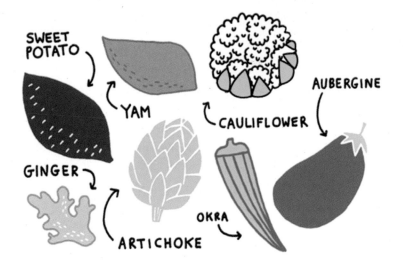

*Can you think of any activities where you could help children to discover a range of vegetables from around the world?*

Where cultural diversity is only acknowledged through posters, or at only particular times of the year through festivals, it could be viewed as **tokenism**. Promoting an understanding of cultural diversity will help to prevent **stereotyping** and reduce prejudice and discrimination.

# Understand the impact of prejudice and discrimination on children and young people

## Describe ways in which children and young people can experience prejudice and discrimination

Everyone working in schools must be aware of ways that children can experience **prejudice** and **discrimination**. Prejudice can occur through lack of knowledge and understanding of diversity. Prejudice is making assumptions about children or young people because they belong to a particular group. For example, a child who has a disability may be assumed to have learning difficulties.

When people demonstrate prejudice, they often go on to label children. A label may be given to an individual or group. It happens when a particular characteristic or label is given because of prejudices. For example, a group of children who receive additional support with reading may be labelled as the 'slow' group. Boys may be expected to be 'noisy' and girls 'quiet'.

Prejudice and labelling can often lead to discrimination. Discrimination happens when children do not receive equality of opportunity. We may all feel that we have been discriminated against at some time in our lives, perhaps because of gender or age.

Some individuals or groups are more likely to experience discrimination. This may happen because of their race, culture, social background, sexual orientation, special educational needs or disability.

## Types of discrimination

Children and young people may experience direct discrimination or indirect discrimination.

### Direct discrimination

This happens when children and young people are not allowed to access part of the curriculum and school activities because of their particular situation such as race, gender or disability. An example is where a school does not accept a pupil because of their special educational need or a group of pupils do not let another pupil join in with them because of their race.

### Indirect discrimination

Staff need to be aware of ways that children and young people experience indirect discrimination. This is often more difficult to spot. Indirect discrimination often occurs when practice and procedures are applied without consideration to individuals' circumstances. A child will not be excluded directly but will be unable to participate because of their personal situation. For example, a school visit to caves where pupils must wear a hard hat will indirectly discriminate against a pupil who wears a turban as part of their religion.

Discrimination can be:

● institutional: this happens when the policies and procedures of an organisation allow practice which directly or indirectly discriminates against someone

● individual: this may be practised by individuals or groups within the school. Individuals could be staff, visitors to the school or other children and young people.

### Over to you!

Research examples of discrimination and identify the type. Is each example institutional or individual? Is the discrimination direct or indirect? Go on to consider the reasons why prejudice or discrimination has happened.

## ✓ Describe the impact of prejudice and discrimination on children and young people

Prejudice and discrimination can only have negative effects on children and young people. As well as affecting academic progress of children, discrimination can negatively impact their overall health and well-being.

When children or young people feel they are being discriminated against they may experience:

- loss of self-esteem
- **disempowerment**
- confusion

- anger
- lack of motivation
- depression.

*How do children feel when they are excluded?*

## ✂ Assess how own attitudes, values and behaviour could impact on work with children and young people

All those working in the school have a legal duty to protect the rights of children and young people. It is important that you examine your own attitudes and values critically, to consider how these may impact on the way you work with children. An individual's background, upbringing and experiences can have an effect on attitudes towards individuals and groups, so it is important to recognise these. Personal prejudices, which may lead to discriminatory practice, can be overcome through developing a greater understanding of diverse groups in society. For example, you can overcome them by finding out about the religious beliefs and cultures of the children you work with, and by knowing about any special educational needs or disabilities.

Do not make assumptions about children and young people. Finding out about their backgrounds, interests, abilities and individual needs will help you to provide more effective, appropriate and personalised support.

## Describe the importance of promoting anti-discriminatory practice in work with children and young people

The promotion of anti-discriminatory practice should underpin all work in schools. It is not sufficient to have policies in place which make statements about anti-discriminatory practice or just to pay lip service to it. Schools must demonstrate anti-discriminatory practice. They must also monitor the ways that positive practice impacts on the education and well-being of the children and young people. As a member of the school team, you share responsibility to ensure that anti-discriminatory practice is promoted. You must also recognise when discrimination is happening.

### Knowledge into action

Research books and reading materials in the class or school library. Do they reflect the range of cultures in society? Are people with disabilities shown in a positive light? Are there examples of females in 'traditional' men's roles and vice versa? Do you ensure that you select and use anti-discriminatory materials with children and young people?

### Key term

**Ethos** — the atmosphere within the school — a positive ethos gives a sense of shared purpose, values and beliefs

### BEST PRACTICE CHECKLIST: Promoting anti-discriminatory practice

- Be a good role model — do not only pay lip service to anti-discriminatory practice, but demonstrate it in everything you do.

- Appreciate and promote diversity and individuality of children and young people by acknowledging their positive attributes and abilities.

- Listen to and involve children and young people in the delivery of services, and respond to their concerns.

- Recognise that the child or young person is at the centre of the learning by treating each one as an individual.

- Have realistic but the highest expectations of all children and young people.

- Support a positive **ethos** within the school.

- Give pupils the confidence and skills to challenge prejudice or racist behaviour of others.

- Recognise and question anti-discriminatory practice.

**Functional skills**

**Mathematics: Analysing**
You could create a tally chart that you can use to log the number of books in your classroom that reflect the range of cultures in society. From this you can then calculate what percentage of books in your room or library promote anti-discriminatory practice.

## Describe how to challenge discrimination

You should always challenge discrimination, but to do this it is essential that you can recognise anti-discriminatory practice. Your role is to protect children from discrimination. If you ignore it when it happens, this will be viewed as condoning (excusing or overlooking) discrimination. Consider how a child may feel if they experience discrimination which is then ignored by a member of staff who is there to support them. The child could feel that you share the view of the perpetrator or believe that the way they are being treated is 'normal'. They may feel that they are in some way inferior. At the very least, they will feel let down that you did not protect their rights.

It can be difficult to challenge discrimination, particularly if it is institutional or practised by a colleague, so it is important that you consider how to deal with different and often difficult situations. To be able to challenge discrimination you require knowledge of policy, procedures and practice. If you feel confident about what is good practice, you will be able to deal more effectively with incidents that arise.

When discrimination happens it may be intentional, but it can also be because of ignorance and lack of understanding. It is not easy to change the views of others but you must challenge discriminatory comments and actions. It is important to learn assertiveness strategies that can help when you recognise discrimination. When challenging discrimination, you should:

1.  explain what has happened or what has been said that is discriminatory

2.  state the effect of this on the individual, group and others

3.  suggest or model ways to ensure anti-discriminatory practice.

When you are concerned about anti-discriminatory practice, whether by staff or pupils in the school, you should speak to your manager or supervisor at the school or college tutor. You must also be aware of the school's policy when racism is happening. The code of practice to promote race equality includes the duty of the school to monitor and report to the local education authority (LEA) on all racist incidents.

## Portfolio activity

Consider the discriminatory practice in the following scenario. Imagine you are present during each event and suggest:

1. why the practice is discriminatory

2. what you would say and do.

### Scenario 1

When assigning responsibilities for the end-of-term production at a secondary school, the teacher assigns the role of making scenery to the boys and the role of producing costumes to the girls.

### Scenario 2

You are in the playground and notice a group of children playing football when they are approached by a boy who has just arrived in the UK from eastern Europe. He asks to play but is told to 'go away' and that he 'shouldn't be at the school'.

### Scenario 3

You attend a meeting to discuss a forthcoming school visit. One member of staff suggests a local wildlife centre. You know the centre well and know that access for those with disabilities is very difficult. It is positioned on a hill and there are a lot of steps. When you mention that it would prevent a pupil who uses a wheelchair from taking part, another member of staff replies that the pupil could stay behind and work with another class.

# Understand inclusion and inclusive practices in work with children and young people

## Describe what is meant by inclusion and inclusive practices

Inclusive practice is a process of identifying, understanding and breaking down barriers to participation and belonging. Inclusion is about ensuring that children and young people, whatever their background or situation, are able to participate fully in all aspects of the life of the school. Inclusive practices will ensure that everyone feels valued and has a sense of belonging. Inclusion is not about viewing everyone as the same or providing the same work, but about providing the same opportunities and access to a high quality of education. In an inclusive environment there is recognition, acceptance and celebration of differences and similarities.

The Special Educational Needs and Disability Act 2001, and statutory guidance in the Special Educational Needs Code of Practice 2001, mean that the majority of children with special educational needs and disabilities are now educated in mainstream schools. This does not exclude children from attending specialist educational setting if that is more appropriate and will provide for pupils with more complex needs.

To understand the issue of inclusive practice for children and young people, it is helpful to understand the medical and social model of disability.

### The medical model of disability

The medical model is based on an assumption that the child must adapt to the environment which exists. This model promotes an atmosphere of 'dependence'.

### The social model of disability

The social model starts with the assumption that the way a school operates, the barriers present and different attitudes can prevent individuals from participating in society. This view of disability works to **empower** children and young people. Inclusive practice is based upon the social model of disability. Legislation requires schools to make 'reasonable adjustments' and remove barriers so that children and young people can take part in educational and social activities within the school alongside other pupils. Pupils with additional needs often require the additional support of a teaching assistant or school support worker, but inclusion for pupils is not only about providing additional support. Adjustments may relate to:

- the physical environment, such as providing lifts, ramps, rails and furniture at the correct height for children with a physical disability, or improved lighting for children with a visual impairment

- providing information, such as worksheet and books with larger print, audio tapes, symbols or alternative forms of communication

- the curriculum, such as groupings, timetabling, additional support, technology (touch-screen computers, trackerballs, text to speech software) or adjustments to assessment (extra time, using different methods to capture evidence).

**Key term**

Empower – enabling the child or young person to make own choices – the opposite of dependency

*How well does your school demonstrate inclusive practice?*

Inclusive practice is not only about the way schools provide for the needs of children with special educational needs and disabilities. Inclusion policies must take account of the needs of all the pupils in the school.

## Describe features of an inclusive setting for children and young people

People often talk about the ethos of a school. It is difficult to sum up what this means. It is something which is often apparent when you enter the school building. There is a feeling that everyone in the school matters and all play their part. Children and young people look purposeful; they approach staff with confidence. The surroundings reflect the diversity of all those within the school. There is a 'buzz' of purposeful activity. Do you remember the feeling you got when you entered the school where you work for the first time? What was it about the atmosphere which made you feel welcome and want to become part of the staff?

An inclusive setting is one which uses a whole-school approach to learning. Barriers are recognised and strategies used to remove them. Where children experience difficulties such as special educational needs or disabilities, there is an approach which focuses on what the child or young person *can* do rather than the difficulties they are experiencing.

### Portfolio activity

Try to look at the school where you work as if through the eyes of a new pupil.

- What is welcoming about the environment?

- What would make you feel that you would be valued for who you are?

Make suggestions for further improvements.

### Key term

**Differentiation** – describes how teachers adjust the learning activities or expected outcomes according to pupils' individual learning needs

### Functional skills

**English: Writing**
Write a reflective account of your support for a group of children involved in a learning activity. Choose an example where you demonstrated inclusive practice and used **differentiation** according to their individual needs. When writing your account, take care with your spelling and make sure that you proofread your work to check that it makes sense.

A school setting which is 'inclusive' will have the following features.

- Barriers are recognised and staff have a good understanding of individuals and groups of children so that they are aware of any difficulties the children may have in accessing the curriculum.

- Barriers are then removed or minimised – the environment is adapted, and personalised support, resources or equipment are provided.

- Pupils are educated alongside their peers and not segregated when they need support. For example, a pupil with English as an additional language will receive language support in the classroom.

- Children and young people are given and use their 'voice' – that is, their own views and opinions are listened to and valued. This may be informal or through a school council or form representatives.

- There are clear policies and procedures and these are reviewed regularly.

● All staff receive regular training relating to inclusion, diversity and equality of opportunity.

● The school works in partnership with stakeholders — staff, governors, parents and children and young people.

● The school works in partnership with other services, for example, speech and language therapists or educational psychologists, to ensure that children and young people receive appropriate professional support.

---

**CASE STUDY: Inclusive practice**

Sean has just qualified as a teaching assistant and has started his new post at a large primary school. It is his first week and so that he gets to know the school, staff and children, he has been asked to work alongside Kira, an experienced teaching assistant who has been at the school for a number of years. Sean joined Kira who was working with a group of 7-year-old children making 3D models. Sean noticed one of the children, Jamie, sitting at the side just watching and asked where his model was. Kira's reply was that because of his disability (cerebral palsy), Jamie had difficulty in using the tools and materials. She said that she asks him to read a book during the art and craft lesson.

• Suggest how Jamie might feel.
• What message does this give to other children in the group?
• Which policies, codes and legislation could Sean refer to when challenging the exclusive practice with Kira?
• Sean will support this group in future weeks. How can he ensure that Jamie is included?

---

## Describe how inclusion works in own sector of the children's workforce

Professionals who work across all children's services must share a common understanding of values and principles of inclusion. The ways in which the values and principles are put into practice may vary depending on the type of organisation and its role in the education and care of children and young people. Whatever the organisation, the child should always be at the centre of all practice.

The Early Years Foundation Stage (EYFS) and the National Curriculum give clear guidance on an inclusive approach to learning and assessment. You will explore the content of each curriculum in other units, but what is important here is to consider how the content is delivered.

The EYFS provides a statement on the duty of settings to meet the needs of all children in relation to their learning, development and personal welfare. This reads: 'Providers have a responsibility to promote positive attitudes to diversity and difference [...] so that every child is included and not disadvantaged.'

According to the National Curriculum Inclusion Statement, schools must implement a whole-school approach to both the national and wider curriculum. Schools must:

● provide a curriculum which ensures active participation and achievement of all pupils

● recognise pupils' entitlement to high-quality learning experiences

● meet the needs and interests of all pupils

● recognise and overcome potential barriers to learning and assessment.

## Personalised learning

In a move to raise standards, schools have adopted a system of personalised learning. This may appear on the surface to be exclusive as it focuses on the needs of individual children and young people. In practice, personalised learning ensures that all children, regardless of their background, special educational needs, disability or culture, receive the support they need to make progress. This works to narrow the gap of educational achievement.

Where personalised learning is successful, children and young people experience:

● a challenging curriculum

● staff who have high expectations

● personal targets

● more focused assessment

● early identification and intervention when targets are not achieved.

*How do you ensure that all the pupils are included?*

## Promoting well-being through an inclusive curriculum

The key role of the school is to provide a good-quality education through an inclusive curriculum, but the school also has a wider role to consider in ensuring the well-being of children. Programmes such as citizenship and personal, social and health education help to build relationships and also prepare children for living and working in the wider society.

## Every Child Matters

The Every Child Matters outcomes were introduced in 2003 in response to the inquiry following the death of Victoria Climbié. The inquiry highlighted the need for services, including schools, to work more closely to protect and support the needs and rights of all children. Schools and other childcare services must demonstrate ways that they work toward each of the five outcomes:

● be healthy

● stay safe

● enjoy and achieve

● make a positive contribution

● achieve economic well-being.

Schools may need to work with specialist services, such as physiotherapy or speech therapy, so that children are able to reach their full potential.

### Reflect

Consider ways that you are able to contribute towards an inclusive environment. How do you build good relationships with children and young people? Do you know about the interests and experiences of children you work with? Having this knowledge and understanding of the children with whom you work will help them to feel valued, develop a sense of belonging and be able to discuss any concerns they may have.

### BEST PRACTICE CHECKLIST: Contributing to an inclusive environment

- Know the individual needs of children and any potential barriers to their learning

- Listen to children and involve them in their own learning.

- Know the background and interests of individual children, and draw on these when supporting their learning.

- Include materials and resources in your work with children which reflect diversity in society.

- Find out about the individual targets of the children with whom you work.

- Use different strategies to support children with their learning.

- Have high expectations of all children.

- Report any concerns that you have about children's progress and/or well-being.

## Getting ready for assessment

You will need to demonstrate an understanding of legislation and codes of practice in relation to equality, diversity and inclusion, and how these are translated into practice within the school setting.

- Write a brief summary of relevant legislation.

- Obtain policies and procedures from the school which relate to equality, diversity and inclusion.

- Discuss these procedures with your supervisor or manager to find how equality of opportunity and inclusion work in practice within the school.

- Find out about adjustments made within the school to include children who have a disability.

- Observe practice within the school and note down examples of anti-discriminatory practice and inclusion.

- Identify ways that you can include materials or resources which reflect cultural diversity in your work with children and young people — for example, a book, art work or music.

## Check your knowledge

1. Name legislation and statutory guidelines which work to protect children and young people from racism.

2. Identify the diverse groups within your school.

3. Give an example of tokenism.

4. What is culture?

5. What must schools do to meet the requirements of the Code of Practice on the duty to promote race equality (2002)?

6. Give one example of direct discrimination and one of indirect discrimination.

7. What is meant by the social model of disability?

8. What are the key features of personalised learning?

### References and further reading

- National Curriculum Inclusion Statement
- Statutory Framework for the Early Years Foundation Stage
- Special Educational Needs Code of Practice

**Websites**

**www.bbc.uk/religion** – information about different religions
**www.equalityhumanrights.com** – Equality and Human Rights Commission
**www.everychildmatters.gov.uk** – Every Child Matters
**www.inclusion.ngfl.gov.uk** – information on supporting individual learning needs
**www.teachernet.gov.uk** – resources for teaching and learning
**www.unicef.org.uk** – UNICEF promotes the rights of all children

# TDA 2.5 Schools as organisations

For this unit you will need to know and understand the structure of schools and how they work, both from your work within the school and also how they fit in at a local and national level.

## By the end of this unit you will:

1. know the different types of schools in the education sector
2. know how schools are organised in terms of roles and responsibilities
3. understand how schools uphold their aims and values
4. know about the laws and codes of practice that affect work in schools
5. know about the range and purpose of school policies and procedures
6. know about the wider context in which schools operate.

71

# Know the different types of schools in the education sector

## Identify the main types of state and independent schools, and describe their characteristics in relation to educational stage(s) and school governance

There are four main types of mainstream state schools which will all be funded by local authorities; these are known as maintained schools. They will all have to follow the National Curriculum. These are as follows.

### Community schools

These are run and owned by the local authority (Education and Library Board in Northern Ireland) which will also support the school through looking to make links with the local community, and by providing support services. They will also usually determine the admissions policy. They may develop the use of the school facilities by local groups such as adult education or childcare classes.

### Foundation and trust schools

Foundation schools are run by their own governing body which determines the admissions policy in consultation with the local education authority. The school, land and buildings will also be owned by the governing body or a charitable foundation. A trust school, although a type of foundation school, will form a charitable trust with an outside partner such as a business. The school will have to buy in any support services. The decision to become a trust school will be made by the governing body in consultation with parents.

### Voluntary schools

These come under two types – voluntary aided and voluntary controlled.

● Voluntary-aided schools will mainly be religious or faith schools, although they can be attended by those of any religion. They are run by their own governing body in the same way as a foundation school, although the land and buildings are normally owned by a religious organisation or charity. They are funded partly by the governing body, partly by the charity and partly by the local education authority which also provides support services.

● Voluntary-controlled schools are similar types of schools to voluntary-aided schools, although they are run and funded by the local authority, which also employs the staff and provides support services. The land and buildings are usually owned by a charity, which is often a religious organisation.

## Specialist schools

These are usually secondary schools which can apply for specialist status to develop one or two subject specialisms. They will receive additional government funding for doing this. Around 92 per cent of secondary schools in England have specialist status (source: TeacherNet, April 2009).

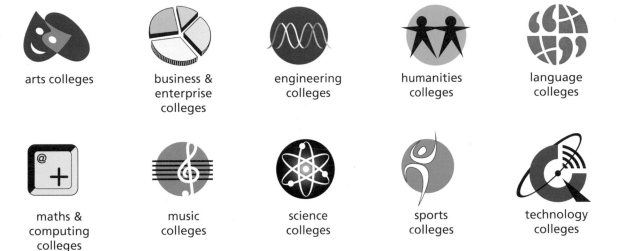

| | | | | |
|---|---|---|---|---|
| arts colleges | business & enterprise colleges | engineering colleges | humanities colleges | language colleges |
| maths & computing colleges | music colleges | science colleges | sports colleges | technology colleges |

*A range of logos from specialist schools (source: Standards site – specialist schools).*

Special schools can also apply for specialist school status to be given for a special educational needs (SEN) specialism under one of the four areas of the **SEN Code of Practice**.

There are also other types of schools which are not funded directly by the local education authority (Education and Library Board in Northern Ireland).

## Independent schools

Independent schools are set apart from the local education authority, since they are funded by fees paid by parents and also income from investments, gifts and charitable endowments. Just over half of independent schools therefore have charitable status, which means that they can claim tax exemption. They do not have to follow the National Curriculum and the Head Teacher and governors decide on the admissions policy. There are approximately 2,300 independent schools in England, which are obliged to register with the Department for Education (DfE) so that they can be monitored on a regular basis, although this may not be by Ofsted but the Independent Schools Inspectorate (ISI).

## Academies

These are set up by sponsors from business and are independently managed schools which jointly fund the land and buildings. They have close links with the local education authority even though they are not maintained by it.

# Know how schools are organised in terms of roles and responsibilities

## Describe roles and responsibilities of members of the school team

### School governors

These are usually a team of 10 to 12 people, although there can be up to 20, who have the responsibility of running the school. They will be made up of a variety of different people who will have links with the school and local community. There should be at least one parent governor and at least one staff governor in addition to the Head Teacher. There may also be a support staff governor. In addition there will be a local authority (LA) governor, appointed by the LA, and a local community governor who will usually work or live in the community served by the school. Governors will work closely with the Head Teacher and Senior Management Team, although you may not see them around the school often during the school day. Governors will be based on different committees which are responsible for various areas of school management – for example, the school site, personnel issues or **community cohesion**. They will meet in these committees and then report back to the full governing body. Their main duties are:

- to set aims and objectives for the school

- to adopt new policies for achieving the aims and objectives

- to set targets for achieving the aims and objectives.

You can find more information on school governorship and governor responsibilities at www.governornet.co.uk

### Senior Management Team

The school's Senior Management or Senior Leadership Team will work closely with the Head Teacher. The team will usually be made up of more experienced staff who have management positions – in a primary school this will probably be the Deputy Head Teacher, year group leaders (if the school has more than one form entry), SENCO (Special Educational Needs Coordinator) and Foundation Stage leader. In a secondary school they may also be year group leaders and SENCOs, but may also be subject area leaders. They will usually meet once a

### Key term

Community cohesion – the togetherness and bonding shown by members of a community, the 'glue' that holds a community together

week or on a regular basis to discuss issues which have come up and to make decisions concerning the running of the school or around the implementation of the **school improvement plan**. They will then discuss how this information will be spread to teachers and support staff.

### Other statutory roles

There will be other staff roles in school which are legally required to be fulfilled in terms of staffing. Apart from the head teacher and deputy, the two main others are SENCOs and, in primary schools, the Foundation Stage manager.

The SENCO is responsible for managing and monitoring the provision for those with special educational needs within the school. They will need to:

● 'ensure liaison with parents and other professionals in respect of children with special educational needs

● advise and support other practitioners in the setting

● ensure that appropriate **Individual Education Plans** are in place

● ensure that relevant background information about individual children with special educational needs is collected, recorded and updated.'

*SEN Code of Practice 2001: 4.15*

The SENCO will also need to monitor and review the provision for pupils with special educational needs and make sure that the paperwork is in place for those who are on Early Years or School Action and Action Plus.

### Foundation Stage Manager

This person must ensure that the Early Years Foundation Stage (that is, Reception and any Nursery classes) is being run according to the statutory requirements of the Early Years Foundation Stage document. They will be responsible for making sure that observations, assessments and record keeping are up to date, as well as ensuring that all staff in the Foundation Stage are trained in its implementation.

### Teachers

All teachers have the responsibility for the planning and preparation of the curriculum for pupils in their class. In a primary school, this will usually be for all subjects under the National Curriculum. As well as being responsible for their own class, teachers will generally also have another area of responsibility in school. This may be as a member of the Senior Management Team, but in a primary school it could also be a subject area. In all schools each subject will need to be represented so that there is a person responsible for it; this means that in a smaller school with fewer teachers, staff may each be responsible for two or three subjects. They will be expected to know about any curriculum developments in their area and to feed back to all staff through staff meetings. They should also be available to advise and support other teachers in their subject, and monitor teaching. The local authority will also arrange subject leader forums which they will be expected to attend.

---

| Role of teacher | Role of teaching assistant |
|---|---|
| • To be responsible for planning and preparing to the National or Early Years Curriculum<br>• To teach pupils according to their educational needs<br>• To assess, record and report on the development, progress and attainment of pupils<br>• To take responsibility for all other adults within the learning environment<br>• To communicate and consult with the parents of pupils<br>• To communicate and co-operate with persons or bodies outside the school<br>• To participate in meetings arranged for any of the above purposes<br>• Usually to be responsible for managing an area of the curriculum, such as Geography, as included in the job description | • To plan and prepare work alongside the teacher<br>• To support learning activities effectively as directed by the teacher<br>• To assess/evaluate pupils' work as directed by the teacher<br>• To report any problems or queries to the teacher<br>• To give feedback to the teacher following planned activities |

*Table 1: Some of the duties around planning and implementing learning activities of the teacher and teaching assistant.*

*What are the different areas of responsibilities of teachers and teaching assistants?*

## Support staff roles

The number of support staff in schools has risen dramatically in recent years. Teaching assistants in England have risen from around 44,500 in 2000 to 130,900 in 2009 (and was predicted to rise again to 140,500 in 2010) (source: DfE). This has been due to an increase in government funding which was based on the reduction of responsibilities on class teachers and a gradual increase in initiatives to raise pupil progress, many of which have been carried out by teaching assistants.

Types of support staff may be:

● breakfast, after-school or extended school staff

● midday supervisors and catering staff

- office or administrative staff
- caretakers or site managers
- teaching assistants and HLTAs
- individual support assistants for SEN children
- specialist or technicians (for example, in ICT)
- learning mentors and parent support workers.

The roles of each of these members of staff may be different and their job descriptions should reflect this.

### Functional skills

**ICT: Developing, presenting and communicating information**
Once you have completed the portfolio activity, you could also create a table of the roles and responsibilities of every member of your school or department.

## Describe the roles of external professionals who may work with a school

There will be a huge range of external professionals who may work with a school on a regular basis. If you are working with an individual pupil and collaborate with your school's SENCO, you are more likely to come into contact with different agencies or individuals. Even if you do not, you still need to be aware of the variety of people who may come into school to work with the head teacher and other staff. These include the following.

*Which of these external professionals are you already familiar with?*

### Educational psychologist

The school should have an educational psychologist allocated to them through the local Special Educational Needs department. They will support the SENCO in providing assessments and observations to pupils who have come into school each year and plan the provision for pupils who have additional needs. They may also lead meetings with parents and write reports giving recommendations for work with individual pupils.

## Speech and language therapist

Speech and language therapists (SLTs) will work with pupils on speech, language and communication problems, both in producing and understanding language. There should be a number of speech and language therapists working in your local area who have links with the school and in some cases are based there. However, most speech and language therapists will work from an alternative location and will come into school to work with children, parents and teachers.

## Specialist teachers

Specialist teachers may come into school to offer advice and support to pupils with a range of needs. These may be:

- behaviour support needs

- social and communication needs such as autism

- English as an Additional Language needs.

## Education Welfare Officer

The Education Welfare Officer (EWO) will usually be based within local authorities and will visit schools and work with the Head Teacher to monitor pupil attendance and to provide support where there are issues around absenteeism. They will also work alongside parents to support excluded pupils on their return to school.

## School Improvement Partner

The School Improvement Partner (SIP) will come into school to advise and support the Head Teacher for three to five days each year. They will have previous experience of school leadership and/or have worked in a senior advisory role in a local authority. They work alongside the local education authority and will support the Head Teacher in looking at ways of developing the school both through the **school self-evaluation** and pupil progress and attainment. This means focusing not only on academic factors but through looking at **extended school provision** and liaison with parents.

## Physiotherapists/occupational therapists

These healthcare professionals may work with pupils outside school but may also be asked to come in for meetings and discussions to support pupil progress.

You will also find that other teachers may visit your school for various meetings such as 'cluster groups'. These are designed to encourage teachers who have similar roles in schools in the local area to meet up and discuss their practice and ideas. This can be very useful, for example, if you are working in a one-form entry primary school and are the only teacher in your school who has expertise in the Foundation Stage.

### Key terms

**School self-evaluation** — document which looks at and evaluates the school's progress

**Extended school provision** — extra out-of-school activities, such as breakfast and after-school clubs

# Understand how schools uphold their aims and values

You will need to understand the following terms as you will see them regularly on school literature and may be asked to define them for your own school. It is likely that your school prospectus or mission statement will outline them with regard to your particular workplace.

## Defining the meaning of aims and values

**Aims** — it is likely that the school's aims or vision will be in the prospectus and in other school literature. They will usually be set by the head teacher in collaboration with parents, staff and the community, and will state what the school sets out to achieve.

## Aims and Objectives

- To provide a caring atmosphere in which our children can develop their skills and abilities in all curriculum areas and fulfil their potential.

- To ensure that staff and children will be able to participate in every aspect of school life, within the school community, whatever their needs or abilities.

- To foster an environment in which children and staff have high self-esteem and the confidence to achieve the highest standards.

- To harness our children's natural curiosity, encouraging a lifelong thirst for learning.

- To stimulate our children to develop enquiring minds and the confidence to pose questions and discuss ideas rationally.

- To help our children to understand that learning is an exciting challenge, part of which is taking risks and learning from mistakes.

- To encourage our children to take a pride in their achievements and appreciate the value of hard work.

- To promote an understanding of and care for the environment both within the school and the outside world.

- To encourage children and staff to have the confidence to grasp opportunities afforded by new technologies.

- To encourage parents to become partners in their child's education and support the school's focus on expected standards of behaviour.

- To enrich our children's knowledge and understanding of the diversity of the world we live in and develop a respect for other cultures, races and religions.

*Your school should outline its aims so that these are clear to all (source: Unicorn Primary School prospectus).*

**Values** – the values of the school are based on the moral code which will inform its development. Core values are at the heart of many communities and belief systems. Although there may be some differences in the way in which people view them, they will usually include respect for self and others and are related closely to Personal, Social, Health and Economic education (PSHE) and citizenship education. They may also be tied in with the school rules. If the school is a church school, this will also be closely linked in with its values.

## Describe with examples how schools may demonstrate and uphold their aims and values

The school's aims and values need to be communicated as much as possible in school literature and on its website as well as in school. This is because these sources are where parents and others gain their first impressions of the school. The school can also demonstrate their aims and values by developing links with the local community and by working together for the benefit of pupils. You will need to make sure that you have considered how schools, in particular your own, communicate their aims and values and whether they do this successfully. Examples of the kinds of links which a school may have could be through:

- pupil fundraising activities for local charities
- developing links with businesses and encouraging visitors from the community
- career information days
- the work of school governors
- encouraging visits and support from parents
- visitors from local churches or other places of worship
- events such as school fairs, which may involve the local community.

Schools cannot work in isolation. It is important that they are able to forge links with the community and to demonstrate to pupils how their learning is relevant to the outside world.

# Know about the laws and codes of practice that affect work in schools

## Identify the laws and codes of practice affecting work in schools and describe how these promote pupil well-being and achievement

Schools, like any other organisation, are obliged to operate under current laws and legislation. Although you may not need to know about these in depth, it is helpful to have some idea about why schools will need to work in a particular way, or why they have to draw up particular policies or documents. The majority of laws and codes of practice which are required in schools are directly linked to the well-being and achievement of pupils, as can be seen from their content. Here is a summary of some of the key pieces of legislation of which you should be aware.

### The UN Convention on the Rights of the Child 1989

The UNCRC was drawn up in 1989 and ratified by the UK in 1991. There are 54 articles included; those which relate directly to schools are as follows.

● Article 2 – children have a right to protection from any form of discrimination.

● Article 3 – the best interests of the child are the primary consideration.

● Article 12 – children are entitled to express their views, which should be given consideration in keeping with the child's age and maturity.

● Article 13 – children have a right to receive and share information as long as that information is not damaging to others.

● Article 14 – children have a right to freedom of religion although they should also be free to examine their beliefs.

● Article 28 – all children have an equal right to education.

● Article 29 – children's education should develop each child's personality, talents and abilities to the fullest. They should also learn to live peacefully and respect the environment and other people.

For more information, see www.unicef.org.uk/crc

### The Education Act 2002

There have been a number of educational Acts and these will continue to be updated with each corresponding year. The 2002 Act brought in several changes to school regulations, staffing and governance, and was further amended in 2006 to include a duty of schools to promote community cohesion. This means that schools are required to work alongside other community-based organisations and to develop links and a shared 'sense of belonging' while valuing the contributions of 'different individuals and different communities'. For more information, see www.teachingcitizenship.org.uk/dnloads/comm_cohesion_doc.pdf

## Children Act 2004 and 2006

The 2004 Act came in alongside the Every Child Matters framework and had a huge impact on the way in which schools address issues of care, welfare and discipline. It took its root from the Victoria Climbié inquiry. Under the joint requirements, agencies such as Social Services and the Department for Education work together to take on more responsibility for pupil welfare. There are five basic outcomes for children and young people under Every Child Matters, as Table 2 shows, which have been built on by the 2007 Children's Plan.

| Outcome | Description |
|---------|-------------|
| Be healthy | Children should be physically, mentally, emotionally and sexually healthy. They should have healthy lifestyles and be able to choose not to take illegal drugs. |
| Stay safe | Children should be safe from neglect, violence, maltreatment, bullying and discrimination. They should be cared for and have security and stability. |
| Enjoy and achieve | Children should be ready for, attend and enjoy school. They should achieve national educational standards at both primary and secondary school. They should be able to achieve personal and social development, and enjoy recreation. |
| Make a positive contribution | Children should engage in decision making and support the local community. They should show positive behaviour in and out of school. Children should be encouraged to develop self-confidence and to deal with significant life changes and challenges. |
| Achieve economic well-being | Children should engage in further education, employment or training on leaving school. They should be able to live in decent homes with access to transport and material goods. They should be free from low income. |

*Table 2: The five outcomes under Every Child Matters.*
*Every Child Matters: Change for Children – DfES-1109–2004*

The Act was also amended in 2006 to place more responsibility on local authorities to:

- improve well-being for young children, and reduce inequalities
- ensure that there is sufficient childcare to enable parents to work
- provide information to parents about childcare
- ensure that local childcare providers are trained
- introduce the Early Years Foundation Stage for the under-5s
- reform of the regulation system for childcare, with two new registers of childcare providers, to be run by Ofsted.

Your work will have been affected directly by the Children Act and you should have had some training or guidance in its implementation. One of its main outcomes for schools is that there is more joined-up work between schools and other agencies for the best interests of children. There have also been many more breakfast and after-school clubs through the introduction of extended schools.

### The Freedom of Information Act 2000

This Act was introduced in January 2005 to promote transparency and accountability in the public sector and is fully retrospective. This means that information can be sought from any time in the past. Any person may request information held by a school, although this must be done in writing. Schools have a duty to provide advice and assistance to anyone who requests information; however, there are some cases in which schools will need to protect information which may be confidential. The Department for Education (DfE) has produced guidance for schools and governing bodies to give advice when dealing with requests for information if and when these are made. For more information, visit www.teachernet.gov.uk and search for 'freedom of information for schools'.

### The Human Rights Act 1998

There are a number of equality laws which may affect schools. These are designed to ensure that inequalities do not exist and that all children will have the same entitlements to education. The Human Rights Act 1998 is linked to the 1950 European Convention on Human Rights. This came in after the end of the Second World War, and although it was a binding international agreement, it was not law. Under the Human Rights Act, individuals in the UK have particular rights and freedoms, but these must be balanced against the rights and freedoms of others. A key provision of the Act is that 'It is unlawful for a public authority to act in a way which is incompatible with a Convention right.'

Some of the articles which have a direct link to school provision are:

● Article 2 – the right to education (although this does not mean the right to go to a particular school)

● Article 8 – the right to respect for private and family life

● Article 10 – the right to freedom of expression.

Restraint of pupils is permitted under the Act, to protect the rights of others or to prevent crime or injury. However, your school or local authority should have a policy on this and you should read it so that you are aware of guidelines for its use. There is a guidance leaflet for schools setting out their responsibilities under the Act: http://nihrc.org/dms/data/NIHRC/attachments/dd/files/42/HRAguide_schools.pdf

### The Special Educational Needs (SEN) Code of Practice 2001 and the Disability Discrimination Act 1995/2005

Under the SEN Code of Practice, parents and SEN children have an increased right to a mainstream education. This has had an impact on the number of children who have special educational needs being included in mainstream schools and also on the number of individual support assistants who support them. It has also had training implications, as in order to support inclusion, schools have been increasingly managing pupils with a more diverse range of needs. However, it has also meant that more children are integrated into mainstream schools, which has had a positive effect on all pupils.

*What are the implications of the SEN Code of Practice?*

The Disability Discrimination Act and subsequent legislation regarding access for all has meant that all schools built from this date have had to make provision for pupils with disabilities. For example, they need to have ramps, lifts and disabled toilets. Existing schools built before this date do not need to do this unless they have modifications to existing buildings, for example, extensions or new blocks. The Act also means that pupils should not be excluded from any aspect of school life due to disabilities, for example, school trips or other outside provision.

### The Data Protection Act 1998

This Act means that schools need to keep and use information only for the purpose for which it was intended. The information also needs to be kept securely on site, either locked in filing cabinets or on password-protected computers. If you are asked to update any pupil information, you should do this while you are on school premises and not take any information off site. You should consider all information about pupils as **confidential** and ensure that you do not share it with others without parental consent. When discussing pupils with others, for example, if you are working as an individual support assistant, you should take care to ensure that you only share necessary information. Adults working with a particular pupil will need to receive information, while those who are merely curious do not!

Legislation will affect how schools work as they will need to comply fully with all legal requirements. It will also affect your work with children, although this may seem to happen indirectly. As laws and codes of practice affecting work in schools change regularly, it is not possible to list them all here. However, you should know that schools may need to seek advice and guidance if and when needed. This will often be through the governing body.

> **Key term**
>
> **Confidential** – information that should be provided only to those who are authorised to have it

# Know about the range and purpose of school policies and procedures

## Describe why schools have policies and procedures

All schools, as with other organisations, are required to have a range of policies and procedures. This is a legal requirement so that all schools meet current legislation and so that parents, staff, governors and others who are involved in the running of the school are able to work from a clear set of guidelines and review and update them regularly. There are likely to be a large number of policies and you should know where to find them in your school so that you are able to find and use them as and when necessary. Although each school will have a slightly different list or they may have different names, each will need to outline its purpose and aims and the responsibilities of staff.

## Identify the policies and procedures schools may have

Schools may have polices and procedures relating to:

- staff
- pupil welfare
- teaching and learning

| Area | Policies |
|------|----------|
| Staff | • Pay policy<br>• Performance management policy<br>• Grievance policy |
| Pupil welfare | • Child protection policy<br>• Health and safety policy<br>• Drugs awareness policy<br>• Behaviour management policy<br>• Personal, social and health education policy<br>• Anti-bullying policy<br>• Attendance policy |
| Teaching and learning | • Curriculum policies (a policy for each subject, such as history, maths, art)<br>• Early years policy<br>• Teaching and learning policy<br>• Special educational needs policy<br>• Planning and assessment policy<br>• Homework policy<br>• Marking policy |

*Table 3: Policies and procedures relating to different aspects of a school's running.*

## Responsibilities

Final responsibility for health and safety within the school lies with the Head Teacher.

The Site Manager (or in her absence the Head Teacher) is responsible for the following areas:

- Admin. areas
- Boiler room
- Classrooms
- Corridors, foyers
- ICT suite
- Kitchen and servery

- Libraries
- Hall
- Deputy Head's room
- Shared learning areas
- Playground and garden areas
- Toilets

It is the duty of every member of staff, both teaching and non-teaching, to report any unsafe conditions to the Head Teacher, Site Manager or the Administrative Officer in their absence. In addition, an attempt should be made to eliminate the danger before reporting it, without causing undue risk to self.

All employees have the responsibility of co-operating with the Head Teacher to achieve a healthy and safe workplace, and to take reasonable care of themselves, pupils and others. Health and Safety issues will be raised as a regular agenda item at the staff briefing meetings, which are held each Friday afternoon.

## Review of Training Needs

The Head Teacher is responsible for keeping under constant review the safety training needs of staff within their jurisdiction. This includes induction and update training. As soon as possible after joining, the induction Co-ordinator ensures new staff are made aware of emergency procedures and fixtures relevant to their place of work, that they receive all necessary documents and are aware of Health and Safety procedures. The deputy is in charge of ensuring Club organisers commit to following these procedures.

*Excerpt from a school's health and safety policy.*

---

### Portfolio activity

Ask your school for a list of current policies. How many of these have you seen and do you know about? Can you find others which could go under the headings above?

### Functional skills

**English: Reading**
Through this portfolio activity you have the opportunity to develop your reading skills.

---

### CASE STUDY: When policies are needed

Marianne was employed in September and took on the role of a teaching assistant in a school for a term and a half before being off with long-term sickness between February and June. Although she supplied documentation from her doctor and was able to inform the local authority how long she would need to be off school, her contract was not renewed for the following year and Marianne felt that this was unfair. She was at home so was unable to access the school's grievance policy to find out what she could have done to prevent this from happening.

- What could Marianne have done in this situation?
- Do you know about your own school's grievance policy?
- Who does a grievance policy benefit?

# Know about the wider context in which schools operate

## Identify the roles and responsibilities of national and local government for education policy and practice

### National government

The role of the Department for Education (DfE) is to be responsible for education and children's services. This means that as well as being responsible for drawing up education policy, for example, in setting the National Curriculum and Early Years Foundation Stage from which schools and nurseries operate, it is also looking into new ways of developing the quality of services available to children under the five outcomes of Every Child Matters. It has also set up and administers the schools' league tables.

Other aspects of its role include:

- funding research into education-based projects and those which are concerned with children and young people

- developing workforce reform such as the 2020 Children and Young People's Workforce Strategy

- promoting integrated working for all those who work with children and young people

- developing the role of the third sector (that is, organisations which are non-governmental — voluntary and community organisations, charities and others which work with children).

For more information see the DfE website at www.education.gov.uk

### Local government

Local government departments for education will provide services to schools in the area in the form of advice and support. The local education authority is responsible for providing accessible local services for:

- staff training and development

- special educational needs

- the curriculum, including Early Years or sixth form

- promoting community cohesion

- school management issues

- behaviour management

- the development of school policies.

Local authorities need to provide documents which set out their own vision and plans for the development of government-based initiatives. This will be through, for example, their local Children and Young People's Plan

(CYPP), which outlines the way in which children's services are integrated and describes how and when improvements will be achieved in the local area. In a similar way to school policies, local authorities also have policies which relate to wider issues, such as their own guidelines for schools for the use of restraint or guidance on the use of medicines.

Most local education authorities will employ specialist advisors to deal with different curriculum areas such as maths or ICT, or to advise on special educational needs or the Foundation Stage. They will also have specifically trained teachers who will provide support for pupils who have, for example, behaviour needs, or who need to be assessed for a specific learning need such as dyslexia. They will sometimes provide these services free to schools, but in some cases schools may be expected to pay for them, in particular if specialist teachers need to come into school to advise teachers or work with specific children.

If there is a change in education policy, for example, which all schools need to know about, the local education authority will be expected to pass on information to schools and offer training to key staff through their local education development centre. They may also come into school and deliver whole school training or INSET (In-Service Education and Training) to all staff if needed.

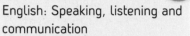

## Functional skills

**English: Speaking, listening and communication**
Before you complete the task opposite, you could plan the questions you are going to ask the Head Teacher. Listen carefully to their response so that you can respond in an appropriate way. You may find it helpful to make notes so that you can look back at what was said at the interview.

## Skills builder

Do you know how much regular contact your school has with the local authority and the DfE? If you can, speak to your Head Teacher or Deputy about how often they receive communications such as emails, phone calls or letters from these organisations. This will help develop your interviewing and questioning skills.

## Describe the role of schools in national policies relating to children, young people and families

Schools are expected to know about and show that they are working from national policies which relate to children, young people and families. An example of this is the Every Child Matters framework, which has had a wide-ranging impact on provision for children and young people nationally. As part of this and community cohesion, schools have been developing their central role in local communities through projects such as the extended schools programme, and Ofsted will also inspect against this criterion. Schools also need to develop their own policies in line with national requirements, such as child protection and safeguarding children, following guidelines from local education authorities.

As well as working from national policies, schools may also be involved in trialling and developing new ideas which can subsequently be rolled out nationally.

## Describe the roles of other organisations working with children and young people and how these may impact on the work of schools

Since there is a wide range of organisations which work with children and young people, it makes sense that they should liaise with one another and share their knowledge and experience. As well as developing links with one another for pupil support and community cohesion, it is likely that meetings will also be held between different services. Although they will work with and alongside schools, they may work in a different way, and all parties will need to be aware of this. However, the impact of a closer working relationship between organisations can only be beneficial to all concerned and in particular in the best interests of the children.

---

**CASE STUDY:** The role of schools in national policies

St Mark's Secondary School has been contacted by the DfE, as it is trialling a fresh community programme to encourage schools from a range of rural areas to develop wider community and diversity links. The school will then be asked to return a report, which will form the basis of a new national policy for schools. The school does not have to take part but is considering whether to do so.

- What do you think the benefits of this might be for the school and for the community?
- Is it a good idea for national government to request this kind of involvement from schools? Why?

---

| Organisation | Description |
|---|---|
| Social services | Social services will link with schools in cases where it is necessary for them to share information or prepare for court hearings. They may also liaise with your school's family worker or have meetings with teachers. |
| Children's services | These are linked to the five outcomes of Every Child Matters, but may be from a range of providers including education, health, social services, early years and childcare. |
| Youth services | These will have more impact on secondary schools but will be concerned with training and provision post-14, the Youth Matters programme and Targeted Youth Support. |
| National Health Service | Many professionals which come into and work with schools may be employed by the National Health Service and Primary Care Trust, including speech therapists, physiotherapists and occupational therapists. |

*Table 4: Organisations which come into contact with schools. Have you been involved with these or any others?*

## Functional skills

**English: Writing**
When writing your report, it is important that you take particular care with your spelling, grammar and punctuation.

## Getting ready for assessment

You will need to show that you understand the aims and values, policies and working practices of your own school and how they fit into the wider community. You can choose to present your evidence in different ways.

- Write a short report about your school and how it is part of the local community.

- Have a professional discussion with your mentor or an expert witness and keep a record of this (this may be a written record or a recording) to use as evidence.

- Find out what other organisations may contact or come into school.

## Check your knowledge

1. Name three different types of schools and say why they have these titles.

2. Which of the following members of staff can be members of a school's Senior Management Team?
   a) classroom teacher
   b) SENCO
   c) year group leader
   d) subject area manager
   e) school governor.

3. In your role, have you had contact with outside professionals? Who have these been? How has this been of benefit to pupils?

4. What do the following mean?
   a) values
   b) policy
   c) code of practice.

5. What is the role of the DfE?

6. Name three other organisations that may work with children and young people.

---

**Websites**

**www.governornet.co.uk** – this site gives useful information for school governors
**www.education.gov.uk** – the site for the Department for Education (DfE)
**www.tda.gov.uk** – up-to-date advice on all areas of education and training
**www.ssatrust.org.uk** – Specialist Schools and Academies Trust (SSAT)
**www.everychildmatters.gov.uk/ete/extendedschools** – advice and information about extended schools provision

# TDA 2.6 Help improve own & team practice in schools

This unit is about your own continuing professional development and how you support the work of your team. As part of your qualification you will need to have some form of professional discussion or appraisal with your line manager which includes thinking about your practice and setting targets for development.

## By the end of this unit you will:

1. be able to reflect on own practice
2. be able to improve own practice
3. understand the work of the team
4. be able to support the work of the team.

**Key term**

**Reflective practice** – the process of thinking about and critically analysing your actions with the goal of changing and improving occupational practice

**Link**

See TDA 2.10 Support learning activities.

# Be able to reflect on own practice

The role of the teaching assistant has in recent years become that of a professional. As part of any professional job role, it is important to be able to carry out **reflective practice**. This will be especially important when working with pupils, as your personal effectiveness will make a real difference to their learning.

## Take note of children and young people's responses to own practice

When working with children and young people, you should think about the way in which they respond to your work with them. This means that in the course of your work, you should evaluate how they have progressed and whether they have met learning objectives. It is likely that you will think about how you handled different situations and whether activities or programmes of work have made a difference to pupil progress. This is for two reasons:

1. because you will need to feed back to teachers on the activity

2. for your own personal development.

---

**CASE STUDY:** Children's responses to your practice

Hasima has recently come to a new school and finds that she is required to fill in an evaluation form following each lesson which she has supported. She is more used to giving verbal feedback to teachers and is not keen to use the forms. However, she does so and finds that they are very useful.

- Why do you think there might be benefits to writing down how pupils have responded to learning activities?
- Can you think of any disadvantages?

---

## Ask for constructive feedback on own practice from colleagues and take note of responses to own practice from others

In all aspects of your role, you will need to be able to think about your practice. Your school will be able to offer you support and will provide you with the advice you need. Taking a step back and looking at things from a different point of view is often an enlightening exercise – the important thing to do is to ask the right questions so that you are learning from the experience. You may also have the opportunity to benefit from other tools such as observations of your practice, peer assessment, and feedback from teachers or other professionals who come into school, or from your assessor. Parents or guardians of pupils may also be able to give you feedback on how you have managed in different situations.

These are all useful ways of helping you to think about how your practice comes across to others.

You may find that some of your reflections come as a surprise and you were not expecting what you find out. If the school has an ethic of personal reflection anyway, it will be easier for you to engage in doing this, as you will be more used to the process. This is particularly true when it comes to uncovering the difference between words and actual practice – if the school has an open and accepting ethos where everyone is engaged in reflection and expects to learn through mistakes, the process will be less threatening.

*How do you think you can learn and reflect best from an appraisal?*

It is important to remember that, in your work with children, you are part of a whole school. If you are reflecting on your practice and find that you need to change or develop the work that you are doing, you will need to discuss this with others with whom you work, as this will also affect them. This could mean that if you are in a school which is less receptive to change or where staff do not reflect on their work as a matter of course, it may be difficult for you to approach others. You may need to be very tactful and sensitive in order to put your ideas across in a way which does not appear threatening to others in your team.

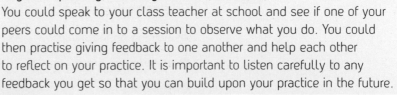

### Functional skills

**English: Speaking, listening and communication**
You could speak to your class teacher at school and see if one of your peers could come in to a session to observe what you do. You could then practise giving feedback to one another and help each other to reflect on your practice. It is important to listen carefully to any feedback you get so that you can build upon your practice in the future.

## Evaluate all aspects of own practice

As you examine your existing practice, you may find that the process is challenging and sometimes hard. You will need to reflect not only on the practical side of your work with children, which can be a difficult process in itself, but also on your own attitudes and beliefs. Reflection can lead you to reconsider issues which you may not even have thought of as relevant to your role in school. When you start to think about all aspects of your role, you may find this hard, as belief systems can be very difficult to change due to your own personal experiences. You may also come across parents who have very different views from yourself or from those of the school. You need to maintain your professionalism at all times and consider the experiences and perspectives of others.

### Functional skills

**English: Writing**
You could complete this task in the form of a report covering all the points (right). When writing your report, you need to think carefully about your layout, grammar, punctuation and spelling.

### Portfolio activity

Think about your own practice under the following headings.

1. How much you share the school's aims and values.

2. How often you think about the work you have carried out with pupils and evaluate how it went.

3. How much you have learned from your experiences in school so far.

4. How you have reacted to different parents and carers, and why.

Why is it important to evaluate your work in this way?

# Be able to improve own practice

Following your reflection on your practice, you will then need to think about how this can lead to improvements. There will always be areas which can be changed and improved, and all members of school staff need to think about how they can improve their practice. This will in turn have a direct effect on pupils' learning and progress.

## Identify possible development opportunities relevant to improving own practice

You should always be on the lookout for opportunities which are available to you for developing and improving your practice. These may be training opportunities which present themselves through your school's programme of development, but may also be through other means.

Development opportunities include:

- training opportunities
- mentoring
- coaching
- e-learning
- open and distance learning.

### Training opportunities

These will come up from time to time, either through the school's programme for training days or through courses which are sent through from the local authority. You may also find that you receive information about training opportunities for support staff through colleges of further education. These may be directly linked to your work in school and your professional development, but may also be for literacy or numeracy qualifications, or for speakers of English as a second language.

### Mentoring

During the course of your professional development you may have a mentor. This is a person who supports and advises you while you are considering or going through a process of change or development such as a training course. Mentors may be formal or informal, and you may decide to set targets with them or simply meet them from time to time for advice or a chat. Your mentor may be:

● a more experienced member of staff, either in a similar role to your own or a member of the Senior Management Team in school

● a college tutor

● an individual who has completed the course which you are undertaking.

### Coaching

Coaching is sometimes used in business and also sometimes in schools as a way of discussing and working through issues with the support of another person. The coach will be a similar individual to a mentor, but will have specific coaching training. This will enable them to guide and support others by encouraging them to think through their own solutions to issues.

### E-learning

E-learning is a term which can cover a number of different methods of training, but is generally used to mean a network which delivers training courses to those who are linked to a particular organisation. For example, colleges or universities may use e-learning to support existing learners through online programmes of study.

### Open and distance learning

Open and distance learning have become effective and convenient development opportunities as they allow you to learn at your own pace and at any time. They existed before the arrival of computers and the main concept was that learning took place at a distance. These types of courses are now available in a large number of different subjects including teaching assistant training. They will always involve some kind of feedback from an instructor and interactions with other learners.

**Over to you!**

What kinds of development opportunities have you come across since you started to work in your school? Are there any other than those listed above? How effective have they been for your own development?

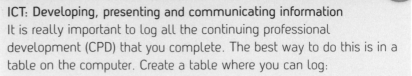

## Describe the importance of continuing professional development

**Continuing professional development** (CPD) is important as it is a way of demonstrating that you are thinking about your own career and that you are interested in progressing and in developing in your role. You should also always keep a record of all courses, qualifications and other ways in which you develop professionally during the course of your career. Your school may be able to track those you have attended since starting, but it is worthwhile keeping your own record. This will be a good reminder for you and also will be useful when applying for jobs or further qualifications.

You should list courses in date order and keep a record of who was running them, and whether there were any qualifications or credits attached in case you need these later. The quickest and easiest way is to keep a file which you can add to and also a Word document on your computer with a list such as the one below. Always keep handouts and other paperwork, certificates or letters of attendance, as you never know when these may be useful.

---

**Sally Robbins — Record of courses attended**

September — December 2003 — DFES Induction Training for teaching assistants
(12 sessions on Monday afternoons)

January 2006 — whole-school INSET on managing behaviour

April 2006 — Early Years numeracy course — twilight 4–6pm with local maths coordinator

September 2007 — Smartboard training for teaching assistants — afternoon as part of INSET

September 2008 — June 2009 — Level 2 NVQ for Support Staff in schools at Bromley College

September 2009 — one-day whole-school Science INSET with John Branston

September 2009 — whole-school Ofsted preparation

July 2010 — Early Years Foundation Stage training — two-day course at local authority

---

*You will need to keep your own record of professional development.*

As part of your CPD, it is also likely that your school will require you to think about setting targets for the coming year. This means that you will be asked to think about strengths, weaknesses and areas for development. This process is sometimes known as an appraisal.

## Work with an appropriate person to identify own strengths, and areas to improve, plan ways to improve and identify goals and targets

Appraisal will usually take place through your line manager. Before the meeting it is likely that you will be asked to think about your role and on areas which you have particularly enjoyed, or those which you have found more challenging. Before you meet with your line manager, you will need to think about your current role and how it matches your job description. You should then note down any aspect of your role which you would like to discuss.

To help you to think about your appraisal, try completing the questions on the self-appraisal form below.

## General self-appraisal

It would be useful if you could bring this information with you to your initial meeting, to help you to identify your needs as part of the appraisal process.

1 Do you feel that your job description is still appropriate? Do you feel that there are any changes that need to be made?

2 What targets were set at the last appraisal/when you started your job? Have you achieved your targets?

3 What are the reasons for not having achieved your targets?

4 What aspect of your job satisfies you the most?

5 What aspect of your job has not been as successful as you had anticipated?

6 Are there any areas of your work that you would like to improve?

7 What training have you received? Has it been successful?

8 What are your current training needs?

*If you have not been given one, suggest to your line manager that you complete a form such as this before your initial meeting.*

You will then need to discuss these strengths and areas for development, and think about how you will be able to relate them to your own continuing progress so that you can turn them into targets for development.

## Take part in continuing professional development that is relevant to own goals and targets

When thinking about the next aspect of your role, which is areas for development, it may help to divide your knowledge and experience into sections. As an example, these might be knowledge and experience of:

● the curriculum

● behaviour management

● ICT

● relevant or new legislation

● health and safety

● working with or managing others

● record keeping

● special educational needs.

You will then need to think about your level of confidence in each of these areas so that you can begin to see areas of strength and those which may need further development. You will need guidance in order to turn these into targets.

Your line manager should be able to work with you to set personal development targets which are SMART (see Table 1).

| **S**pecific | You must make sure your target says exactly what is required. |
|---|---|
| **M**easurable | You should ensure that you will be able to measure whether the target has been achieved. |
| **A**chievable | The target should not be inaccessible or too difficult. |
| **R**ealistic | You should ensure that you will have access to the training or resources which may be required. |
| **T**ime-bound | There should be a limit to the time you have available to achieve your target. This is because otherwise you may continually put it off to a later date! |

*Table 1: SMART targets.*

When thinking about these targets you should not usually set more than three or four in total, so that they will be achievable. You should also ensure that you look at the targets between appraisal meetings to make sure that you are on course to meet them. There is little point in setting them if you have the meeting and then put the paperwork away again until next year!

You may find that because of the school development plan there are already training programmes planned over the next 12 months, for example, on the use of a new ICT programme in school (see below) and that you will be attending this anyway. This will therefore form one of your targets. You may also like to think about training courses which will be useful to attend.

New targets for professional development:

1. To attend whole-school training on ICT numeracy programme ..................
2. To attend course on Early Years Foundation Stage ..........................
3. To complete level 3 qualification in Supporting Teaching and Learning in schools. ...

*Part of a completed appraisal form.*

## Review own personal development and identify new areas of skill and knowledge to achieve new goals and targets

At the end of a set period, usually one year, you will meet up again with your line manager to review your progress and to think about how you have developed over the past year. This will include looking at previous goals and targets to see whether they have been met. It may be that you have achieved them all, but in some cases work may be ongoing, your role may have changed or targets may not have been achievable — for example, if a course has been cancelled or if illness or another priority in school has prevented you from meeting your goals. You may then need to carry these over to the following year. During this final part of the appraisal meeting, you will identify how you are going to develop your skills and knowledge over the coming months, and set new targets for development.

# Understand the work of the team

## Describe why teamwork is important in schools

Teamwork is important in any group of people who work together, as it means that they have a shared purpose and the sense of a common purpose. Whatever size the school you work in, you will be part of a group of people who each have a different role to fulfil while working to support individuals or groups of pupils. While each member of the **team** should know and understand their own role, they should also know and understand the roles of others in their team, and how they fit together.

In a school, it would be easy for members of the team to become very busy and preoccupied with the number of things which they need to do, and therefore to lose sight of the wider picture. This is why it is important for the team to meet regularly and prioritise how they work together for the benefit of the pupils.

### Key term

**Team** — people with whom you work on a long-, medium-, or short-term basis, relating to the support provided for a specific pupil or group of pupils

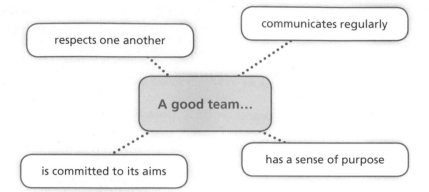

*Characteristics of an effective team. Does your school team do these things?*

## Describe the purpose and objectives of the team in which you work

As well as working together and having shared roles, the team must have a clear purpose and objectives. You may be part of several different teams within your school, each with different objectives. You should know what these are and how each team works together:

● to support a named child – assistants who work with individual children may work alongside others such as the SENCO, or other professionals who come into the school to support a child who has special educational needs (see TDA 2.5 Schools as organisations for the types of professionals who may come in to schools)

● to give general support within a specific class or department – in a primary school, assistants will work with the class teacher but there may also be other adults or assistants within the class who work together. In secondary schools it is more likely that you will be attached to a particular department or subject, such as maths, as you may have strengths in that subject. You should plan and discuss learning activities alongside teachers or at least have access to plans so that you have a clear understanding of what you are expected to do within the class on a weekly and daily basis. Plans should show the role of other adults as well as learning intentions and whether activities are whole class, group or individual (for more on planning with teachers, see TDA 2.10 Support learning activities)

● within a year group – the school may be large and have a number of classes within a year group. Year groups may work very closely together and support one another in planning and moderating pupils' work

● as part of the whole school team – all members of staff within a school are part of a team and will support one another. For example, the maths coordinator will be able to offer help and advice to any member of staff on any maths activities.

*What help and advice do you think different teachers will be able to offer to each other?*

Sometimes you may find that you are part of a team which is only together for a short time – for example, if you are on a working party to organise the Christmas production or the summer fair. In this situation it is also important for someone to take charge and ensure that different members of the team are able to work together efficiently.

**Skills builder**

Consider the team or teams to which you belong in your school. Write a reflective account to outline your role and consider how you work with others as part of that team. This task will help to develop your reflective practice skill.

## Describe own role and responsibilities and those of others in the team

In each of these situations, members of the team will need to understand their role and how it fits in with the role of other members of the team. The most important part of any role within a team is communicating effectively with others. There should be clear and consistent methods of communication, so that all members of the team feel that their opinions are valued. As part of this process you should

### Reflect ?

Think about a team to which you belong in school. How often does the team meet and are the meetings formal or informal? Do you think that this method is the best way to ensure that each team member is clear on what they have to do?

attend regular meetings which should give you a clear idea of how what you are doing fits in to the school or team as a whole. If you have a team leader, they should identify action points in any meetings you attend and give a deadline by which they will need to be carried out.

## Describe the importance of respecting the skills and expertise of other practitioners

You should remember that all members of the team are equally important, and that your expertise and that of your colleagues is unique to each person's experience. You should always respect the opinions and knowledge which others bring. This is because in order to have a good working relationship with them you will need to show that you consider their opinions and expertise. If a member of your team has been working in schools for a long time and a new person comes in and tells them that things should be done in a different way, it will cause bad feeling and resentment. These can quickly cause problems and unrest within teams.

---

**CASE STUDY:** Respecting the expertise of other practitioners

Saul is a new member of staff working in a large secondary school. He is working within the modern languages department and has recently returned from some time abroad. He has been given a mentor, Jodie, who has been at the school for some years and is the most senior assistant in the department. As part of her role, Jodie has been asked to support Saul in ensuring that he has all the training and information he needs. She is very helpful and offers to support Saul in any way she can. After being in school for half a term, Saul decides that it would be a good idea to run a languages group and form contacts with schools in other countries, so that pupils can develop relationships with them and communicate regularly using emails and Internet links. He does not tell Jodie about his idea but informs a group of Year 11 learners, who ask her about it. Jodie finds that during a lesson she is supporting she is being asked questions about something she knows nothing about, and is unable to tell the teacher about it either.

- How do you think Jodie feels?
- Why should Saul have spoken to her first?
- Do you think that he should have done anything else before speaking to the pupils?

---

As you become more experienced yourself, you may find that others come to you for help or advice. You should always think about your role and others within the team when doing this, while remaining supportive. Where you do not feel that it is appropriate for you to deal with a particular issue, you may need to refer to someone else within the team. You must remain non-judgemental about others and not allow your own opinions to intrude or cloud any decisions you may have to make.

# Be able to support the work of the team

These assessment criteria must be assessed in the workplace by your assessor. You may choose to use a simulation activity for assessment criterion 4.6 (Respond to differences of opinion and conflict constructively). See page 105 for an example of a simulation activity.

## Support the purpose and objectives of the team, and carry out own role and responsibilities within the team

As part of your qualification, you will need to show that you support the purpose and objectives of the teams to which you belong. This means you should be able to give examples of ways in which you have carried out activities and supported others to achieve the aims of the team. You may have documents such as minutes of meetings which show that you have done this, or your assessor may be able to speak to an expert witness who is able to relate how you have supported others in achieving team objectives.

### Over to you!

When your assessor comes into your school, be ready with examples of work you have carried out in your team which supports the work of others.

### Functional skills

**English: Speaking, listening and communication**
This activity provides a very useful topic for discussion. Once you have had your discussion with your assessor, you could also bring the work into your sessions to share with your peers. You may get some good ideas from other people in your class that you could carry out in your setting.

---

**CASE STUDY:** Supporting the purpose and objectives of the team

Marianne is working within a speech and language unit which is attached to a mainstream school. She has been asked to work as part of a group which is trialling a new six-week programme for pupils who have been making limited progress. Alongside class teachers, Marianne and other assistants have chosen eight pupils of varying ages who they feel will benefit from the intervention. At the end of the six weeks, Marianne has to write a report on the progress made by the two pupils she is supporting and the level of success which the pupils have achieved. This is then discussed alongside the progress of the other six pupils who are in different classes.

- How is Marianne's work supporting the team objectives?
- Why is it important that she writes her report and goes to meetings about the programme?

---

## Communicate clearly with team members and others, making sure they have the information they need

When working with others in your team, you will need to make sure you listen to them and take on board what they are saying. You should also ensure that you pass on any information which you have been given so that they have all the information they need. This is important — often people do not really hear others' views because they are too busy thinking about their own or are too eager to put their ideas across.

You should remember that all contributions are important and valid, and take time to listen to them.

## Interact with others in a way that supports good teamwork

In order for individuals to work co-operatively, it is important for members to have good interpersonal skills. These are sometimes the most difficult skills to have, as within any team there will be a number of personalities. Individuals will need to have the skills to relate to one another well and be sympathetic, supportive and helpful. Members of the team should be sensitive to the needs and feelings of others, and encourage those who they know are finding work challenging or difficult. This may be due to other issues which they have to deal with outside school.

There may be a combination of factors which makes it difficult for individuals to focus and tackle problems in the work environment. This may mean reading others' body language at times or realising that now may not be a good time to approach another member of the team with a problem. There may also be a member of the team who is much more of a speaker than a listener. This can be a problem if the person does not give others the chance to have their say.

As part of your team, you should always be supportive to others and try to balance responsibilities so that individuals do not have more to do than their colleagues.

## Identify and suggest ways in which the team could improve its work

If you are relatively new to the role of a teaching assistant, you may not feel that it is your place to suggest different ways of working or

*Why is it important to be sensitive to the needs and feelings of others in the team?*

to challenge ways in which things are done. However, although you will need to be sensitive to others, you should still be invited to put your ideas across and give your own suggestions from time to time. In education, regular changes occur and it is likely that when you are training, you will be finding out about new initiatives and ideas through your contacts outside school. On the other hand, you should not criticise the way in which others work or how they have done things in the past.

## Functional skills

**English: Speaking, listening and communication**
This case study provides a good opportunity for some role play in your class. Try out different ways that Ryan could have approached this situation and discuss the outcomes as a group. When carrying out this activity, it is important to listen carefully to what others have to say, so that you can respond in an appropriate way.

## CASE STUDY: Suggesting ways in which the team could improve its work

Ryan is working as a support assistant in a Foundation Stage class. He has recently attended updated Foundation Stage training and has been given a number of useful ideas and **pro formas**. The trainer had stated that these had all been sent out to schools in the local authority and that they should be used for all timed observations that are carried out in Reception classes. Ryan goes back to school and at the next Foundation Stage meeting, tells the year group leader that she should have been using these materials before. He asks her why the rest of the team were not informed about them.

- How do you think Ryan's comments will affect the team?
- What might have been a better way of approaching this?

## Respond to differences of opinion and conflict constructively

## Key terms

**Pro formas** — standard documents or forms

**Issue** — situation or circumstance that hinders or prevents effective team performance, such as poor co-operation between members of the team or interpersonal conflicts between members of the team

However well your team works together, it is likely that at some stage there will be an **issue** or problem within it. This will need to be resolved before the team can move on and continue to progress.

There may be a number of reasons for this, including:

- incomplete information given to team members
- team members resisting change
- a team decision which some individuals do not like
- dominant team members taking over
- inability of individuals to accept feedback
- competition between team members.

Using the bullet points as guidelines, devise a scenario to simulate the issue described and present it to your assessor with other candidates. This can then be written up by your assessor and used for your portfolio.

As part of a team, you should remember that you will always get along with some personalities more than others. However, this should not mean that you cannot relate in some way to all members of your team, as you will have a common purpose. Also, in the course of your work you may find that work or home pressures may affect the way in which team members relate to one another. It is important to try to minimise conflict so that bad feeling and resentment do not build up over time. In order to ensure this, you should make sure that you try to resolve any issues as soon as possible through the appropriate channels. Communication is the most important factor, as many conflicts arise due to either misunderstandings or lack of time to discuss what is happening. If you find that another member of your team appears to be making the course of your work more difficult due to their attitude or opinions, you will need either to try to resolve the situation or to refer the issue to a senior member of staff.

You should be familiar with your school's policy for dealing with difficulties in working relationships and practices. This is usually known as the grievance policy. The policy will give you information and details about how to approach any problems you may face when working with others. As an example, most policies will advise a set way of dealing with issues as they arise. There should be separate guidelines for individuals wishing to raise a grievance and for collective disputes.

# GRIEVANCE POLICY

**Informal procedure** (recommended course of action)

1) Speak directly and confidentially to the person or persons with whom you have a grievance. If agreement is not reached the issue should be taken directly to the Head Teacher. If the grievance is with the Head Teacher take the issue to the Chair of Governors.
2) The Head Teacher or Chair of Governors will act as mediator and encourage both parties to resolve the issue as soon as possible and to avoid using the more formal procedure. Parties may be represented by a trade union representative or colleague if required. If the issue is not resolved within seven days of the grievance being raised, it should progress to the next level, i.e. the formal stage.
3) A record of the mediation meeting and any agreed actions by both or either party should be kept on file so that it can be referred to if required.

**Formal procedure**

1) If the informal procedure does not resolve the issue or it has not been resolved to the satisfaction of both parties, a letter should be sent to the Clerk to the Governors outlining progress so far. This should then be addressed by the grievance subcommittee of the governing body.
2) A meeting will be called between all parties by the grievance subcommittee and each person given the opportunity to put forward their side. There will be opportunities for questioning and responses by all.
3) If there is still no resolution, the matter may be passed to the Director of Education of the local authority and/or the unions.

*Excerpt from a school's grievance policy.*

> **BEST PRACTICE CHECKLIST:** Working in teams
>
> - Be considerate and respectful towards others within your team.
> - Be clear on your role and the roles of others.
> - Carry out your duties well and cheerfully.
> - Do not gossip or talk about other people in your team.
> - Make sure you discuss any problems as they arise.
> - Speak to the appropriate team member if you need help.
> - Prepare for and contribute to meetings.
> - Acknowledge the support and ideas of other team members.

## Seek advice and support from relevant people when needed

The school may have policies and procedures in place for dealing with difficulties and conflicts within working relationships. This will include areas such as confidentiality and all members of teams should be aware of issues surrounding the exchange of information. You should be aware of whom you need to speak to if you find that there are problems within your team or group which are affecting your work. If you find that you are in a difficult situation while carrying out your duties, you may need to refer to other members of staff. This may be a named person, but if the situation is sensitive and you do not feel able to discuss it with them, you may need to go to someone to whom you are more able to talk.

### Portfolio activity

Reflect on an issue or problem which you have encountered when working in a team. You may wish to have a professional discussion with your assessor about how you resolved the problem so that they can record it for your portfolio. Alternatively you can write a reflective account to show how you have dealt with any issues which have arisen. If you write it up, be careful how you do this if your portfolio is likely to be seen by others in your team.

## Check your knowledge

1. Why is it important for you to reflect on your practice in school and what areas should you think about?

2. What kinds of opportunities might be available for you to develop your practice?

3. Where might you be able to get feedback on your progress?

4. What should you do before sitting down with your line manager to set targets for your continuing professional development?

5. Name three things that you should remember when you are working as part of a team.

6. What kinds of factors may cause conflict within teams?

### Websites

**www.ofsted.gov.uk** – Ofsted
**www.napta.org.uk** – the National Association of Professional Teaching Assistants
**www.teachernet.gov.uk/ wholeschool/supportstaff** – guidance for support staff
**www.qcda.gov.uk** – the Qualifications and Curriculum Development Agency

## Getting ready for assessment

If your school does not usually carry out a professional appraisal for teaching assistants, you may like to use the example below. You can then use this in your portfolio.

---

**Professional Review Meeting**

Name: ..................................... Date: ...................

Line manager: .......................................

Areas discussed:

Review of last year's targets:

1. ............................................................. target met/not met

2. ............................................................. target met/not met

3. ............................................................. target met/not met

New targets for professional development:

1. .......................................................

2. .......................................................

3. .......................................................

To be reviewed on: ...........................................

Signed: ......................................... (TA)

Signed: ......................................... (Line manager)

---

The appraisal meeting as a whole should cover much of the assessment criteria for the first part of this unit, although you should check with your assessor to make sure that your awarding body will accept this. If your assessor can be present at your appraisal interview and witness it, this will be even better evidence for your portfolio, although this may be difficult to arrange.

### Target-setting examples

1. Some candidates choose to have one of their targets as completion of their award by a set date.

2. Include any INSET (In-Service Education and Training) that your school will offer during the next 12 months, for example, whole-school training on safeguarding children. In this way you are including something you will be doing anyway rather than setting additional work for yourself.

3. Include any training you have requested specifically for yourself, for example, a sign language course or a qualification to upgrade your maths or English skills.

Remember that targets will all need to be SMART. If your line manager has written a target which is not clearly achievable within the timescale, or which is not clear, it is important that you point this out.

If you are having some difficulty in setting a meeting in your school, speak to your assessor. You may be able to set and review some targets of your own through your college course.

# TDA 2.7 Maintain & support relationships with children & young people

This unit is about how you contribute effectively to the relationships you have with children and young people in school. You also need to show that you support them in their relationships with their peers and in the way in which they work together.

All of the assessment criteria for this unit must be assessed in the workplace as this unit requires you to demonstrate the competence required to maintain and support relationships with children and young people.

## By the end of this unit you will:

1. be able to communicate with children and young people
2. be able to develop and maintain relationships with children and young people
3. be able to support relationships between children and young people and others in the setting.

# Be able to communicate with children and young people

## Communicate with children and young people in a way that is appropriate to the individual, using both conventional language and body language

You will need to demonstrate a number of skills in order to **communicate** effectively with children and young people. Although it is very likely that you will do this every day without thinking, it is worth reflecting on the ways in which you do this and in how you make it appropriate to the individual. Children learn to communicate through the responses of others: if they do not feel that their contribution is valued, they are less likely to initiate communication themselves. Responding appropriately to children reinforces self-esteem, values what they are saying and is a crucial part of building relationships. Making conversation and finding out the answer to questions also builds on the language skills that are vital to a child's learning.

You should always ensure that you consider pupils' needs when communicating with them – for example, if they have communication difficulties such as a speech and language disorder or a sensory impairment.

It is likely that you will use different forms of communication with children on a regular basis. Although spoken language will be appropriate for most pupils, in school we often need to use body language and gestures to get our point across. This is particularly true in situations where a teaching assistant needs to communicate with a pupil from the other side of the classroom – for example, through giving

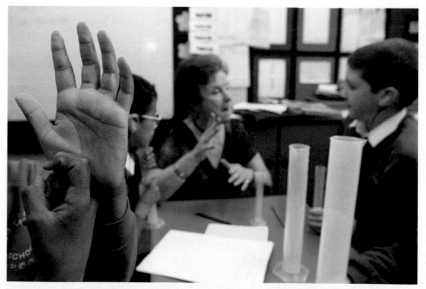

*Do you know British Sign Language or Makaton?*

## CASE STUDY: Using methods appropriate to the individual

Melanie is working with a group of Year 2 pupils who have different needs.

1. Charlie is immature for his age and has a limited attention span.

2. Josh has problems with his receptive language, which means that he can find it difficult to understand what has been said.

3. Hannah has a slight hearing impairment, although she does not wear a hearing aid.

Melanie needs to ensure that she includes each pupil during her work with them and that they are all involved.

- How can she make sure that she does this?

### Knowledge into action

Take some time to look around the school at the different ways in which adults actively listen to pupils. You can take brief notes and include context (for example, lesson time, going to office, out on playground) to back up what you have seen. Share this with the rest of your group.

them eye contact and raising their eyebrows to let them know they have seen them talking! In order to communicate with pupils, you may find that in some cases you will need to go for additional training — if a child or young person that you support uses sign language or Braille, for example, or uses electronic methods of communication. You may also need to speak to the class teacher or SENCO if you have concerns about a particular pupil around issues of communication; even if speech is the most appropriate form of communication, some pupils may have speech and language difficulties and need additional support.

## Actively listen to children and young people and value what they say, experience and feel

When communicating with children and young people, you will need to show them that you are actively listening to them. This means that you are showing that you are interested in what they are saying in different ways. If we do not actively listen to children and young people, we are giving them the message that we do not value what they are saying and thinking.

Examples of active listening include the following.

- Give children and young people your full attention when listening to them. Make sure you demonstrate that you are listening to pupils. If you say that you are listening but are looking away or are busy doing something else, this gives the child or young person the message that you are not really interested in what they are saying.

- React and respond to what they say. While listening to pupils, make sure that you respond to what they say by reacting to it, through speaking or by using body language or appropriate expressions, so that they can see that you have understood.

- Use non-verbal communication to support what you are saying. Body language can be a very powerful communicator. We can use it to reinforce what we are saying through facial expressions, eye contact, body stance and gestures. Always bend down to the level of younger pupils to speak to them, so that you are not intimidating and they can see that you are listening to them.

- Give them time to express themselves. Always remember when working with pupils that they may benefit from having thinking time or discussion time with a partner so that they can decide how they are going to respond. Many children or young people need the reassurance that an adult will wait and give them time to think and say what they want to say. You should also encourage them to do the same for one another, so that they learn to be patient and not interrupt others.

- Take their feelings seriously. When listening to pupils, and in particular if they are very upset or anxious about something, you should make sure that you take their feelings seriously and listen carefully to their concerns. Even if it is unlikely that their worries will actually come to anything, reassurance is very important and you must never ridicule them or laugh, even if their worries seem very unfounded. (See also page 115.)

## Check that children and young people understand what is communicated

There are a number of ways in which we can check that children and young people have understood what has been communicated.

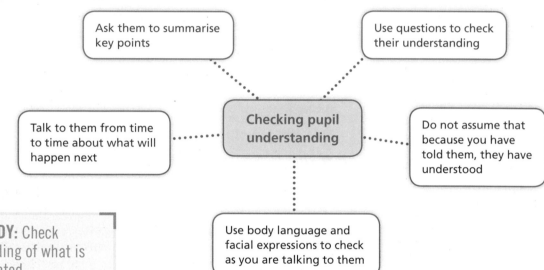

*Do you use these methods to check pupil understanding?*

### CASE STUDY: Check understanding of what is communicated

You have been asked to work with Year 1 on some data handling. As part of the exercise, the pupils need to draw a table and a tally chart to log their information as they are working. You ask them to draw the table and then send them off to gather the information in pairs. When one of the children comes back, you see that she has drawn a piece of furniture for her table and written her data underneath.

- How could you have avoided this?
- What might you say to her after you see what she has done?

### Ask them to summarise key points

It is always worth repeating and summarising key teaching points to pupils when you are working with them in case they have not picked them up. When giving children instructions, go over what they need to do or ask them to do it for you. In this way, you can be sure that they have understood the requirements of the task.

### Use questions to check their understanding

You should always use questions to check that pupils understand key points and know what they are required to do. It also helps if you avoid asking closed questions which require 'yes' or ' no' answers, in order to encourage children to respond in more depth.

### Talk to them from time to time about what will happen next

Pupils will benefit from the reassurance of an adult going over with them what will be happening next as they are working, so that you can be sure they are approaching a task in the right way.

### Use body language and facial expressions to check as you are speaking to them

You will probably do this without thinking — raising your eyebrows will usually mean that you are asking a question, whereas a nod or a smile will be encouraging. In the same way, you should look at pupils to see if their body language and expressions back up their understanding.

### Do not assume that because you have told them they have understood

Pupils will often say that they have understood something even if they have not, in particular if they do not want their peers to know. You may find that while you are speaking to them, it is clear that they have not understood, particularly if they are anxious. You should also make sure that language you have used is appropriate for the age range and needs of pupils.

# Be able to develop and maintain relationships with children and young people

## How to establish rapport and respectful, trusting relationships with children and young people

Understanding and trust for others is a crucial part of being able to have a positive relationship with them. We cannot do this unless we value others and respect their views. As well as taking time to listen to all pupils, one of the key things to remember in school is that you are the responsible adult and you should not try to be 'friends' with pupils in order to gain their trust and develop a relationship, as this does not work. Children and young people will need to know and understand the boundaries of their relationships with adults in school; they will respond to authority as long as you are clear about this from the beginning. This does not mean that you will not be able to form good relationships with them — in fact your relationships will probably be better as a result.

We can show that we trust and respect pupils in a number of ways.

- Listen to all pupils and let them put their ideas forward — encourage discussion.

- Find out how individuals like to be addressed and then speak to them in the correct way — remember any nicknames or chosen names.

- Encourage pupils to respect other children and adults by acting as a good role model.

- Give children and young people the opportunity to have responsibility and develop independence.

- Celebrate diversity through assemblies, stories and displays.

- Do not be afraid to praise and have fun with pupils if they have worked hard!

---

**CASE STUDY:** Establishing rapport and trusting relationships

Angela is about to start working with a new group of pupils in Year 9. She has only worked with Year 7 before and is a bit anxious about starting to work with older pupils. Before starting the first session, she says to the group, 'We are all here to work, and I am going to help you to do your best. Let's start with some ground rules...'

- Do you think this is a good start?
- Why do you think Angela has done this?
- How do you think she should end the session?

---

**Functional skills**

**English: Speaking, listening and communication**
This case study provides an excellent opportunity for discussion. You could share your ideas on how you would have approached a challenge similar to Angela's. Listen carefully to what others have to say so that you can make relevant contributions and share ideas with each other.

## Give attention to individual children and young people in a way that is fair to them and the group as a whole

When you are working with groups of pupils, you may find it difficult to balance the needs of individuals with those of the group. This will be because often children and young people seem to require different levels of attention: some may be able to work and organise themselves independently, whereas others may need the reassurance of an adult. When speaking and listening, some may be constantly trying to contribute their ideas, while others may be very quiet. Make sure you give all pupils the opportunity to contribute to discussions. Part of the reason for this is that you will not be able to assess what they know or be able to challenge their ideas unless you know what these are. You can give pupils opportunities to contribute in different ways, by:

- aiming your questioning at different pupils to ensure that all have had the chance to contribute
- asking the group a question or giving them a task and then inviting them to discuss it with a talk partner or buddy before seeking a response
- giving pupils 'thinking time' and then asking the group so that they are more confident before responding: this also avoids the more enthusiastic pupils having opportunities to call out
- giving the group small whiteboards and pens, and asking them to write down the answer and then hold these up at the same time
- asking the group a question and then telling them all to find out the answer, if they do not know it, from someone who does. You will need to give them a little time to do this. You can then ask the group the question again and be sure that everyone knows the answer. This is very effective in helping those pupils who do not have the confidence to answer questions in a group situation.

You will need to arrange the position of different pupils in the group, as well as your own, so that you are able to give this reassurance at times just by your physical proximity. If you can encourage pupils to work and make decisions for themselves, they will not need as much adult support and will have more confidence.

### CASE STUDY: Giving attention to individuals

Myra is working with a Year 7 class in a mixed-ability geography lesson. The class are finding out about their local area and have been asked to discuss in their groups their likes and dislikes about their neighbourhood. Myra is working with a group of six, two of whom are not engaged at all in the discussion.

- How would you approach this situation?
- Why is it important to ensure that all of the group have a chance to contribute?

**BEST PRACTICE CHECKLIST:** Giving attention to individuals

- Encourage all children and young people to put forward their own ideas.
- Know the names of all pupils.
- Acknowledge that some pupils will have strengths in a particular area and encourage this.
- Know the needs of all pupils (for example, any special educational needs or SEN).
- Enable children and young people to express themselves in different ways — for example, through creative activities.
- Sit close to pupils who need more reassurance.
- Be sympathetic if individuals find some things difficult.

## Demonstrate supportive and realistic responses to children and young people's questions, ideas, suggestions and concerns

### Functional skills

**ICT: Using ICT**
You could discuss with your class teacher the possibilities of using a voice recorder to record dialogue between you and a child. You can then play this recording back to see how you responded to the child and reflect on what you would do differently next time.

When responding to children and young people, you should ensure that you demonstrate supportive responses to them. This means that whatever your own feelings about what they are saying to you, you should show them your support. Children and young people are at the early stages of developing their skills of communication and their ability to relate to others. They are adding to their vocabulary as well as looking at the ways in which the adults around them respond to others. If pupils do not feel that adults are listening to them, they may be affected in different ways, and this may have an impact on their confidence or behaviour.

### Questions

Usually, questions are a good thing as they demonstrate that pupils are interested and want to know more, so you should be supportive and answer them as much as you can. If the question is not suitable, or pupils should already know the answer or are asking at an inappropriate time, you should not be impatient. Ask them to think about what they have just said and whether they might be able to answer their own question.

### Ideas and suggestions

If pupils are putting forward ideas, you should be supportive, as this shows that they are thinking about what they have been asked to do. If you make fun of what they are saying or laugh at their ideas, they will start to lose confidence in their own abilities and be less keen to say what they think next time.

### Link

See page 111 for more on actively listening to children and valuing what they say, experience and feel.

## Provide children and young people with reasons for actions when appropriate

In order to support your relationships with pupils, you will at times need to give them reasons for your actions. This is particularly required if they do not understand why you may have reacted in a particular way to something which has happened in school. An important example of this could be where a child or young person has confided in you and you need to pass this information on if it is a child protection issue and a child or young person is at risk. You should at all times tell the pupil that you will not be able to keep confidentiality if they disclose anything of this nature. You may also need to give pupils reasons for your actions in the following situations.

- You have reported them to a teacher or senior manager for something that they have done. If you have good relationships with pupils, and in particular if you get on well with a particular child or young person, they may see this as a way of acting inappropriately without being told off and try to 'push the boundaries'. You will need to speak to them and explain why it is important that they do not do this.

- You need to speak to pupils sternly because they have put themselves or others at risk. Pupils may not be aware if they have acted dangerously or have not seen a hazard. You may need to move quickly to avert an accident or incident and need to discuss this with pupils afterwards.

- You may sometimes need to talk through the reasons for doing things if you are planning something out of the ordinary, such as a school trip or visit, and are unable to comply with what pupils would like to do.

## Encourage children and young people to make choices for themselves

An important part of learning is for children and young people to be able to learn to make choices for themselves. In the earliest stages of school, making choices is part of the curriculum and they are given opportunities to practise this in their selection of play activities. They are encouraged to have some control within the boundaries of the setting. As they become older, pupils should continue to be encouraged to participate in decision making. This is because a strict and authoritarian structure is likely to cause problems later on, as children and young people will become frustrated by constantly being told what to do. One strategy which is often used with pupils is discussing targets for work and behaviour and involving them in setting their own, so that targets are not imposed on them without their involvement. Another strategy, which is regularly used with older pupils, is the use of school councils. These work very effectively in encouraging pupils to think about and discuss different sides of an issue, and come to a decision which will then be adopted by the school.

### Knowledge into action

Can you think of other times when you may need to provide children and young people with reasons for your actions? In each case, show why you have had to explain your actions to pupils. Why was it important to give pupils reasons for what you had done?

### Functional skills

ICT: Developing, presenting and communicating information
You could present your examples in the form of a presentation that you could share with the rest of your group to show what you do in your setting.

### Reflect

Think about the ways in which pupils in your school are encouraged to make choices for themselves. It is an important skill that children need to have. Describe how these examples will help pupils.

**CASE STUDY:** Encouraging children to solve conflict themselves

You are on duty at playtime and are on 'football patrol'. Today some of the Year 7s have had a dispute during the game, which has led to two of them coming over to you and each complaining about what has happened.

- What would you say to the children who came to speak to you?
- Is there any way in which you could prevent this kind of thing from happening?
- Give an example.

*What skills do you think pupils develop from attending student councils?*

# Be able to support relationships between children and young people and others in the setting

## Support children and young people to communicate effectively with others

As adults working with children and young people, we need to help them to understand the value and importance of positive relationships with others. Pupils will over time learn to do this in different ways in school. They will be encouraged to work in pairs, groups and as a class to listen to one another and acknowledge ideas. They will learn to think of others and have respect for their feelings. They will also find out how positive relationships with others will enhance what they do.

We can support children and young people by showing them how our own positive relationships are beneficial. If we are able to show them that we value and respect others, they are much more likely to learn to do the same. You should be consistent in your behaviour and relationships so that children and young people learn to do this. By observing our interactions with children and other adults, pupils should be able to see the effects of positive relationships and effective communication with others.

We will also need to support children and young people through the way in which we manage any disagreements or conflict which they have with their peers.

> **CASE STUDY:** Support children and young people to communicate effectively with others
>
> Year 6 are working on a group activity. They have been given a brief for a design for a bridge which they will later have to build using construction materials. Peheli, who is a support assistant, has been asked to support those groups who need it during the afternoon. After some time, she notices that most of the groups have settled to the task, but that one of them still seems to be in disagreement. She goes over and finds that they are arguing about the design and that one of the group, Dane, seems to be taking over, while several of the others do not agree with him.
>
> • What should Peheli do in this situation?
> • What should she say to Dane?

> **CASE STUDY:** Encouraging diversity
>
> You are a member of staff at a small village primary. At your school, many religious festivals and celebrations are discussed and shown through lessons and assemblies. During one open evening, a parent is looking at one of the Diwali displays and comes up to you and asks why the school needs to have a display like this 'when it is not even English'.
>
> • What would you say to the parent?
> • Why do you think that this kind of comment should not go unchallenged?
> • How do you encourage children in your school to understand others' individuality?

## Encourage children and young people to understand other people's individuality, diversity and differences

It is important that schools encourage pupils to learn to value and embrace diversity and individuality. The learning environment should be one in which all cultures, ages and personalities are valued and respected. Often as pupils become older and form friendship groups, they can become nervous about being different and standing up for what they think. Adults will need to encourage them to speak confidently and listen to what they have to say.

## Help children and young people to understand and respect other people's feelings and points of view

It is important for children and young people to learn to understand and respect the feelings of others. Young children will find this harder as their understanding will not be developed enough for them to put themselves in the position of others. By school age they may have a greater or lesser experience of this and older pupils will enjoy opportunities to debate and discuss different points of view. We often speak to them in school about thinking about the consequences of their actions and how they might have affected others. Through stories, assemblies and role play, we might encourage them to think about considering others' feelings.

Children also need to be able to understand how their own feelings might affect their behaviour and you may need to talk to them about this. For example, saying to a pupil, 'I know you are upset because you could not do cooking today' will help them to make the link between emotion and behaviour. In this way, they will be more able to understand how to think about others.

It is the beginning of the school year. The class teacher and yourself need to speak to your new class about the kind of behaviour you expect to see. You have decided that you will involve the pupils in discussing a set of class rules.

- Why might this be a worthwhile exercise?
- What support would you need to give pupils?
- Have you been involved in similar activities in your own school?
- Is there anything else you should take into account when doing this?

# Support children and young people to develop group agreements about the way they interact with others

When first starting to work with pupils, you should encourage them to discuss ground rules about how they will work together. This does not need to take long, but should encourage them to consider how they react to one another and the meaning of the word 'respect' when working together. In this way you will be proactive in establishing how pupils will work together.

# Demonstrate ways of encouraging and supporting children and young people to deal with conflict for themselves

Conflicting points of view and ideas will be a natural outcome of encouraging children's individuality. We will all have our own thoughts and feelings, and children and young people need to learn how to deal with this. They will also have to learn what behaviour is acceptable in the school environment, and be able to listen to and respect the thoughts of others. Older children should be encouraged to have discussions and debates around different points of view, as this will give them perspectives other than their own. Learning to talk through and resolve issues themselves will give them a valuable skill.

You will need to recognise that adults should not always intervene when there are areas of conflict and that if we want pupils to learn to resolve issues, we need to give them opportunities to do so. The best strategy is for them to discuss or negotiate issues themselves. However, there are times when you need to intervene and speak to pupils – for example, if at any time they become aggressive or unkind. Children who are very young or immature may find it hard to put themselves in the place of others. You may need to point out how important it is to be considerate of how others may be feeling. For example, if they want to take part in an activity which another child is doing, they will have to wait. Learning to share can be difficult for some children who may not have had much experience of this before coming to school.

If children have specific needs or abilities, for example, if they are autistic, they may find empathy with others very difficult. You will need to adapt how you respond in order to support them and you may need to ask for specialist advice. Where pupils have limited understanding due to their needs, it may be more difficult to explain to them and you may have to speak to them sensitively to resolve conflict.

## Getting ready for assessment

As all of the assessment criteria for this unit must be assessed in the workplace, you will need to plan a school visit carefully to maximise opportunities for your assessor to observe the ways in which you maintain and support relationships with children and young people. You can do this by planning a visit which includes group work and a playtime observation, so that they can see you dealing with any issues which occur. You may also find it useful for one of your witnesses to verify that you have good relationships with pupils who you support on a regular basis.

## Check your knowledge

1. Give examples of three different methods of communication.

2. How can we show that we are actively listening to pupils when speaking to them?

3. Here are some of the ways in which we can check children and young people's understanding:

   a) asking them to repeat back to us    c) using questions to check

   b) getting them to tell each other    d) using positive body language.

   Can you think of any further ideas? Why is it important to check and not to assume that children and young people have understood what we have said?

4. Describe some ways in which we can encourage all members of a group to participate in an activity.

5. Why is it important for adults to always be supportive of pupils' questions and concerns?

6. Give three examples of ways in which we can support and encourage pupils to make choices for themselves.

7. How can we encourage children and young people to understand individuality and diversity?

8. Why might it be more difficult for some pupils than for others to learn how to resolve conflict for themselves?

---

**Websites**

**www.teachernet.gov.uk/teachingandlearning** – teaching and learning strategies at Teachernet

# TDA 2.8 Support children & young people's health & safety

This unit requires you to know about current legislation and procedures which exist in your school for keeping children and young people safe in the learning environment, whether this is the classroom or other areas of the school. They will need to be taught how to manage risk for themselves and others.

## By the end of this unit you will:

1. know the legislative and policy framework for health and safety

2. be able to recognise and manage risks to children and young people's health, safety and security

3. be able to support children and young people to assess and manage risk

4. be able to respond to emergency situations.

# Know the legislative and policy framework for health and safety

## Describe how current health and safety legislation, policies and procedures are implemented in the setting

The piece of legislation which affects health and safety in schools the most is the Health and Safety at Work etc. Act. Under this Act, which came into effect in 1974, individuals in any organisation are required to ensure that they:

- report any **hazards**
- follow the school's safety policy
- make sure that their actions do not harm themselves or others
- use any safety equipment provided
- ensure equipment is safe and appropriate.

### Report any hazards

Everyone should be alert to any hazards which are likely to cause injury to themselves or others in the school. The school is required to carry out an annual risk assessment to determine which areas and activities of the school are most likely to be hazardous, the likelihood of specific hazards occurring, and those who are at risk. Pupils and staff need to be vigilant and immediately report any hazards which they notice to the appropriate person. This may be the school's health and safety representative, the Head Teacher or another member of staff. You should be aware of the designated person to whom you should report health and safety matters.

### Follow the school's safety policy

The school is required to have a safety policy which should give information to all staff about procedures which the school has in place for ensuring that the school is as safe as possible. All new staff joining the school should receive induction training in safety procedures and what to do in case of emergencies. Safety should be a regular topic at staff meetings and staff should sign the health and safety policy to state that they have read it.

> **Key term**
>
> Hazard – anything that has the potential to cause harm

> **Knowledge into action**
>
> Look at a copy of your own school's health and safety policy. What references can you find to current legislation? How does the school ensure that all staff have read and implement correct procedures?

> **Functional skills**
>
> English: Reading
> By using the health and safety policy to look at the links to the current legislation, you will develop your reading skills.

# HEALTH AND SAFETY POLICY
## INTRODUCTION

### Health and Safety at Work etc. Act 1974

The Health and Safety at Work Act etc. 1974 places a primary duty of care on all employers to ensure, as far as is reasonable, the health, safety and welfare of all their employees. In addition, employers are required to adopt a statement of safety policy. The council has done this. The Education Department has issued its policy to extend and particularise the general aims and objectives of the Council's statement.

Part One of the Education Safety Policy deals with the responsibilities of Head Teachers in individual establishments and the requirement for them to issue a local statement of safety policy and the arrangements for ensuring it is implemented correctly.

### GENERAL STATEMENT OF SAFETY POLICY

Our policy is to provide and maintain safe and healthy working conditions, equipment and systems of work for all employees, and to provide such information, training and supervision as they need for this purpose. We also accept responsibility for the health and safety of pupils and other people who may be affected by our activities.

The allocation of duties for safety matters and the particular arrangements which we will make to implement the policy are set out below.

The policy will be kept up to date, particularly as the curriculum, staff and procedures change. To ensure this, the policy and the way in which it has operated will be reviewed bi-annually.

This document must be read in conjunction with the Bromley and Education Department Safety Policies. Copies of all three documents will be available in the Staff Room for all staff.

These policies will form part of the induction training given to staff.

Signed ..................................................................................................................

Date ...................................

Head Teacher

Signed ..................................................................................................................

Date ...................................

Chair of Governors

*Part of a school's health and safety policy.*

### Make sure that their actions do not harm themselves or others

Staff also need to ensure that any actions which they take are not likely to harm or cause a danger to others in the school. This will include tidying up and putting things away after use. You also need to consider the effects of *not* taking action – for example, if you discover a potential danger, it is your responsibility not to ignore it but to report it as appropriate.

### Use any safety equipment provided

Staff need to ensure that safety equipment which is provided for use when carrying out activities is always used. This includes safe use of tools which are used for subjects such as design and technology, or gloves when handling materials in science activities. There should be guidelines in the school's policy for the safe use and storage of equipment.

### Ensure equipment is safe and appropriate

All materials and equipment used in schools will need to fulfil recognised standards of safety. The most widely used safety symbol is the Kitemark, which shows that an item has been tested by the British Standards Institution. Products are not legally required to carry a Kitemark, but many do so in order to show that they meet these requirements. However, European regulations require that many items must also meet their legal requirements before they can be offered for sale within the European Union. These items will carry a CE symbol to show that they meet European rules.

*How many of these safety symbols do you recognise?*

Always make sure that the equipment you are offering for use to children is age and ability appropriate. The guidelines which are given by manufacturers are intended to be a realistic means of checking that equipment is not misused. A pupil who is too young or too old may be unable to use the equipment appropriately and may hurt themselves and others as a result.

All staff working within a school have a responsibility to ensure that children are cared for and safe. The Children Act (1989) and Children

(Scotland) Act 1995 also require that we protect children as far as we can when they are in our care. This includes preventing any **risks** which may occur.

> **CASE STUDY:** Making sure pupils do not harm themselves or others
>
> Maria is working in a special school for pupils who have learning difficulties. She is supporting a cookery lesson during which some liquid has been spilled on the floor. Maria tells one of the pupils to put a chair in front of the spillage so that others will be aware of it, but then forgets to get it cleaned up and the chair is put away. During the following lesson, the floor is still wet and a pupil in another class slips over.
>
> - What should Maria have done?
> - Why is it important to act immediately in situations like this?

## Describe how health and safety is monitored and maintained in the setting and how staff are made aware of risks and hazards

The person responsible for health and safety in your school should carry out safety checks routinely or make sure that these take place on a regular basis. There should be regular walk-rounds or other means of making sure that hazards are not being left unreported. Where hazards are discovered — for example, items stored on top of cupboards which could fall down when the cupboard is opened — these should be recorded and reported immediately. Safety checks should also be made on all equipment which could be hazardous if neglected. All electrical items which are used in school, for example, should have annual checks carried out by a qualified electrician. Equipment such as fire extinguishers should be checked annually and this should be recorded on the outside of the extinguisher.

Health and safety should also be a regular discussion point at any meetings which you attend in the school, and staff regularly reminded about any issues. If a specific hazard has arisen and all staff need to be notified quickly, there should be a procedure for doing this.

*How many hazards can you find in this classroom?*

## Identify the lines of responsibility and reporting for health and safety in the setting

As well as being aware of the name of your school's health and safety officer, you should know about how health and safety issues are reported in your school. Although the Head Teacher will ultimately be responsible for all issues within the school, your health and safety officer and site manager should be able to give you details of the different procedures you should follow. They should also be in your school's health and safety policy, which should have been read by all staff. Table 1 details lines of responsibility, but this may vary depending on the school's policy.

### Portfolio activity

What would you do if you found the following in school and would you need to report them?

- A broken chair in a classroom
- An electrical problem
- A piece of faulty equipment
- Fox mess outside a door into the school
- A pupil being sick.

| Role | Responsibility |
|------|----------------|
| Head Teacher | Ultimate responsibility for health and safety |
| Health and safety officer | Monitoring and ensuring procedures for reporting and recording potential hazards are understood by all |
| Site manager | Dealing with or removing hazards |
| All staff and pupils | Reporting health and safety issues |

*Table 1: Roles and responsibilities.*

# Be able to recognise and manage risks to children and young people's health, safety and security

The assessment criteria for this learning outcome must be assessed in the workplace.

## Demonstrate how to identify potential hazards and deal with risks to the health, safety and security of children and young people

In the course of your work with children and young people, you should always be aware of potential hazards and how you should deal with them. As an adult it is your responsibility to ensure that pupils are not subjected to any unnecessary danger while in your care. You must ensure that you are vigilant at all times and do your best to prevent accidents and emergencies from occurring. There is a number of areas which you will need to consider when looking at the learning environment.

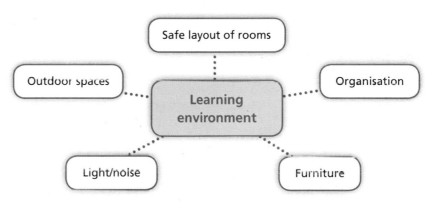

*There is a number of physical hazards you need to look out for in the learning environment.*

### Safe layout of rooms

Rooms should be organised safely and there should be adequate space so that the number of people who will be using them will be able to move around comfortably. Everyone should be able to access materials and equipment as required without causing risk to others. If you notice that something might be better from a safety point of view in a different position, you should always say something.

### Organisation

Equipment should be stored safely and well organised so that it does not present a hazard. Drawers and storage should be properly marked so that it is clear where different equipment is kept and pupils are able to find it easily. Always replace equipment in the correct place after use.

### Furniture

This should be an appropriate size for the age of pupils so that they are able to sit comfortably when working. Pupils should not be hunched over tables or desks which are too small or have difficulty in sitting and working comfortably.

### Light/noise

There should be sufficient light for pupils to work without discomfort. You should be aware that harsh lighting (for example, from fluorescent bulbs) can sometimes be uncomfortable after a prolonged time and cause headaches in some individuals. You may also find that an area which you had thought was suitable in which to work with children is inappropriate — for example, it may be too cramped or too noisy during lesson time.

### Outdoor spaces

Outdoor areas which are to be used by children and young people should be secure and boundaries regularly inspected to ensure that they are safe. When pupils are going outside, the area should be checked first to ensure that it is tidy and any litter, broken glass or animal mess has been cleared up. If you are taking pupils outside, make sure that they are aware how any equipment is to be used and reinforce rules wherever possible to remind them how to behave. If you are working with younger children, remember that ponds and sandpits should be covered when not in use, as sandpits left uncovered can attract foxes and dogs, and can also be hazardous if children are unattended. Any toys or equipment should always be appropriate to the space available and should be put away safely. Plants can also be dangerous — thorns or nettles should be kept back and any poisonous plants noted and/or removed.

*What should you check before children can play outside?*

## Functional skills

**Mathematics: Interpreting**
Have a go at drawing your classroom to scale and then add the cupboards and storage to your plan. Label on your plan where you store hazardous items so that you are protecting the children. For example, you may draw a locked cupboard and label it as where you keep your scissors so that the children cannot use them unsupervised.

In the normal course of your practice, it is likely that you will be involved in risk assessment at some stage, whether this is because you have some responsibility for health and safety or because you are going on a school trip or visit. There will usually be a member of staff responsible for ensuring that all risk assessments are carried out and the paperwork completed in good time before the trip or activity is carried out. The representative and the head teacher then need to check and sign this to show that it has been completed correctly. The forms will give some guidance as to the kinds of checks that should be carried out.

**Risk Assessment – Transport (Contract Vehicle)**

| Hazard | Who may be affected? | Control measures | Further Action |
|---|---|---|---|
| Condition of vehicle/driver | All | If the condition of either the vehicle or the driver is considered to be dangerous the venture is not allowed to proceed. | Ask the company to confirm that vehicle to be used has appropriate documentation, is roadworthy and drivers hold relevant qualifications and experience prior to booking. |
| Unexpected movement/ braking of vehicle | All | Pupils sitting in seats with seat belts fastened at all times when the vehicle is in motion. Pupils must not distract the driver when the vehicle is in motion. All baggage stowed securely. | Staff supervision to ensure that this is complied with throughout the journey. |
| Road Accident | All | **If the accident is not serious.** On normal road keep pupils on the vehicle if it is safe to do so. If not, move the pupils to a safe location protected from traffic. When moving follow the highway code and use staff to supervise the pupils to avoid danger. **If the accident is serious** Move those able to walk away from the scene of the accident keeping them safe throughout. This will have to be assessed at the time. Deal with casualties as best as you can until emergency help arrives. | Control communication between pupils and parents/carers. Contact school as soon as possible. Control communication between pupils and parents/carers. Contact school and Emergency Contact at the LEA as soon as possible. Co-operate with the emergency services and at least one member of staff accompanies an injured young person to hospital. They remain there until parents or guardians arrive. |

*A risk assessment form.*

**CASE STUDY:** Identifying potential hazards and risks

Tim is taking a group of six Year 2 children on a maths walk which will be both inside and outside the school.

- What should Tim do to ensure that the children are safe before he sets off?
- Should he take anything else with him?

## Security hazards

Security hazards exist when the school procedures are not followed and visitors are able to enter the school without going in through the main door and being signed in there. This is likely to happen on days when, for example, doors are left open due to hot weather, or a member of staff who usually signs people in is absent. You should be alert to these kinds of situations and redirect people or make others aware of their presence if necessary. You should also report any security issues such as holes in fences, broken gates and so on.

## Fire hazards

If you are working in an environment where fire is an additional hazard, you should have had some training in what to do. For example, you may be working with pupils in a kitchen in a food technology class or in a science laboratory during a chemistry lesson. It is likely that you will have regular fire drills and know how to evacuate the building, but you should also know about different kinds of fire extinguishers and fire blankets, and when and how to use them. Fire hazards may also exist when electrical equipment is misused or is not safety checked. You should not bring your own electrical equipment into school and use it unless it has been checked. (See also page 136 on procedures for fire.)

## Food safety

School kitchens will need to comply with health and safety requirements, as will other areas in the school which carry out any cooking with pupils. If you are asked to cook with pupils, make sure that you only use safe ingredients, as many children have food allergies, and check that you know how to use any equipment before use and that it is safe for pupils. You should be a good role model for children and always follow good practice yourself with regard to hygiene. This will include washing of hands before any activity involving foodstuffs, such as lunchtime or prior to cooking activities. You should also make sure that you do not leave young children alone near items such as sharp knives, hotplates or ovens.

## Personal safety

You should be aware of risks to pupils' personal safety at all times when you are supervising them. These may be due to their ages, needs or abilities. For example, younger children will need you to point out risks more regularly than older pupils, who should be more aware. You should take the specific abilities and needs of pupils into account when working with them. You should in particular take note of any pupils who have special educational needs (SEN).

## Demonstrate ways of supporting children and young people to take responsibility for their own health, safety and security

When you are working with pupils, you should always ensure that you talk through any health and safety preparation if you are carrying it out. This is because children and young people need to be taught to think these things through and do them for themselves. If they are used to talking them through, this will become part of the learning process and raise their awareness. Very young children in particular may not always understand immediate dangers and will need more supervision until they increase in awareness as they grow older. They will need to learn not to rely on adults to tell them what to do but to develop their own responsibilities so that they learn to be independent. You can support children and young people to take responsibility for health and safety by giving them as many opportunities as possible to do this.

### Portfolio activity

Give an example of a time when you have given pupils an opportunity to discuss and evaluate risk within your setting or on a school trip or journey. Show how you have supported them in the activity and what you consider the benefits to have been.

### CASE STUDY: Taking responsibility for health, safety and security

Duncan, a teaching assistant, has been asked to take part of a school journey with a Year 6 class who are going to spend a week on the Isle of Wight. He is one of two male staff who are to accompany the group. Before they set off, the group have a meeting with the children and their parents to talk through rules for the trip and how they should keep safe.

- How do you think the school could approach this so that they encourage the children to take responsibility?
- Do you think that the parents should be involved?

## Be able to support children and young people to assess and manage risk

### Outline the importance of taking a balanced approach to risk management

It is important for all those who work with children and young people to take a balanced approach to risk management. Children should learn to be able to take some risks, and most activities will carry some element of danger. Many educationalists now believe that the current tendency for many parents to keep their children indoors and take them everywhere by car has negative effects and is overprotective, as it does not allow them to explore and discover the world for themselves or assess elements of risk. If children's experiences are limited due to adults' anxieties, it is likely that they will find it difficult to assess and manage risk when they become adults.

When children are given more independence, they are more likely to grow in confidence — they should be encouraged to think about risks which may arise and act accordingly. In school, while it is important to be vigilant and avoid excessive risk taking, we can help pupils to think about risks in the environment and what we can do to avoid them. Although you are making sure that learning environments in which pupils can work and play are safe places, you can also encourage them to think about why certain courses of action, such as playing football close to other pupils, may not be sensible. As pupils grow older, they should have more opportunities, both in school and through extra-curricular activities, to consider how their decisions will impact on themselves and others. They should also have opportunities to discuss potential risks and problems with one another and with adults.

A balanced approach to risk management means:

● taking into account the child or young person's age, needs and abilities

● avoiding excessive risk taking

● not being excessively risk adverse

● recognising the importance of risk and challenge to children and young people's development.

### Portfolio activity

Think about the areas of risk for the following groups. How does the risk involved balance with the learning experience?

• Taking a group of pupils with learning difficulties to the park

• Working with a Reception group in the outside classroom

• Taking Year 8 on a skiing trip

• Working with Year 4 on a design & technology activity using hot glue guns and hacksaws

• Sending Year 10 on a modern languages exchange visit.

### Functional skills

**English: Speaking, listening and communication**
You could use the portfolio activity above as an excellent topic for discussion. Why not discuss these areas of risk in your class and share your ideas with each other? Take care not to speak over someone else and listen carefully to what they have to say so that you can make a relevant contribution. You could plan your thoughts carefully before the discussion so that you know what you are going to say.

## Demonstrate ways of supporting children and young people to assess and manage risk for themselves

This assessment criterion must be assessed in the workplace.

You will need to be able to give examples from your own practice of how you have supported pupils in assessing and managing health and safety risks to themselves. This will show that you have an awareness of the kinds of situations in which you should be vigilant, but also how you are able to pass this awareness on to pupils. The more that pupils are encouraged to think about the kinds of issues which may pose a risk, the more likely they are to learn to do this. The kinds of things your school might do to encourage this could include:

1. signs and reminders on plugs and electrical equipment

2. notices on cupboards to remind pupils about safe storage

3. discussing safety issues with pupils as part of day-to-day practice

4. washing hands after using the toilet or after handling animals or plants

5. talking through the reasons for fire practice and other safety requirements

6. reminders on outside doors to close them and fire doors to keep clear.

**Over to you!**

Can you think of other things which schools can do to support children and young people in assessing and managing risk for themselves?

---

**CASE STUDY:** Supporting children to assess and manage risk

Jackie is working with a group of Year 5 children who are about to go pond dipping. The pond is some distance from the school and it is used for educational purposes by the school and their partner infant school. Although the group will be going with the class teacher, Jackie has been asked to talk through the risks with the children before they go and has been given a list of the kinds of issues of which they should be aware. She has to ask them to draw up their own risk assessment. The issues she has been given are:

1. informing the school who they are taking with them

2. safety when crossing roads

3. importance of sensible behaviour

4. tripping and other hazards close to the pond

5. danger from poisonous plants or hazardous litter

6. falling into the pond

7. danger of infection from cuts if uncovered (Weil's disease).

- Do you think that this is a good exercise? Why?
- How might this help both the children and staff while they are off site?

**Functional skills**

**English: Writing**
You could develop your writing skills by writing a letter home to the parents of the children who are going pond dipping, explaining the risks to them so that they know what their child is doing and can enforce the rules at home. Take care with your choice of language and make sure that you structure your letter in a logical way.

# Be able to respond to emergency situations

The assessment criteria for this learning outcome may be assessed through simulated activities. This means that you may carry out an observed emergency situation which may be observed and recorded by your assessor.

## Recognise and respond to emergency situations

In any environment where children are being supervised, it is likely that there will be illness, incidents or injuries at some time. You may find that you are first on the scene in the case of an accident or in an emergency and need to take action. If you are the only adult in the vicinity, you will need to make sure you follow the correct procedures until help arrives. You may also have to deal with an accident or emergency which involves one of your colleagues or another adult. It is vital to send for help as soon as possible. This should be one of the school's qualified first aiders and an ambulance if necessary.

Emergency situations include:

- accidents
- illness
- fires
- security incidents
- missing children or young people.

Warning! If you are not trained in first aid, and if you are at all unsure about what to do, you should only take action to avert any further danger to the casualty and others.

## Follow the setting's procedures for dealing with emergency situations

All schools need to ensure that they take measures to protect all adults and pupils while they are on school premises and undertaking off-site visits. This means that there will be procedures in place for a number of situations which may arise. These include the following.

### Accidents

There should be enough first aiders in the school or on the trip at any time to deal with accidents. First-aid boxes should be checked and replenished regularly, and there should be clear lines of reporting so that accidents are recorded correctly. If you are off site you should always have a first aider with you, along with a first-aid box and any inhalers, EpiPen®s or other medical requirements of pupils you are with.

### Illness

It is likely that the school will usually deal with incidents of illness by sending pupils or adults directly to the office, sick room or first aider. However, if you need to deal with an illness which has come on suddenly, you may need to take action yourself while sending for a first aider. You should make the casualty comfortable and ensure that they are warm, but should not attempt to carry out any further treatment.

There is also an increasing number of pupils in schools who have allergic reactions to foods such as nuts or intolerances to foods such as wheat. All staff in the school should be aware of the identities of these children and there should be clear instructions readily available about how to deal with each case. Lunchtime supervisors in particular will need to be kept informed. There may be a book containing photographs of the children, contact telephone numbers and information about the food intolerance. In some schools, photographs and information may be displayed on staff room walls, although care should be taken with this due to confidentiality.

*How do you deal with children with allergies?*

---

**CASE STUDY:** Dealing with an allergy

Jemma is supervising Class 3 and a new child started in Class 2 a few weeks ago. At lunchtime, the child starts to have difficulty breathing and his friend calls Jemma over. She finds out that the child has a nut allergy and is sitting close to a child who has peanut butter in her sandwiches.

• What should Jemma do first?
• What should have happened to prevent this situation from occurring?

*Fire notices must be displayed prominently*

## Fires

Schools may need to be evacuated for different reasons — for example, a fire, bomb scare or other emergency. Your school is required to have a health and safety policy which should give guidelines for emergency procedures and you should make sure that you are aware of these. The school should have regular fire drills — around once a term — at different times of the day (not just before breaks for convenience!) so that all adults and pupils are aware of what to do wherever they are on the premises. These may be, for example, at lunchtime if midday supervisors are present, or during after-school or breakfast clubs when there may be different staff on site and pupils may be in a different environment. Fire drills and building evacuation practices should be displayed and recorded, and all adults should know what their role requires them to do and where to assemble pupils. If you are on a school visit, you should have been briefed as to what to do in case of fire or evacuation of the building.

## Security incidents

This aspect includes making sure that all those who are in school have been signed in and identified. Schools may have different methods for doing this; for example, they should have secure entry and exit points, and visitors should be issued with badges. If staff notice any unidentified people in the school, they should challenge them immediately. If you are on duty outside and notice anything suspicious, you should also send for help.

### Portfolio activity

Using a copy of your school's health and safety policy, highlight the procedures your school has in place for the areas above. If it is not documented in the policy, find out whether it is recorded elsewhere. If you are unable to find the information recorded anywhere, you will need to speak to your head teacher or health and safety representative in order to find out and then write a reflective account under each heading.

### CASE STUDY: Following school procedures around security

Khaled works as an ICT technician in a mixed secondary school. He is on his way out one day when he notices a man who he does not recognise walking off the football pitch with a group of pupils and talking to them. He goes over to speak to the man and to find out what he is doing. As it turns out, the man had come into school to speak to a group of learners and, after signing out, had decided to go and watch the football practice and talk to the teams about their fixtures.

- Did Khaled do the right thing?
- Do you think he should deal with this matter on his own?
- Should he say anything to anyone after the incident?

## Missing children or young people

Fortunately it is extremely rare for children to go missing, particularly if the school follows health and safety guidelines and procedures. On school trips you should periodically check the group for whom you are responsible as well as keeping an eye on children who are being supervised by helpers. If for some reason a child does go missing, you should raise the alarm straight away and make sure that you follow school policy.

## Give reassurance and comfort to those involved in the emergency

You will need to support and reassure not only the casualty but also others who may be present. Children and young people, as well as other adults who are nearby, may become distressed and, depending on what they have witnessed, may be in shock themselves. If possible, ask another adult to remove any children who may be present and to supervise and stay with them while you remain with the casualty in order to reassure them.

## Give other people providing assistance clear information about what has happened

When first aiders or the ambulance arrives, you will need to pass on clear information about the circumstances of what has happened. You need to ensure that you do not omit any important details. You should include:

- the time of the incident
- exactly what happened and whether you saw this yourself
- who was present
- any medication the casualty may be on if you know this
- exactly what assistance you have given to the casualty.

This will enable the first aiders to manage the situation and to carry out the appropriate treatment.

## Follow the procedures of the setting for reporting and recording accidents and emergencies

Even if you are not a first aider, you should know the correct procedures for recording and reporting injuries and accidents in your school, as you may be called upon to do this. Remember that following all injuries or emergencies, even minor accidents, a record should be made of what has happened and the steps taken by staff who were present. You should also report verbally to senior management as soon as possible.

In addition to recording accidents, your school will also need to monitor illnesses which are passed around the school, as in some cases these will need to be reported to the local education authority (LEA). It is likely that your school office or sick bay will have a Department of Health poster showing signs and symptoms of some common illnesses so that staff know what to look for. All staff need to be alert to physical signs that children may be incubating illness. Incubation periods can vary between illnesses, from one day to three weeks in some cases. Remember that young children may not be able to communicate exactly what is wrong. General signs that children are off colour may include:

- pale skin
- flushed cheeks
- rashes.
- different (quiet, clingy, irritable) behaviour
- rings around the eyes

## Accident report form

Name of casualty ....................................................................................

Exact location of incident .......................................................................

Date of incident ......................................................................................

What was the injured person doing? .......................................................

How did the accident happen? .................................................................

What injuries occurred? ...........................................................................

Treatment given ......................................................................................

Medical aid sought ..................................................................................

Name of person dealing with incident ....................................................

Name of witness ......................................................................................

If the causualty was a child, what time were the parents informed?...........

Was hospital attended? ............................................................................

Was the accident investigated? ............................. By whom?...................

Signed ....................................................... Position...............................

### Knowledge into action

Investigate your setting's procedures for recording and reporting accidents, incidents, injuries and illness. Are all staff aware of the location of the appropriate paperwork when the need arises?

*Find out where accident forms are kept in your school and the procedures for completing them.*

| Illness and symptoms | Recommended time to keep off school and treatment | Comments |
|---|---|---|
| Chickenpox – patches of itchy red spots with white centres | For five days from onset of rash. Treat with calamine lotion to relieve itching | It is not necessary to keep the child at home until all the spots have disappeared |
| Rubella (German measles) – pink rash on head, trunk and limbs; slight fever, sore throat | For five days from onset of rash. Treat by resting | The child is most infectious before diagnosis. Keep them away from pregnant women |
| Impetigo – small red pimples on the skin, which break down and weep | Until lesions are crusted and healed. Treat with antibiotic cream or medicine | Antibiotic treatment may speed up healing. Wash hands well after touching the child's skin |
| Ringworm – contagious fungal infection of the skin. Shows as circular flaky patches | None. Treat with anti-fungal ointment; it may require antibiotics | It needs treatment by the GP |
| Diarrhoea and vomiting | Until diarrhoea and vomiting has settled and for 24 hours after. No specific diagnosis or treatment, although keep giving clear fluids and no milk | |

| Illness and symptoms | Recommended time to keep off school and treatment | Comments |
|---|---|---|
| Conjunctivitis – inflammation or irritation of the membranes lining the eyelids, red eyes, watering eyes, sticky coating on the eyelashes, sore eyes | None (although schools may have different policies on this). Wash with warm water on cotton wool swab, lubricant eyedrops can be purchased over the counter. GP may prescribe antibiotics | |
| Measles – fever, runny eyes, sore throat, cough; red rash, which often starts from the head, spreading downwards | Give rest, plenty of fluids and paracetamol for fever | This is now more likely with some parents refusing MMR inoculation |
| Meningitis – fever, headache, stiff neck and blotchy skin; dislike of light; symptoms may develop very quickly | Get urgent medical attention. It is treated with antibiotics | It can have severe complications and be fatal |
| Tonsillitis – inflammation of the tonsils by infection. Very sore throat, fever, earache, enlarged red tonsils, which may have white spots | Treat with antibiotics and rest | It can also cause ear infection |

Table 2: Common illnesses and their characteristics.

Children often develop symptoms of illness more quickly than adults, as they may have less resistance to infection. Most schools will call parents and carers straight away if the child is showing signs or symptoms of illnesses. If children are on antibiotics, most schools will recommend that they stay off school until they have completed the course.

## Functional skills

ICT: Developing, presenting and communicating information
You could select one bullet point from the checklist and convert it into a poster to be displayed in your class. Think carefully about the age of the children in your group so that you can adapt the language that you use. Include colour, text and images in your poster.

## BEST PRACTICE CHECKLIST: Health, safety and security arrangements

- Always be vigilant.
- Use and store equipment safely.
- Check both the indoor and outdoor environment and equipment regularly and report anything that is unsafe, following the correct procedures.
- Challenge any unidentified persons in school.
- Check adult–child ratios in all situations.
- Always encourage pupils to assess risks for themselves.
- Ensure you are aware of security procedures at the beginning and end of the day.
- Make sure you are thoroughly prepared when carrying out unusual activities or when going on trips.
- Use correct procedures for clearing up any bodily fluids.

## Getting ready for assessment

In order to gather evidence for this unit, you should plan your assessment visit carefully. As part of it, you should arrange to go for a health and safety walk-round with your assessor and do the following.

- Identify and act on any risks you can find in your school by reporting them to the appropriate person and recording them appropriately.

- Point out safety equipment and talk through the procedures for fire drills and school security.

- Show the accident book to your assessor and in particular point out any entries which you have made.

- Talk to your assessor about any examples of how you have encouraged pupils to assess and manage risk for themselves.

## Check your knowledge

1. Who should you ask or where would you find out about health and safety procedures in your school?

2. What is the main piece of legislation around health and safety of which you should be aware?

3. What obligations do you have under the Act to:
   a) have first aid training?
   b) report any hazards?
   c) use safety equipment?
   d) write down any health and safety issues?

4. What kinds of potential hazards should you be aware of in school?

5. Name three aspects of health and safety you should consider when going on a school trip.

6. Why should all incidents and accidents be reported?
   a) So that schools can keep track of how many they have.
   b) So that if there is any further development, there will be a record of what happened.
   c) To inform parents.
   d) To ensure that they know who carried out any treatment.

7. You should not carry out any kind of first aid unless you are a qualified first aider — true or false?

8. How can children and young people be encouraged to learn how to manage risk for themselves?

## Websites

**www.bbc.co.uk/health/treatments/first_aid** – information from the BBC on first aid

**www.sja.org.uk** – St John Ambulance

**www.hse.gov.uk** – Health and Safety Executive

**www.redcross.org** – the Red Cross

**www.nhs.uk** – National Health Service

**www.hpa.org.uk** – Health Protection Agency

# TDA 2.9 Support children & young people's positive behaviour

For this unit you will need to show that you support good behaviour in school and respond to inappropriate behaviour. This will be in a variety of contexts, including around the school, on school trips and in different learning environments.

## By the end of this unit you will:

1. know the policies and procedures of the setting for promoting children and young people's positive behaviour
2. be able to support positive behaviour
3. be able to respond to inappropriate behaviour.

# Know the policies and procedures of the setting for promoting children and young people's positive behaviour

## Describe the policies and procedures of the setting relevant to promoting children and young people's positive behaviour

When managing pupils' behaviour, all staff need to be aware of school policies. This means that you should know where they are and have read them, so that pupils will understand when you apply sanctions and behaviour management strategies. Although the main policy dealing with behaviour is the behaviour policy, other school policies will also have an impact on managing behaviour, for example, the health and safety, child protection and anti-bullying policies.

Policies and procedures of the setting relevant to promoting positive behaviour cover:

- behaviour
- code of conduct
- rewards and sanctions
- dealing with conflict and inappropriate behaviour
- anti-bullying
- attendance.

### Behaviour policy

The school's behaviour policy is important as it gives guidelines to all staff on how they should manage pupil behaviour. All staff need to be familiar with school policy so that it can be consistently applied in the school.

### Code of conduct

It is likely that your school will have a set of rules or **code of conduct**. It is imperative in any school for pupils to have guidelines so that they have a clear understanding of how to behave. Children and young people need to be aware of the boundaries within which to manage their behaviour so that they know what is expected of them.

These rules should be written in such a way that the pupils are given positive targets, for example, 'I will walk quietly around the school' rather than the negative 'Do not run in school'. Where the language may be difficult for very young children to understand, for example, 'treating others with respect', staff should make sure that the children understand its meaning. The rules should be discussed frequently with pupils, both in class and during assembly times, and displayed around the school so that they remember them.

**Key term**

Code of conduct – an agreed set of rules by which all children are expected to behave

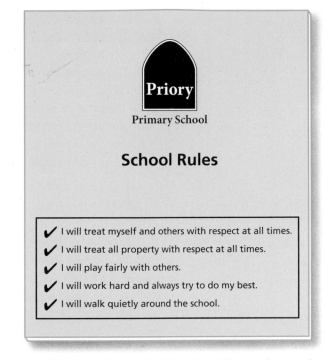

*A simply and attractively laid out code of conduct will appeal to pupils.*

As well as this list of school rules, pupils should be encouraged to behave in a positive way through watching the behaviour of adults. Children and young people will soon notice if an adult is not acting in a way that they would expect, or if there are inconsistent expectations between adults. When a child is behaving particularly well, you should remember to praise this behaviour so that it is recognised. Children and young people need to be praised for work, behaviour, effort and achievement genuinely and frequently. This will reinforce good behaviour and build self-esteem.

## Rewards and sanctions

Your school should have a scale of sanctions for instances when behaviour is undesirable, despite modelling and encouraging good behaviour. All staff should be able to apply these and pupils should be aware of this. There should be a structured approach, which is clear and defines what is expected and the consequences of inappropriate behaviour.

Consequences could be:

- time out or name on the board

- miss one to five minutes or longer of break time

- be sent to the deputy head or year group leader

- be sent to the head teacher or for staff to speak to the parents.

Your school's behaviour policy should give a clear indication of the procedures you can use when implementing rewards and sanctions. You should make sure that both you and pupils are aware of what will happen if their behaviour is not acceptable.

**English: Writing**
**ICT: Developing, presenting and communicating information**
You could produce a leaflet for the parents of the children that outlines how their child's behaviour will be dealt with in your school. This will give the parents the opportunity to use the same rewards and sanctions at home. Think carefully about the layout of the leaflet and your choice of vocabulary.

All adults in the school should be able to give rewards and sanctions, although some will be specific to certain members of staff. An example of this might be certificates, which may only be handed out by the Head Teacher in Friday assembly. If, as a member of support staff, you are not sure about what you can pass on to pupils, you need to find this out so that you are ready at the appropriate moment!

---

**CASE STUDY:** Using rewards and sanctions

At Meerham Primary School, there has been a number of recent issues around pupil behaviour. As a result, the behaviour policy is about to be updated. You are working with the SENCO to investigate what is current practice in the school. You find out that although there is a set of school rules, the rewards and sanctions which are applied by staff vary depending on the teacher. In other words, when pupils' behaviour is inappropriate, in Year 5 the teacher will put a pupil's name on the board followed by sending them to another class, but in Year 3 a different strategy is applied.

- Why do you think this may cause problems in the school?
- What should the new behaviour policy include?
- How could you work with other staff to decide on an update to the policy?

---

### Dealing with conflict and inappropriate behaviour

It is likely that your school policy will give you guidance and information about how you should manage more difficult behaviour. It is important that pupils see a clear structure in what will happen if they choose not to pay attention to the school rules that are in place. They will be much more likely to adhere to the rules if they know exactly what will happen if they do not. In this situation, adults are prepared for the types of behaviour which may occur and are teaching pupils that they are responsible for their actions.

### Anti-bullying

This policy may be addressed as part of the behaviour policy but should set out school procedures for dealing with any incidence of bullying within or outside the school. Bullying can take many forms, particularly

## Link

For more on this, see TDA 2.2 Safeguarding the welfare of children and young people.

through cyber-bullying with the increase in technologies such as mobile phones and the Internet, and increasing numbers of younger children have access to these.

### Attendance

The attendance policy will set out how the school manages issues around attendance. In all schools, attendance is monitored closely and recorded on computer systems so that patterns can be noted and parents or carers informed if attendance falls below a certain percentage. In some cases, schools will award certificates to classes or individual pupils for full attendance during a term or half term.

### Over to you!

Using your school's behaviour policy, find and photocopy for your portfolio:

- any school rules or codes of conduct
- rewards and sanctions used within the school
- your responsibilities under the policy.

If you are unable to copy the policies, you may wish to write a reflective account to explain both your responsibilities and the school's procedures.

### Functional skills

**English: Reading and Writing**
This activity promotes both your reading and writing skills. It is really important that you read the policies carefully so that you can use the information in the policies to write your account. When writing your account, it is important that you take care with your layout, spelling and punctuation.

## Describe the importance of all staff consistently and fairly applying boundaries and rules for children and young people's behaviour

All staff in your school need to know and apply the rules consistently, and behaviour should be closely monitored in the school by senior managers. This is because children and young people need to be shown fair and consistent boundaries and respond well when they know what is expected of them. If all members of the school community are using the same principles and strategies when managing behaviour, it is far more likely that pupils will respond positively. Also, if behaviour is not managed well in a school, it is likely that pupil learning will suffer, as more lesson time will be wasted. Pupils should know the scale of rewards and sanctions, and the order in which they will be applied, whoever is speaking to them about their behaviour.

Workforce remodelling has had an impact on the number of different professionals who are now working in schools. Support staff and midday supervisors, as well as those running extended school provision, should know the importance and impact of consistent strategies. It is also important that support staff are given status within the school so that they are respected in the same way as teaching staff. This will in turn lead to better behaviour management and clearer boundaries for pupils.

### Reflect ?

Look at the way in which pupils interact with and respond to different adults in your school. Do you notice any difference in the way in which they do this? Why do you think this may be?

### CASE STUDY: Consistent boundaries and rules

Sue has just started working in a junior school as a midday supervisor and a part-time teaching assistant. She mainly works in Year 3 but is sometimes asked to work in Year 2 when needed. Because she is not in the classroom as often as other staff, she is not aware of how much she should 'let them get away with', as she confides to a colleague.

- What should have happened when Sue started in her role?
- Should there be any difference in the way in which midday supervisors and teaching assistants apply behaviour management strategies?

# Be able to support positive behaviour

## Describe the benefits of encouraging and rewarding positive behaviour

It is important for all pupils, but especially for those who tend to be 'told off' more than others, that their positive behaviour is recognised and rewarded. Even as adults we like to be noticed for something good that we do. Research has shown that we need to be given six positives for every negative in order to balance this out. It is always much easier for us to focus on negative aspects of a child's behaviour and react to those. When recognising and rewarding positive behaviour, however, you must not forget to notice those children who always behave appropriately.

These ideas are linked to Behaviourist Theory, which was developed by B.F. Skinner in the 1940s. He suggested that children will respond to praise and so will repeat behaviour that gives them recognition or praise for what they do. This may take the simple form of verbal praise, which is very powerful, or physical tokens of praise, such as stamps, stickers or merit marks. Children who receive praise or attention for positive behaviour, such as kindness towards others, are much more likely to repeat this behaviour.

Children and young people may also attempt to gain attention through undesirable behaviour. You will need to be aware of this and try to ignore it where possible, instead giving attention to pupils who are behaving well.

**CASE STUDY:** Promoting positive behaviour

Ray works with pupils of all ages in the music department of a mixed secondary school. He finds that the behaviour of pupils varies between the different age groups, with those who have selected music as a GCSE or A level option being much easier to supervise. He is working with a group of Year 8 pupils on some composition work and finds that they are not at all on task or engaged in the activity. Two of the boys are distracting the rest of the group with their behaviour.

- What kinds of strategies do you think Ray could apply here?
- Is there anything else he could do in the long term to encourage more positive behaviour in those groups which are less engaged?

## Apply skills and techniques for supporting and encouraging children and young people's positive behaviour

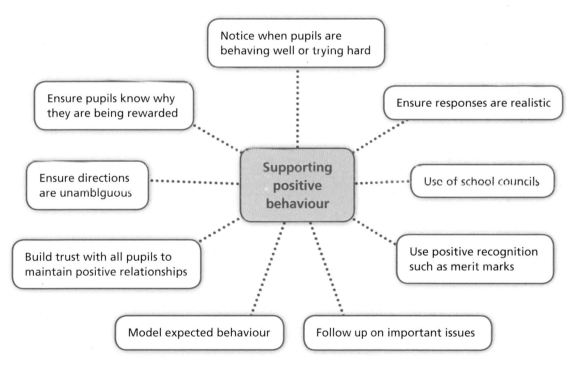

*How many of these strategies do you apply in your school?*

### Notice when children are behaving well or trying hard
This is important because it will help to build positive relationships and shows that you care about the pupil. If you do not notice, they may not think that it is worth repeating the behaviour or that it is not important.

### Use positive recognition such as merit marks

Most schools use these kinds of systems and will have assemblies and evenings to celebrate work and behaviour.

### Follow up on important issues

You should always make sure you follow up, particularly if you have said that you will. There is little point in saying to a pupil that you will be telling their teacher how pleased you are with their behaviour if you forget to do so. The pupil will then think that you do not really think it is important.

### Build trust with all pupils to maintain positive relationships

Do all you can to show pupils that you are interested in and value them. As you get to know them, you will remember particular things about them. Giving your trust to pupils encourages them to take more responsibility, for example, allowing younger children to take the register down to the school office, or allowing older pupils to organise their own school events.

### Ensure children know why they are being rewarded

You must be clear about exactly what you are praising or rewarding, for example: 'I am giving you this merit mark because you have been so helpful to others this morning.'

### Making sure directions are unambiguous

You should make sure that you communicate clearly to pupils so that they know what you are asking of them. Young children may find directions confusing, especially if there are too many instructions at once or if they are occupied doing something else. If you communicate through questioning, for example, 'Would you like to get ready to...?', pupils may think that there is some choice involved. If we want children and young people to do as we ask, we need to say things as though we mean them.

### Making use of school councils

School councils are also being increasingly used in both primary and secondary schools and are linked to the citizenship curriculum. In Wales they have become a compulsory part of school life, following legislation by the Welsh Assembly. They discuss a range of issues, but a report by Ofsted in November 2006 cited them as having one of the most positive impacts on whole school behaviour, as pupils have a voice in managing issues which affect them. Councils are comprised of an elected representative group of pupils who play an active role in dealing with issues such as bullying. An organisation called School Councils UK has the support of the Department for Education (DfE) and gives advice and guidance for setting up and running councils.

## Demonstrate realistic, consistent and supportive responses to children and young people's behaviour

As well as applying skills and techniques for supporting and encouraging positive behaviour, you also need to be able to show how you support children and young people consistently and realistically when responding to any inappropriate behaviour. Being realistic means that when you are managing behaviour, you should ensure that you do not give pupils unattainable targets — depending on factors such as their age and their needs. Depending upon these, your rewards and sanctions may be very different — this is to ensure that they are appropriate for the pupils concerned. Pupils in Year 7 and Year 8, for example, will probably not be as worried about having their name put on the board as younger pupils — in a similar way, very young pupils will be unlikely to receive a detention! Your school should have a scale of sanctions for you to use with pupils when behaviour is inappropriate. However, pupils should be able to achieve any requirements which are set so that they do not become disheartened and stop trying. They will need to know that you are supporting them and want them to succeed.

You should consider the following.

### Physical stage of development

You may have to take pupils' physical stage of development into account when managing behaviour. Sometimes, if children's growth patterns are very different from their peers, this may have an effect on their behaviour. For example, children in the last two years of primary school may start to become taller and develop some of the first signs of puberty. Girls in particular can become much taller than boys and this can put pressure on them to behave differently. There may need to be additional provision made in this instance, for example, when getting changed for PE. If there are physical difficulties, such as a visual or hearing problem, these may affect the way in which children relate to others and cause a delay in their overall development which you may need to take into consideration.

### Social and emotional stage of development

The social and emotional development of children is directly linked to the way in which they begin to relate to others. Children need to interact with others so that they have opportunities to gain confidence. For example, they may withdraw socially, find communicating difficult or suffer a language delay. All of these could have a negative effect on their developing self-esteem and on their behaviour, and you may need to take this into account. The rate at which a child will develop socially and emotionally will also depend on the opportunities they have received to interact with others. Where a child has come from a large family, for example, there may have been many more opportunities to play with others and form relationships. If a child has had very little contact or social interaction with other children, it may be more difficult when at the earliest stages of starting at a school or nursery to understand how relationships with others are formed. There may also be less understanding of social codes of behaviour such as taking turns or waiting for others to finish speaking, or alternatively negative behaviour in order to gain attention. As pupils become older, immature behaviour will usually take other forms of attention seeking.

## The needs of the pupil

In some cases you may be supporting pupils who have specific behaviour needs. These pupils will need to have targeted support and you should have been given advice and guidance for the most appropriate strategies which you should use when managing their behaviour. If this does not happen, you may need to ask your SENCO or others who have worked with the pupil in the past for the best kinds of strategies to use so that you can adapt your responses and manage their behaviour in the most appropriate way.

*You may need to seek advice from others when managing the behaviour of pupils with specific needs.*

### Portfolio activity

Write an account of a situation in which you have had to manage pupils' negative or inappropriate behaviour. Consider whether you took into consideration the ages, needs and abilities of the children. Make sure you include your school's strategies and how you have implemented these in stages.

**CASE STUDY:** Developing supportive responses

Cassie works in Year 3 of a large primary school, supporting Della, who has some behaviour issues. Della has Attention Deficit Hyperactivity Disorder (ADHD) and finds it very difficult to stay focused on written activities, although she wants to succeed, and can become very frustrated. Cassie has been working alongside the teacher and they have the support of Della's parents.

Cassie is working with Della during a science session in the class with another teacher as the class teacher is absent. The teacher tells the group that none of them will be going to lunch until they have written up their work on rocks. Della is finding this very difficult and is starting to disturb the rest of the class with her behaviour.

- What should Cassie do in this situation?
- How could it have been avoided?

## Provide an effective role model for the standards of behaviour expected of children, young people and adults within the setting

You need to demonstrate that you are a good role model in all areas of behaviour within the school. Pupils take their lead from adults and need to see that they too are behaving appropriately and responsibly. We cannot ask them to behave in a certain way if our own behaviour is not appropriate and it is important to keep this in mind. This is also true for good manners. Be careful when speaking to other adults and pupils that you are showing the same respect that we are asking them to show others.

**CASE STUDY:** Providing an effective role model

Mariam works in a unit for pupils who have behaviour needs which is attached to a mainstream school. There are a number of assistants in the class who are accompanying the pupils to the hall for a PE lesson. On the way to the hall two of the assistants are laughing and joking with Mariam about a social activity which they are all going to after school. Some of the children in the group are also talking in loud voices in the corridor.

- What do you think about this?
- Why is it important for adults to show appropriate behaviour in all areas of the school?

# Be able to respond to inappropriate behaviour

## Select and apply agreed strategies for dealing with inappropriate behaviour

You should be aware of the school's strategies for dealing with inappropriate behaviour so that you are able to do this when the time comes. Inappropriate behaviour is behaviour which conflicts with the accepted values and beliefs of the setting. Inappropriate behaviour may be demonstrated through speech, writing, non-verbal behaviour or physical abuse. You and all other staff in the school will need to work together to ensure that you are using agreed behaviour management strategies. An error which is often made when first starting to work with children is to try to befriend them as a way to first gain their approval. This not only does not work, but will make behaviour management very difficult. It is more important to set boundaries and limits first so that pupils know where they stand and this will ultimately make your job easier — there is plenty of time to be friends later! As well as being aware of school policies and any scale of sanctions which you are able to use, you should also be able to show that you mean what you say — never use empty threats, as this will prevent pupils from listening to you in the future. (See also the Best practice checklist on page 155 for more strategies.)

### Functional skills

**English: Speaking, listening and communication**

You may be able to relate to the case study opposite or have some excellent ideas on what John should have done. Why not hold a discussion in your class to discuss this case study further? Listen carefully to what others say so that you can respond in an appropriate way.

### CASE STUDY: Agreed strategies for dealing with behaviour

John is working in Year 6 for the first time — in the past he has only worked in Key Stage 1. Today he has been given a literacy group to work with for the first time; some of the pupils have started to talk over him and not listen to what he is saying. John asks them to stop and says that if they do not he will have to send for the teacher. They do not stop and he threatens to keep them in at playtime.

- Why will John's second strategy not work either?
- Do you think he considered the policy of his school in this case?
- What should John have done?

When working within classes or with individual pupils who have particularly negative behaviour on a regular basis, it may be helpful to keep a log of any situations which they find difficult or any triggers to their behaviour. If you become aware of triggers to inappropriate behaviour, you should always mention it to others so that the situation can be avoided if possible. You may need to remove the pupil from the situation or speak to them if you see the warning signs that they are becoming distressed. If you are supporting a pupil who has behavioural needs, you should be able to discuss with them the kinds of situations which they find difficult to manage. In this way you may be able to support them in managing their own behaviour. Alternatively you may discuss the situation with your SENCO and decide to bring in help from an outside professional in order to evaluate different strategies.

*How can you support children in identifying the situations which trigger their behaviour?*

## Describe the sorts of behaviour problems that should be referred to others and to whom these should be referred

You may find that you need to deal with behaviour or discipline problems which are difficult to manage or with which you have not had experience. Depending on your experience, confidence and how long you have been in the school, you may feel comfortable in dealing with inappropriate behaviour yourself. However, there are some situations in which support staff should always refer to others. These are:

● when pupils are a danger to themselves and/or others

● if you are dealing with a difficult situation on your own

● if you are not comfortable when dealing with a pupil, for example, if they are behaving unpredictably

● if pupils are not carrying out your instructions and you are not in control of the situation

● if the incident is serious enough to warrant the involvement of a senior member of staff.

Depending on the situation, you may have to refer to different people — sometimes it may be enough just to have support from another adult within the school. However, there is also a wider range of specialist support you may be able to call upon which is available:

- within the school:
  - ○ SENCO or supervisor — this should be the first point of contact for behaviour support and devising additional strategies for use within the classroom. They will also contact other professionals outside the school
  - ○ other teachers or members of support staff may also be able to offer advice, particularly if they have had to deal with similar behaviour patterns
  - ○ Head Teacher or Deputy — you should be able to speak to those in the Senior Management Team of your school if you have particular concerns about a pupil or situation

- outside the school:
  - ○ Behaviour Unit — this unit is usually run by the local authority and will offer support and suggestions for dealing with pupils who have behaviour problems. They may also come into schools to observe or work with specific pupils
  - ○ educational psychologists — these professionals visit all schools regularly to support pupils and the adults who work with them. They offer help and advice on a variety of special needs problems, and may assess pupils and devise individual programmes. They are also involved with assessing those pupils who may need a statement of special educational needs.

## Skills builder

In pairs, look at the scenarios below. Decide which of these you would be comfortable dealing with yourself and which you would need to refer to others.

1. A Year 7 child has gone home, because he does not feel well, without telling an adult.

2. A Reception child has a temper tantrum because she does not want to get changed for PE.

3. A pair of Year 6 boys got into an argument at break which they have brought into the classroom.

4. You discover that a pupil has brought some inappropriate material into school.

5. A Year 4 special needs pupil is upset as he has misread a social situation and thinks that a group of pupils are bullying him.

How would you deal with the situations you could manage yourself?

This task develops your skill of collaborative working.

**BEST PRACTICE CHECKLIST:** Managing unwanted behaviour

- Intervene early so that the problem does not escalate. If a situation arises where you are the first to be aware of unacceptable behaviour, intervene straightaway.

- Repeat directions calmly rather than reacting to what the pupil is saying or doing, for example, 'I have asked you to line up by the door.'

- Make sure you send for additional help if needed, especially if there are health and safety issues.

- Make eye contact with the pupil who is misbehaving. Sometimes all that is needed is a stern look so that they see an adult is aware of what they are doing.

- Relate any negative comments to the behaviour, rather than the pupil, for example, 'Simon, that was not a sensible choice' is more acceptable than 'Simon, you are not a sensible boy.'

- Remove items that are being used inappropriately. If a pupil is using a piece of equipment to hurt or threaten another individual, this should be gently taken away. You should then tell the pupil why the item has been removed and when they will be able to have it back.

- Use proximity; move closer to a pupil who is misbehaving so that they are aware of an adult presence. This will usually prevent the behaviour from continuing. You can use this practice in whole-class teaching time, when the teacher is at the front, to calm or prevent inappropriate behaviour by having an awareness of who to sit beside.

- Time out is sometimes used when older pupils are consistently misbehaving and need to be given some time to calm down before returning to a situation. It can be applied within the classroom or on the playground.

- Use an agreed scale of sanctions of which all in the school community are aware.

## Functional skills

### English: Writing
Completing the reflective account opposite allows you the opportunity to develop your writing skills. Think carefully about the tense of your writing and the way you lay out your work.

## Getting ready for assessment

Write a reflective account of a situation in which you have had to manage pupil behaviour. Outline the background and events leading up to what happened. Make sure you indicate how you followed school policy, assessed and acted on any risk involved, and took into account the needs of the pupils. You should also show how you promoted positive behaviour and demonstrated fair and consistent responses to pupils.

## Check your knowledge

1. Name three school policies which are relevant to behaviour management.

2. Why is it important for staff to be consistent when managing behaviour?

3. Why is it important to intervene as soon as possible when managing inappropriate behaviour?

4. How might sanctions and rewards be different in a primary and a secondary school?

5. Give three examples of how you might be an effective role model for pupils.

6. What kinds of things can schools do in order to promote positive behaviour?

7. Who else might you speak to if you need support in managing pupil behaviour?

8. Why is it important to follow up anything which you say to pupils when managing their behaviour?

   a) Because pupils will quickly pick up on empty threats.

   b) Because pupils will take no notice of you next time.

   c) Because pupils need to be clear about what will happen if their behaviour is inappropriate.

9. What would you do if you had to manage a situation in which a pupil was becoming aggressive and which you felt was unsafe to them and to others?

### Websites

**www.everychildmatters.gov.uk** – Every Child Matters
**www.schoolcouncils.org** – School Councils UK
**www.teachernet.gov.uk** – TeacherNet
**www.nspcc.org.uk/pbb** – information on NSPCC EduCare programme to prevent bullying

# TDA 2.10 Support learning activities

This unit examines how you can most effectively support pupils and teachers. This is one of the most important aspects of your role. All learning will take place under the direction of a teacher, but you may be asked to support both individuals and groups if you are working at Level 2. The unit identifies what you will need to do to support, plan, deliver and review learning activities. It applies not only to classroom activities but to any environment where teaching and learning takes place.

## By the end of this unit you will:

1. be able to support the teacher in planning learning activities

2. be able to prepare for learning activities

3. be able to support learning activities

4. be able to observe and report on learner participation and progress

5. be able to support the evaluation of learning activities

6. be able to evaluate own practice in relation to supporting literacy, numeracy and ICT.

# Be able to support the teacher in planning learning activities

## How a learning support practitioner may contribute to the planning, delivery and review of learning activities

In your role as a teaching assistant, you will be contributing to **planning**, delivery and review of learning activities alongside teachers. This may take place formally or informally. However planning takes place, there should be some opportunity for you to discuss and review pupils' work with teachers. Planning, teaching and **evaluation** follow a cycle which gives structure to the learning process.

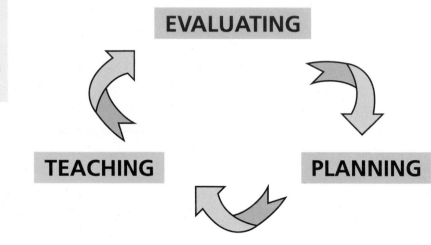

*The cycle of planning, teaching and evaluating.*

It could be that the teacher plans for the long and medium term, and that you are involved in short-term or daily plans, or plans for individual sessions. You should know the learning objectives so that you are clear about what pupils will be expected to have achieved. You may be asked to put forward some ideas of your own at this stage, for example, if you have strengths in a particular subject or area. (See also 'Own strengths and weaknesses' below.)

Although teachers will have completed long-term plans for classes and groups, you may be asked to work with them to discuss and plan activities for the week, and time may be set aside for you to do this. You will need to work with teachers to ensure that the work you are covering fits in with activities and topics planned. Alternatively, you may not be involved in planning but speak to the teacher and look together at what will be happening to see whether you have some suggestions of your own. In some schools, particularly in secondary, it is more difficult for teaching assistants and cover supervisors to have time to plan

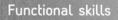

### Key terms

**Planning** – deciding with the teacher what you will do, when, how and with which pupils, to ensure that planned teaching and learning activities are implemented effectively

**Evaluation** – an assessment of how well the teaching and learning activities achieved their objectives

### Functional skills

**English: Writing**
**ICT: Developing, presenting and communicating information**
Planning is an important part of your role. The computer can be a great help as it allows you to make changes easily. When planning you could use Word and insert a table to keep your planning organised.

| Stage of planning | Purpose | Content |
|---|---|---|
| Long term (curriculum framework) | Shows coverage of subject and provides breadth | Summary of subject content |
| Medium term (termly or half termly) | Provides a framework for each subject | Shows overview of activities and/or topics. Links to national strategies |
| Short term | Provides a plan for the week's lessons which can be broken down by day | Should include:<br>• learning intentions<br>• activities<br>• organisation/differentiation<br>• provision for special educational needs (SEN)<br>• use of other adults<br>• rough time allocations<br>• space for notes |

*Table 1: There are three different types of planning which you may be involved with in school.*

with teachers, particularly if they are working in a number of different classes. Some support staff in secondary schools are now attached to departments or curriculum areas so that they have the opportunity to become familiar with schemes of work and have more time to talk through plans with particular staff.

Following the session, both you and the class teacher should reflect on the effectiveness of the teaching and learning activities, and their success in relation to the learning objectives.

When evaluating, you will need to look at whether the children you were working with were able to meet the learning objective through their task. If the majority did but one or two found certain aspects difficult, it would be appropriate to record by exception, for example: 'This group were all

| Role of teacher | Role of teaching assistant |
|---|---|
| • To be responsible for planning and preparing to the National or Early Years Curriculum<br>• To teach pupils according to their educational needs<br>• To assess, record and report on the development, progress and attainment of pupils<br>• To take responsibility for all other adults within the learning environment<br>• To communicate and consult with the parents of pupils<br>• To communicate and co-operate with persons or bodies outside the school<br>• To participate in meetings arranged for any of the above purposes<br>• Also usually to manage an area of the curriculum, such as Geography – this will be included in their job description | • To plan and prepare work alongside the teacher<br>• To support learning activities effectively as directed by the teacher<br>• To assess/evaluate children's work as directed by the teacher<br>• To report any problems or queries to the teacher<br>• To give feedback to the teacher following planned activities |

*Table 2: Roles and responsibilities of the teacher and teaching assistant.*

**CASE STUDY:** Identifying strengths and weaknesses

Emil is working as a learning support assistant for a pupil in Year 7, although today the pupil is absent. His line manager asks him if he can work with a group of Year 9 pupils to carry out a guided reading activity during the first part of the morning, as it will benefit them to have some extra sessions. As he has only been at the school for a term and this is his first job as a teaching assistant, he is not sure about whether he will be able to do this effectively as he has not been trained in guided reading approaches.

- What would you do in this situation?
- What would you need to take into account?

able to complete the task and had a good understanding, but George and Bayram could not understand the representation of 2p and 5p coins.' Similarly, if a child completes the task quickly, this should also be recorded. You may also be involved in meetings with others in the year group during which you discuss topics or long-term plans for the year and whether you should repeat the same ideas the following year.

## Own strengths and weaknesses in relation to supporting learning activities and how these may impact on the support that can be provided

In primary and secondary schools, teachers and support staff have to work in many different subjects and situations. You are not just teaching the subjects of the National or Foundation Stage Curriculum, but also social skills and relating to others, being part of a school and so on. You are likely to feel more confident in some areas and this will subsequently impact on learning activities. However, if you are asked to do something which you are unsure of, you should always speak to teachers about it at the planning stage if possible. You should be absolutely clear about what you are required to do and what pupils are going to learn. If you are not sure, the outcome is unlikely to be satisfactory.

## Use own knowledge of the learners and curriculum to contribute to the teacher's planning

When planning, we should take account of pupils' experiences and interests in order to engage them and keep them motivated: we need to be able to relate what we are doing to their experiences. As you get to know pupils and grow in experience, it will be easier for you to do this. You may also take into consideration different learning styles of pupils, which may mean that you approach the task in a way which is most appropriate for them. Howard Gardner developed the theory of 'multiple intelligences' as a way of considering how individuals learn best in a particular style of learning. You may know, for example, that a pupil in your group needs to approach tasks in a practical way in order to succeed and you should discuss this with the teacher at the planning stage if possible. For more on this, look at www.thomasarmstrong.com/multiple_intelligences.htm (see also page 166 – Apply skills and strategies to engage and motivate learners).

### Functional skills

**ICT: Finding and selecting information**
You can search the Internet for games that help you to identify your learning style. This will help you to support the children in working out their learning styles.

## Identify and obtain the information required to support learning activities

Information required includes:

● the learning objectives

● the learning resources required

● own role in supporting learning activities

● any specific information or instructions relating to the learners and/or activities.

If you plan with teachers or have copies of their plans, this should be given to you in advance of the lesson. If you do not have time to look at the plans, you should at least have a discussion with the teacher. You may need to write things down to remember what you are going to be doing and what preparations you need to make.

● **Learning objectives:** You must always be clear on the learning objectives of the lesson, or what pupils are expected to be able to do following learning activities. These should also be displayed for the benefit of pupils and/or written on their work.

● **Learning resources required:** The lesson plan should detail any materials which are different from those which are normally found in classrooms or which are specific to the activity, for example, technologies or curriculum-specific items.

● **Own role in supporting learning activities:** It should be clear to you exactly what you are required to do, for example, supporting an individual or group, the kinds of key questions you should be asking pupils.

● **Specific information/instructions relating to the learners or activities:** You should have access to school records about pupils' learning, and be able to refer to paper or electronic-based records if required. This will give you details about pupils' educational background and will be particularly useful if you do not know the children well.

Sometimes changes need to be made to plans and this may happen at the last minute due to unexpected events. You will need to be flexible. Any changes to pupils' routine or timetable may affect their behaviour and you also need to take this into consideration.

You should always make sure that you know in advance when your assessor will be coming into school to observe you working with pupils and that you are able to tell them the objectives and organisation of the lessons you will be supporting.

## Lesson Plan    YEAR 10 MIXED ABILITY

| Objectives | Analysing exam questions<br>Using marks to guide answers<br>Finding answers in the text | | |
|---|---|---|---|
| Resources | GCSE AQA for English P54–57<br>Activity sheets<br>Teacher<br>2 x T/A | | |
| Starter | Discuss in class around the aims<br>Elicit from pupils reasons for aims | | |
| Main Teaching | Differentiated groups: Pupils open envelope 1 – guided by teacher – read the questions (T. checks understanding)<br>Pairs: Pupils open envelope 2 – working in groups, answer first 4 questions. (Teacher checks answers as a class)<br>Pairs & group: Pupils now answer the questions proper after reading the text together – answers in exercise books. Teacher goes over answers as a group. | | |
| Development in groups or individual | (AA) Group<br>Working on activity sheets independently with some input from teacher | (A) Group<br>Working with T/A for less able pupils | (BA) Group<br>Working with T/A for EAL pupils |
| | All groups complete same activity | | |
| Plenary | What skills have you learnt?<br>Teacher recap on aims of lesson. | | |
| Homework | N/A | | |

| Visual | Auditory | Tactile | Kinaestheitc | Literacy | Numeracy | ICT |
|---|---|---|---|---|---|---|
| ✔ | ✔ | ✔ | | ✔ | | |

*Lesson plans should set out the information you need in order to support learning activities effectively.*

## Identify and agree with the teacher the opportunities for using information and communication technology to support learning

When supporting learning activities, it is likely that you will be required to use **ICT** to support pupils' learning. Technologies should be used wherever possible to support learning, through the use of everyday equipment such as interactive whiteboards or computers, but also using digital cameras or programmable toys. Always ensure that you have located any equipment and trialled it before starting learning activities with pupils so that you do not come up against any unexpected difficulties, such as equipment not working properly.

### Link

For more on ICT resources, see page 293.

# Be able to prepare for learning activities

## Select and prepare the resources required for planned learning activities

The school should have different resource or curriculum areas where members of staff will have access to equipment for each particular subject area, for example:

- science **resources**
- maths equipment
- design and technology tools and equipment
- art resources and musical instruments
- PE equipment
- geography/history resources
- CD-ROMs, software and other equipment for computers
- RE resources
- Personal, Social, Health and Economics education (PSHE) resources
- textbooks and resource books for all curriculum areas.

Some of these, such as PE equipment, may be immediately apparent. However, if there is a small subject area which you are not often required to support, you may need to ask other members of staff. You should also make sure that you are familiar with how different items of equipment work before you come to use them.

You will also be responsible for more general classroom preparation, for example, ensuring that there are sufficient resources for planned activities within the classroom on a daily basis. If there is anything

### Functional skills

**ICT: Using ICT**

You could open Excel and produce a spreadsheet of all the different ICT equipment you have access to and how many there are of each item. This spreadsheet would not only help you but also other members of staff who may not be aware of new ICT equipment in school.

### Key terms

**ICT** – information and communication technology; this covers a range of different activities, equipment and technological devices, such as programmable toys, telephones, videos, timers, keyboards, keypads, computers, software, digital cameras, interactive whiteboards as well as new technologies as they become available

**Resources** – furniture and equipment needed to support the learning activity, including classroom furniture and curriculum-specific equipment such as computers or PE, science or mathematics equipment

**Functional skills**

**Mathematics: Analysing**
You could do a scale drawing of one of the classrooms in school where you spend a lot of your time and label where in the room you store all the necessary resources. This plan may be helpful to visitors to your room, for example, supply staff or students.

**CASE STUDY:** Select and prepare the resources required

Melissa is new to the role of the teaching assistant. She is working in a Year 3 class and has been given a lesson plan and asked to set out resources. As she arrived early, Melissa is fully prepared for the morning and now has some time before school starts. The teacher has gone to collect the class from the playground.

- What could Melissa be doing in this situation?
- Why is it important that she uses all her time effectively?

specific or unusual required, for example, anything that is topic-based, this should have been discussed and directed by the teacher. You will also be expected to maintain the learning environment during and in between lessons, for example making sure there are adequate sharp pencils or pens, or keeping stocks of paper ready for use. It is important for you to be aware of items such as these, which are constantly in use and which may run out quickly. There will always be something to do in a classroom and when the class teacher is unable to speak to you, you should have the initiative to keep busy.

The types of materials which may be needed might include:

- written materials: books, worksheets
- equipment for different curriculum areas
- general classroom items: pencils, paper, scissors, glue sticks
- specific items, for example, artefacts for an 'Egyptians' topic
- outdoor equipment
- large equipment such as sand and water for early years classes.

## Adapt resources as directed by the teacher to meet the needs of learners

You will need to consider the needs of learners when planning learning activities, as some children will need to have specific resources to enable them to access the curriculum. Teachers or the SENCO may need to advise you if you have to support a child who has very specific needs. The school may already have some of the resources required or they may be available through catalogues or online. However, in some cases, you will need to develop or adapt some of your own. You may also need to adapt resources for learners if it is clear that they are not appropriate or adequate for their needs.

## Ensure the learning environment meets relevant health, safety, security and access requirements

You should always be aware of health and safety issues, in particular when working with young children. It is a duty of all school employees to keep pupils safe, as many young children or those with additional needs are not aware of hazards which may occur or the possible consequences of their actions. Schools will also have in place security measures, such as gates and procedures for identifying any visitors. If you encounter unfamiliar persons on school premises you should always challenge them politely, for example, by saying, 'Can I help you?'

It is important that storage areas are locked and kept tidy so that they do not present an additional hazard. Spaces such as cleaning cupboards or areas where resources are kept can sometimes be left untidy due to lack of time or if staff are unsure where items should be stored.

> **CASE STUDY:** Meeting health and safety requirements
>
> Steven has just set up an area outside the classroom to work with a group of pupils on some maths intervention. One of the teachers walks past and gets chatting to him and points out that it might not be a good area to work on the activity there because they will be blocking an external door which is a fire exit. Steven can see that this is not a good idea, but it had not been pointed out to him before.
>
> * Should someone have drawn Steven's attention to this?
> * What should he do?

# Be able to support learning activities

## Use a range of learning support strategies to support the needs of learners

It is likely that as you work with pupils, you will develop a range of different strategies to help you to support them more effectively. As well as encouraging them to carry out tasks as independently as possible, pupils may need you to challenge them further and motivate them to learn. Depending on the way that tasks have been set, you should encourage pupils while allowing them to develop their own self-help skills. There are different ways in which you can support pupil learning. The following list will give you some ideas, but it is likely that you will develop your own as you grow in experience.

### Before pupils start the task
Make sure pupils understand what they have to do and give them a starting point so that they are able to focus. Ensure the environment is positive and conducive to learning. Check their understanding of any specific vocabulary and model it yourself during the task.

### When pupils are on task
Use open-ended questions (for example, 'what', 'why' and 'who') with pupils rather than questions that prompt them to answer 'yes' or 'no'. Rephrase questions if necessary. Encourage pupils both by using praise and by involving them in discussion about what they are doing. Make sure you involve pupils in any further learning opportunities that become available as you are working. Modify or change the task if pupils are finding it hard — they may work better if it is presented differently.

### When the pupils are finishing the task
Question the pupils to check on their understanding before you feed back to the teacher. Ask them to look again at the learning objectives to consider whether these have been met and to evaluate their own work against them. If they tell you that they have finished, it is always worth keeping an additional challenge or related task in mind for them to do once they have checked their work.

If you are working with an individual pupil, it is likely that you will develop an understanding of their likes and dislikes as well as identifying the kinds of strategies that will help to support and motivate them. Pupils will also have their own learning targets and both you and the pupil should be aware of these.

When working with groups, your main consideration must be involving all pupils and making sure that some individuals do not take over question-and-answer sessions. In particular you may need to discuss with the teacher additional strategies for supporting those children who are reticent about putting ideas forward, particularly if they lack confidence in larger groups.

*How can you support quieter pupils to speak up when in large groups?*

## Apply skills and techniques to engage and motivate learners

**Knowledge into action**

Ask your line manager if you can observe an experienced teaching assistant working with a group of pupils. Look in particular at how they encourage and motivate learners as they are working.

As you will be working with pupils as they are learning, it is vital that you use praise and encouragement to keep them motivated and on task. It must be clear to pupils why they are being praised. It is important, as you get to know pupils, to praise their efforts as well as their achievements. Children and young people need to have recognition for what they do, just as adults do, and this may take different forms.

● **Verbal praise:** This could be simple praise while pupils are working, for example, by saying, 'Well done, that's a great introduction', or by asking the pupil to show their work to another adult at a convenient moment. Verbal praise can be a very powerful motivator as it gives the pupil instant recognition that they are doing well.

**Functional skills**

**Functional skills**

**English: Speaking, listening and communication**

Once you have carried out your observation of an experienced teaching assistant, you could hold a discussion as to why they do things in the way they do, or maybe get some good tips from them that would support you in your role. It is important that while you observe them you make a note of any questions that you would like to ask.

● **House points, merit marks, stickers and charts:** You should be aware of the school policy on how these are used. Some schools leave it to teachers to use reward systems that they find the most beneficial, whereas others may not like individuals using them in this way.

● **School recognition of effort:** If the pupil is rewarded during an assembly or gains a school certificate or recognition in front of their peers, this will offer motivation at all stages of learning.

## Ways of supporting learners to develop literacy, numeracy and ICT skills

When supporting learning, whatever the subject, you should at all times encourage pupils to develop their skills in the areas of literacy, numeracy and ICT. There will always be some overlap in what children are required to do. If you have opportunities for example, to include ICT in a learning activity for another subject area, you could discuss ways of doing this with the teacher. When your assessor comes to see you working with pupils, you will need to think about how you show that you support these subjects in different ways, as well as through literacy, numeracy and ICT sessions.

## The sorts of problems that might occur when supporting learning activities and how to deal with these

You may encounter problems when supporting learning activities. They could take different forms, but could relate to any of the following.

### Learning resources

The task will usually require certain resources such as pencils, paper, worksheets or textbooks, mathematics apparatus, paints, science equipment, etc. If you have been asked to set up for the task, make sure that you have enough equipment and that it is accessible to all the pupils. Check that you know how to use equipment, that it is functioning and that pupils will be able to use it. If the teacher or another adult has set up for your task, it is still worth doing a quick check to ensure that you have everything you need. You will avoid potential problems before they arise.

### Learning environment

This relates to the suitability of the area in which pupils will be working. Problems may arise in the following circumstances. (See diagram over page.)

● **Insufficient space to work:** You should always ensure that you have enough space for the people and equipment before you start. Check that there is enough space around the table or work area for the number of individuals that you have been asked to work with. If pupils are working on weighing, for example, and there is no room for them all to have access to the equipment, they may quickly lose their focus on the task.

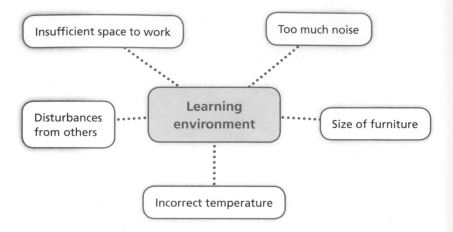

*Problem areas within the learning environment.*

- **Too much noise:** The pupils may be working with you in a corner of the classroom, but any other kind of noise will be a distraction, whether it is from others in the room or an outside disturbance such as grass cutting or a nearby road. It may be possible for you to investigate another area in the school that is available and free from this kind of noise. Alternatively, inform the teacher that the noise level in the classroom is preventing pupils from being able to benefit from the activity.

- **Size of furniture:** Furniture in schools, particularly in primary classes, may be different sizes for various age groups. You should ensure that the space you are using is suitable for the age and size of the pupils you support so that they are able to work comfortably.

- **Incorrect temperature:** If the room is too hot or too cold, you will need to rectify this or move to another area, as pupils will not be able to work.

- **Disturbances from other pupils:** This can often be a problem if you are working in the classroom, because tasks with close adult supervision can often seem more interesting to other pupils than what they are doing. They may be curious to find out what the guided group or individual is doing. If there is a continual problem, the teacher should be informed.

## Learning activities

As you are working on the activity with pupils, you may find that it is too easy or too hard for them, or you do not have enough information. Although teachers will plan carefully, it may be that tasks are set at the wrong level for the pupils you are supporting. In this situation, you may either need to adapt the work so that pupils are able to achieve, or extend them in some way so that they are given more of a challenge. You may also be working with a group whose wide range of abilities means that some pupils finish before others. You may need to have something else ready for them to move on to. Always inform the teacher after the activity if you had to do this.

## Learners

There may be a variety of reasons why pupils are not able to achieve. This may be caused by the following.

- **Poor behaviour:** If any pupils are not focused due to poor behaviour, you will need to intervene straightaway. If pupils are able to continue interrupting, they will do so and you will be unable to continue with the task. Always praise the good behaviour of any pupils who are doing what is required of them, as this sometimes makes the others try to gain your attention by behaving well. As a last resort, if one particular pupil is misbehaving and disturbing others, remove them from the group and work with them later.

- **Pupils' self-esteem:** Sometimes a pupil with low self-esteem may think that they are not able to complete the task that has been set. Some pupils are quite difficult to motivate and you need to offer reassurance and praise wherever you can to improve their self-esteem. However, it is very important to remember that your role is one of a facilitator and that you are not there to complete the task for the pupil. Some may just need a little gentle reassurance and coaxing to 'have a go', while others may be more difficult to work with and require you to use your questioning skills.

- **Lack of concentration:** There may be a few reasons for pupils finding it hard to concentrate on the task that has been set. The work set may be at the wrong level and you may need to modify it (see above). Some pupils, particularly younger children, have a short concentration span and the task may be taking too long to complete. You will need to stop the pupil and continue the work later. Pupils may also be unable to concentrate because of worries at home or because they have fallen out with friends. You may need to take time to talk to them on their own if they are unable to focus, as there may be an underlying problem.

**Reflect**

Think about and discuss a problem you have faced when supporting a learning activity. How have you dealt with it? Would you do the same thing next time?

# Be able to observe and report on learner participation and progress

When you are supporting learning, you will also be observing how pupils are working and coping with the activity so that you are able to feed back to teachers. However, you should not confuse this with more formal observations which require you to sit away from pupils and not interact with them. Observations are important, as through them we can assess and evaluate pupil participation and progress even more closely.

## Skills and techniques for monitoring learners' responses to learning activities, and how well learners are participating in activities and the progress they are making

Your role is such that you will need to be constantly monitoring pupils' responses to learning activities and finding new ways to engage them where necessary. Pupils will find some subjects more stimulating than others or need help to achieve learning objectives. It is important that you monitor their responses and check what they know because you need to feed back to the teacher whether pupils have achieved the learning objective. You might monitor and promote pupil participation in the following ways:

| Method | How to do it |
|---|---|
| Instructing pupils | • Talk through with pupils what they have to do.<br>• Give pupils a starting point so that they are able to focus. |
| Questioning pupils | • Use open-ended questions.<br>• Find out what the pupils already know or remember from last time.<br>• Involve all the pupils in a group.<br>• Probe, using questions, if pupils are unable to understand the task. |
| Explaining to pupils | • Explain any words or phrases that pupils are not clear about.<br>• Remind pupils of key teaching points.<br>• Model the correct use of vocabulary.<br>• Ensure all pupils understand the teacher's instructions. |
| Asking pupils to demonstrate their learning | • Invite pupils to tell you at the end of the session what they have learned.<br>• Ask pupils to 'teach' what they have learned to someone else so that you can assess how much they know. |

Table 3: Promoting pupil participation.

As you are working with pupils, you may need to note down specific things they say – a good guide is to record anything uncharacteristic for the pupil or that shows either a good or a poor understanding of the task. This is because you may not have time to record a comment for every pupil and if the activity has gone as expected, the majority of pupils should have achieved the learning objective.

As well as looking at learner progress, you should also note whether they are participating throughout the activity and are engaged in the task. If pupils are distracted or are not carrying out the activity as they should, it is important that you make note of this so that it can be followed up.

## Record observations and assessments of learner participation and progress in the required format

The teacher with whom you are working should give you information about the **format** of the observation you are carrying out and your method of recording. More formal observations may be presented in a number of ways depending on their purpose. Some different types of recording are listed below.

### Free description

This enables you to write everything down during the period of the observation (usually 5–10 minutes). The observation will be quite short as it will be very focused on the pupil. Free descriptions need to include what the pupil says to others, how they express themselves non-verbally and the way in which the activity is carried out. They are used when a lot of detail is required and are usually written in the present tense.

### Structured description

This type of description may require the observer to record what the pupil is doing against specific headings or in response to predetermined questions. Structured descriptions are to be used to guide the observer on what needs to be recorded, for example, a series of steps towards achieving a task.

### Checklist

These are used to check and record whether pupils can carry out a particular activity quickly and in a straightforward way. They usually require the observer to make a judgement on whether a pupil is able to achieve a task; the focus is not on how they do it but whether or not they can. Checklists may take different forms and schools can devise their own easily, depending on what is being observed.

### Event sample

This method is used to record how often a pupil displays a particular type of behaviour or activity. Event samples need to be carried out without the observer participating in the activity to retain objectivity.

### Informal observations

You may be asked to 'just keep an eye' on a pupil or to watch them during break time, especially if there have been any specific concerns, and then feed back to teachers. In this case you can make your own notes, but you should be careful about confidentiality if you are writing things down. Remember not to leave notebooks lying around, particularly if you have recorded pupils' names.

Alternatively, you may just be asked to jot down any observations you have made during the session in a separate column on the lesson plan or on a feedback sheet. You will need to speak to the teacher about the most appropriate method of recording.

# Be able to support the evaluation of learning activities

## The importance of evaluating learning activities

When you have carried out your work with pupils, you will need to evaluate what you have done so that you can feed back to the teacher and think about your approach. Evaluation means reflecting on how the activity has gone and why things may have gone a certain way. You may ask yourself the following types of questions in order to help you to evaluate activities.

1. What went well? How do you know it went well? (For example, think about the resources, learning environment, pupils' reaction to the task and how much time was available.)

2. What did not go so well? How do you know?

3. Did you need to change any aspect of the activity as you were working? How?

4. Would you change your approach if you carried out the activity again? How?

Evaluation is important, as it feeds into the planning cycle and enables both pupils and teaching staff to think about the learning that has taken place. When evaluating teaching and learning activities and outcomes, look back to the learning objectives. We cannot measure what pupils have learned without knowing what we are measuring against. If we have not thought carefully about learning objectives at the planning stage, it will not always be possible to evaluate whether pupils have achieved them. Learning objectives need to be clear for this to be possible.

● Learners must understand what they mean.

● They must be achievable.

● We must be able to assess pupils against them.

## Provide constructive feedback on learning activities in discussion with the teacher

You will need to give **feedback** to teachers after you have carried out learning activities with pupils so that they are aware whether pupils have achieved the learning objectives and how much support was needed. Finding time to give feedback to teachers can be very difficult and you may need to make sure you give it at an appropriate moment. There is often little time to sit down in school and discuss pupils' work with teachers. Some teachers and teaching assistants will discuss each day's activities on the phone on a daily basis. Others will come into school early in order to plan and give feedback together.

Another way in which feedback can be given if there is not time for verbal discussion is through the use of feedback forms. If these are planned and set out correctly, you will be able to show:

● whether pupils have achieved learning objectives

● how they responded to the activity

● how much support they needed.

With this information, feedback forms can be an effective time-saving device.

# Teacher/TA Feedback Sheet

**Class:** Year 7

To be filled in by teacher:
**Teacher's name:**
**TA's name:**

### Brief description of activity

Revision of Year 6 work on plotting different points and shapes using co-ordinates on x and y axes.
Follow up to revise reflecting shapes.

### How session is linked to medium-term plans

Departmental schemes of work — revision of work on shape carried out in Year 6.

### TA's role

To check understanding of how to plot co-ordinates.

### Important vocabulary

Axis, perimeter, shape, diagonal, co-ordinate, edge, corner names of shapes

### Learning objectives

To be able to plot points using co-ordinates.
To identify and reflect shapes.

### For use during group work

| Children | D | H | Feedback/Assessment |
|----------|---|---|---------------------|
|          |   |   |                     |
|          |   |   |                     |
|          |   |   |                     |
|          |   |   |                     |
|          |   |   |                     |
|          |   |   |                     |
|          |   |   |                     |

D = Can do task
H = Help required to complete task

*A feedback form.*

## Identify any difficulties encountered in supporting learning activities

For whatever reason, you will sometimes encounter difficulties when supporting learning activities. It is important that you are able to feed back to teachers about what happened and how you dealt with these. You may need to be tactful; there may be a number of reasons why an activity has not gone well — for example, if the environment was not ideal for the task. However, if the problem is clearly due to planning or if the pupils have not found the task engaging, it may be difficult to suggest this to the teacher. Depending on their personality and how well you get along with one another, this may or may not present problems. If you have a relationship that allows you both to give suggestions to one another, you will find it easier. The most important thing to remember is that even if you are sure you are right, it is better to give your feedback in the form of suggestions.

## Provide the teacher with feedback on learners' participation and progress

When giving feedback to teachers, you should also ensure that you include details about how pupils participated in the activity and whether they made progress during the session. It is likely that this too will be part of the general feedback which you give to teachers. You should make sure that you include details of any marking which you gave pupils during the activity. Some teachers prefer that you mark pupils' work and give your feedback through comments in their books followed by your own initials, but you will need to check which method teachers prefer.

If you have carried out more formal observations as detailed on page 171, you may not need to give the teacher as much verbal feedback, as their purpose is different and they will give all the detail required. You should consider the following questions.

- Have pupils met the learning objectives?
- Have they participated fully in the session?
- Have they understood the vocabulary or terminology used?
- Were the resources you used appropriate for the session?
- Were you in control of the session and did the pupils respond well to you?
- How could you have improved what you did?
- What will you do now?

### Functional skills

**English: Speaking, listening and communication**

The scenarios below could be done in pairs in the form of role play. Take turns at giving and receiving the feedback. Carrying out short role-play activities like this can help to build your confidence in speaking and listening.

### Reflect

Consider how you would give feedback to the teacher on the following.

- A pupil has shown no interest in the learning activity because she did not want to work with the assigned partner the teacher put her with.
- A boy has been unable to access the task as it has been too difficult for him.
- A group of pupils, as you suspected, have not worked well together on a task.
- A task has not gone well due to inadequate time and resources.

## DVD activity

**Video clip 3 – Understanding shape or measures**

In this clip, the teaching assistant is working with a group of Year 1 pupils on an activity to encourage them to name and describe the properties of different 2D and 3D shapes.

1. While watching the clip, consider the following questions.

   - What evidence is there that the assistant has a clear plan for the activity?

   - What positive teaching and learning strategies does she use throughout the task? Are there any negative aspects?

   - How will the teaching assistant be able to assess whether the learning objective has been met?

   Make notes on how you might carry out the activity differently if you were asked to work on it with pupils.

2. What do you think about the method of feedback used in this clip? Trial this method with your class teacher if you have not done this already and use as evidence for your portfolio, including the teacher's signature to confirm this as performance evidence. Remember to remove the children's names.

3. Watch DVD clip 6 SEN (physical impairment) and answer the same questions for the teaching assistant supporting the PE lesson.

# Be able to evaluate own practice in relation to supporting literacy, numeracy and ICT

## Ways in which own knowledge, understanding, and skills in literacy, numeracy and ICT impact on practice

### Over to you!

Consider your own knowledge, understanding and skills in these three areas of literacy, numeracy and ICT. How do they impact on your practice?

You should have a good level of competence in literacy, numeracy and ICT. Increasingly, schools are requiring those who support teaching and learning to have at least a Level 2 qualification (GCSE level) in these three areas. This is because pupils should receive the best possible support in their learning. It is also of benefit to you as it will improve your own confidence when working with pupils.

## Opportunities to improve own knowledge, understanding and skills in literacy, numeracy and ICT

You will need to consider how you can improve your own knowledge, understanding and skills in literacy, numeracy and ICT, and develop a plan. Discuss this with your line manager or other member of the Senior Management Team so that you can develop a plan together. Failing this, you should have access to a college representative, such as your tutor or assessor, who will know about the opportunities in your local area. Some local authorities offer additional literacy, numeracy and ICT courses at convenient times for support staff to encourage them to undertake the training.

## Getting ready for assessment

Write a reflective account of a learning activity you have undertaken with a group of pupils, and include the plan. Drawing closely on the assessment criteria for this unit, include:

- information you had before the activity, such as the learning objective, the needs of the pupils, and any specific criteria you needed to follow
- whether you had any input or suggestions to make at the planning stage
- how you included all the pupils in the group and why you need to do this
- why it is important to plan and evaluate learning activities you have done with pupils
- any problems that have occurred and how you dealt with them.

## Check your knowledge

1. Why is it important for you to have copies of plans or to have talked them through with teachers before you start working with pupils?

2. What kind of information should you have before you start to support a learning activity?

3. What should you do when working on learning activities with pupils to ensure that you are able to feed back effectively to teachers?

4. List three learning support strategies which you have used to support the needs of learners.

5. How can you motivate and encourage learners while working with them?

6. Why is evaluation important?

7. How should you feed back to teachers following learning activities?

---

**Websites**

**www.everychildmatters.gov.uk** – Every Child Matters (Green Paper)

**NATIONAL CURRICULUM DOCUMENTS**
England: http://curriculum.qcda.gov.uk
Northern Ireland: www.ccea.org.uk
Scotland: www.ltscotland.org.uk
Wales: http://old.accac.org.uk

# TDA 2.11 Contribute to supporting bilingual learners

This unit is for staff who support bilingual and multilingual pupils in the target language (English or Welsh), and looks at the way in which pupils develop their language skills. You will need to be aware of the way in which all pupils process language, and the importance for bilingual and multilingual pupils of retaining their identity through valuing and promoting their home language.

## By the end of this unit you will:

1. be able to interact with bilingual learners
2. be able to support bilingual learners to develop skills in the target language
3. be able to support bilingual learners during learning activities.

# Be able to interact with bilingual learners

According to government statistics, over 200 languages are now spoken in the homes of pupils who attend British schools. If you have been asked to support **bilingual learners** and multilingual learners, you need to be able to think about how you can promote the development of the **target language** (English or Welsh), while valuing each pupil's home language and culture. This is particularly important if there is only one bilingual or multilingual pupil learning the target language in the class or group.

Bilingual learners include both those who are newly arrived and are new to the language used to deliver the curriculum, and those who are more advanced and can communicate confidently in the target language, but who need further support with language use in academic contexts.

Many schools also now have a governor and/or designated teacher with overall responsibility for EAL pupils, whose role is to advise other staff on the kinds of strategies that are the most effective.

## Interact with bilingual learners in a way that demonstrates respect for their first or home language(s), values, culture and beliefs, and sensitivity to individual needs

As part of your work for this unit, you will need to be able to show that you demonstrate respect for bilingual learners' home languages, values, culture and beliefs. It is very important for bilingual pupils that their home language and heritage is recognised in school. Children and young people need to know that their culture and status is valued, as this helps them to feel settled and secure, factors which contribute to their being able to develop skills in a new language. Children and young people need to want to learn; if they feel isolated or anxious, it is more likely that this will be difficult for them. If you are a bilingual teaching assistant, you can encourage pupils to speak their home language in school. If you have two or more pupils in the class who speak the same language, encourage them to use it together — by discussing things in one language, this will also help the development of the target language.

Cultural awareness has become more important as schools recognise the value of bilingual pupils' experiences and knowledge. The status of other languages should be recognised in school through assemblies, displays, school trips and cultural events. Personal, Social, Health and Economics education (PSHE) activities may also focus on the importance of valuing individuals and celebrating diversity.

As well as being aware of their language needs, you should also be able to show sensitivity to pupils' own circumstances and individual backgrounds. As you get to know them, you will find out about their individuality and the kinds of adjustments that they are having to make.

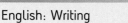

*You will need to be sensitive to the needs of bilingual pupils.*

The primary need of all pupils, especially those who speak English as an additional language, is that they should feel safe and settled, and have a sense of belonging. Bilingual pupils may have to make significant adjustments to life in a new country. They will often have found it a real culture shock and have great anxiety, not only about communicating with others, but also in adapting to their new environment. However, it may also be an advantage to them to be in a structured and secure environment if they have experienced trauma or an unsettled period.

The kinds of effects could be that the child:

- becomes withdrawn
- is frustrated by being unable to communicate and displays behaviour problems
- is anxious and reluctant to participate in class activities.

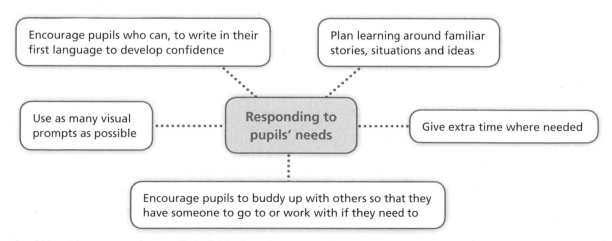

*You should be able to respond to pupils' individual needs.*

**Reflect** **?**

Have you worked with any bilingual pupils who are finding it difficult to participate in class activities? What methods did you find most useful to support them, if so?

All of these effects make it difficult for pupils to participate in class activities. You will need to make sure that you develop as many strategies as possible for pupils who need emotional support.

---

**CASE STUDY:** Showing sensitivity to individual needs

You are working in a Year 2 class as a teaching assistant with Agnieszka, who arrived in the country from Poland last term. Although she is doing very well and her language has really developed during the time she has been in school, you have noticed that during the weekly spelling test she consistently gets very poor marks as she finds this very difficult. She is starting to be more reluctant to come into school on Tuesdays as a result.

- What could you do to support her?
- Are there any additional strategies which you could use?

---

## Use language and vocabulary which is appropriate to the learner's age, level of understanding and proficiency in the target language

Children and young people from all backgrounds, whether they are learning one or more languages, need to be given opportunities to develop their language skills in a variety of different ways. When developing speaking and listening skills with pupils who speak English as an additional language, you will need to use language and vocabulary which is appropriate to their age and level of understanding. If pupils come to school only speaking their home language and needing to develop their English or Welsh, they will need to have more support in order to do this.

Table 1 below shows the stages of language development in children. Adults will need to support children through all of these stages in order to encourage and promote language development. At each stage, the role of the adult may be different. For example, a pre-school child needs positive recognition of their attempts to communicate through eye contact and speech. A 5- or 6-year-old child may need adults to help them to extend their vocabulary through the use of open-ended questions or 'what if?' strategies. An older pupil may need to have specific vocabulary explained or guidance around the different nuances of how language may be interpreted.

Learning more than one language will mean that children will progress more slowly through these stages of language development. You will therefore need to ensure that you use language and vocabulary which is appropriate to the individual's age and level of understanding. If a teacher speaks to the group and uses language which may be difficult for them to understand, you may need to clarify what has been said for them.

| Age | Stage of development |
| --- | --- |
| 0–6 months | Babies try to communicate through crying, starting to smile and babbling. They start to establish eye contact with adults. |
| 6–18 months | Babies start to speak their first words. They start to use gestures to indicate what they mean. At this stage, they are able to recognise and respond to pictures of familiar objects. |
| 18 months–3 years | Children start to develop their vocabulary rapidly and make up their own sentences. At this stage, children enjoy simple and repetitive rhymes and stories. |
| 3–8 years | Children start to use more and more vocabulary and the structure of their language becomes more complex. As they develop their language skills, they are able to use language in a variety of situations. |
| 8+ years | Children continue to develop the complexity of their language skills and their confidence in the use of language should begin to flourish. The attainment targets in the English National Curriculum set out the specific language skills expected of pupils at the different Key Stages. |

*Table 1: Stages of language development in children and young people.*

A pupil's age may also make a difference when starting to speak a new language and you should be aware of this. Older pupils may find it more challenging due to the demands of the curriculum and the fact that they need to learn to speak, read and write in English in order to access it. They may also be more self-conscious than younger children and as a result, less likely to attempt to speak. A younger child may be more relaxed and less anxious about acquiring language. Research has shown that the younger the child, the easier it is for them to learn additional languages. For children to attempt to initiate language, they will need to feel relaxed and confident that their contributions will be valued. However, you should also remember that when learning a new language, it is normal to have a 'silent phase' when the learner is 'tuning in' to new sounds and vocabulary. It is important not to push pupils into speaking before they are ready.

Also, a pupil's ability to speak additional languages is not a reflection of their overall abilities. Although speaking two or more languages is a gift and should be celebrated, all pupils can be of higher or lower than average ability overall. It may take longer to determine if pupils have any additional needs or are gifted and talented; this is another reason why it is important to monitor pupils' development in the target language closely.

> **CASE STUDY:** Giving support appropriate to the learner's needs
>
> You are working with a group of three pupils, who all speak Gujarati. Although they have the language in common, their needs are all different.
>
> 1. Ahmed is in Year 3, speaks very little English and has just come to this country.
>
> 2. Mahir is in Year 4, has lived here all his life but has always spoken Gujarati at home and needs extra support with his English. He is of average ability.
>
> 3. Marian is in Year 1 and is bilingual and able in her work, but is very anxious and reluctant to speak English, although she is able to.
>
>    - How might you approach your work with these pupils?
>    - Do you think they should be taught together just because they speak the same language?

> **BEST PRACTICE CHECKLIST:** Interacting with bilingual learners
>
> - Create a secure and happy environment where pupils and their families feel valued and part of the school.
>
> - Raise cultural awareness in school in different ways.
>
> - Reinforce language learning by giving pupils immediate verbal and non-verbal feedback and praise.
>
> - Give pupils time to think about questions before they respond.
>
> - Create more opportunities for speaking and listening, such as paired conversations with others.
>
> - Remember that learning more than one language does not mean that the pupil should be put with groups of lower-ability learners.

# Be able to support bilingual learners to develop skills in the target language

## Use knowledge of the needs of individual learners to support development of the target language

When children and young people are learning a language, it is important for those around them to support them wherever possible. They will need the encouragement and support of others in order to develop their skills in the target language. Part of the support that you give to pupils will need to come from getting to know individuals and finding out what support they need. When a pupil from a different background, culture or language from others in the class or year group enters school, it may be a difficult experience for them, particularly if they have not been to

## Portfolio activity

Think about the different ways in which you have obtained information about the pupils you support. How does your school make this information available to colleagues who need it without compromising on confidentiality?

---

**CASE STUDY:** Using knowledge and needs of the individual to support language development

You have been asked to work with Olwenyo in Year 7, who has come up from primary school but four years ago came to the UK from Nigeria with his parents. Although his English is good, he did not reach the expected level in his SATS and has found the transition to secondary school very difficult.

- What kinds of issues do you think there might be in this situation?
- What might you do initially with Olwenyo in order to support him?

---

school before. They may find it hard due to lack of confidence or self-esteem, and staff need to be sensitive to their needs. The different backgrounds and needs of individual pupils as they come into school will all influence their learning, and you will need to find out as much as you can about each pupil in order to support them fully.

Usually the school will have systems in place when pupils first enter the school so that they are aware of those who speak English or Welsh as a second language. Parents will have been asked to provide information about pupils and in the case of primary schools, staff may have been on home visits or visited nurseries in order to gather information. Secondary schools will usually have been passed on information from primaries. Sometimes bilingual assistants may be employed by the school, in particular if there are a large number of pupils who speak one particular language. Specific assessments or observations may also be carried out on pupils to find out more about them.

As you get to know the pupils you are supporting, you will also gather your own information about the pupil or pupils, such as their personalities, interests and ambitions. These will all help you to support the target language as they will enable you to discuss particular aspects of their lives.

QCDA has also produced guidance, *A language in common: Assessing English as an additional language*, on how to assess pupils who are in the early stages of learning English. This is so that there is some standardisation in how bilingual pupils are assessed, although individual local authorities may have produced their own versions. It enables teachers to track pupil progress in speaking and listening, reading and writing. The guidance comprises detailed descriptors for features of English language use up to level 1 of the National Curriculum. It can be found under resources on the QCDA website: www.qcda.gov.uk

## Techniques for supporting learners in developing language skills in the target language

In order to support learners in developing language skills, you should have both background knowledge of the pupil and an idea of their current level of skill in the target language. You will also need to have some support from the school as to what you are required to do in order to encourage and develop the language skills of those pupils you are supporting. However, in a general sense, you should be giving them support in a number of ways, including:

- giving praise where possible
- modelling correct language when speaking to them
- repeating back to them what the teacher is saying
- explaining what has been said by others
- encouraging them through smiles, nods, gestures and body language.

As with all situations, effective use of praise is very important when working with pupils who speak English as an additional language. You will need to provide them with encouragement and support, as they will not be confident in the target language. Through the use of a positive learning environment and opportunities for them to develop relationships with others, you will be able to encourage and support their learning.

## Ways of encouraging and supporting bilingual learners to interact with others using the target language

As language is a way in which we communicate, you will need to encourage and support bilingual learners to interact with others in the target language. In this way they will develop their language skills in a meaningful way. You will need to find as many opportunities as you can for doing this, through individual and group work as well as including pupils in working alongside their peers as much as possible.

| Method | How this helps |
|---|---|
| Using opportunities to talk | Speakers of other languages should be given as much opportunity as possible to talk and discuss ideas with others. At a very young age, this would include opportunities such as role play, whereas older pupils may enjoy discussions. |
| Through physical cues and gestures | These might include gestures such as thumbs up, thumbs down or facial cues, which will enable pupils to make sense of the situation more quickly. |
| Songs and rhymes | Younger children develop concepts of pattern and rhyme in language through learning nursery rhymes and songs. These are also an enjoyable way of developing pupils' language skills as well as being part of a group. You may also be able to introduce rhymes and songs in other languages for all pupils to learn and so develop their cultural awareness. |
| Games | Opportunities for games are useful as they help pupils to socialise with others as well as practise their language skills. |
| Practical examples | These can help pupils when they are being given instructions, for example, showing a model when a group is going to work together. |
| Talk partner/discussing with others first | This may help speakers of other languages to gain confidence before telling their ideas to others in the group or class. They should work with a variety of other pupils so that they are provided with a range of language models. |
| Develop specific areas of language | If pupils have come into school with very limited experience of the target language, you may be asked to work with them to develop specific areas of understanding. For example, the pupil may need to focus on positional vocabulary such as behind, above, below, next to and so on. You may need to work with pictures or other resources to help pupils to develop their understanding of these words. |

Table 2: Supporting bilingual learners to interact with others in the target language.

*Have you seen evidence of pupils developing their socialisation skills during games?*

## Be able to support bilingual learners during learning activities

### Learning resources to meet the needs of bilingual learners

If you are responsible for supporting EAL pupils in your school, you should have access to appropriate resources. You may already have a number of these in school and your school or local authority can put you in touch with sources of additional materials. The Internet can be an excellent resource, although you may need to have time to look for appropriate sites and programs to use (see also page 190 for a list of websites).

## Key term

**Resources** — teaching and learning resources to provide effective access to the curriculum, including written materials, videos or DVDs, bilingual and pictorial dictionaries, and bilingual software

You may be asked to produce **resources** yourself, especially if you are bilingual, in order to support pupil learning. These might include displays or word banks for pupils, as well as dual language texts and story sacks for younger pupils. If you find additional resources, always check with teachers before using them with pupils. You may also start to develop a bank of resources which you can share with others.

### Knowledge into action

Complete a table like the one below to show the kinds of resources you have used with or produced for bilingual and multilingual pupils.

| Type of resource | Source |
|---|---|
| Bilingual reading program for computer | Local EAL advisor |
|  |  |
|  |  |

### Functional skills

**ICT: Using ICT**
You could produce this table on the computer and then save it with an appropriate file name. You can come back to this table again in the future and add more things to it as you develop your skills.

## Skills and techniques for including bilingual learners in learning activities

Although you may be working across the curriculum, in particular if you are in a primary school, language will be the vehicle through which pupils are learning and many of the strategies you should use will be similar to those used to develop literacy skills. If pupils have access to a broad and balanced curriculum, they will develop their language skills all the time during learning activities. After consultation with teachers, you may find that you need to adapt or modify the activities which pupils have been asked to do in order to help them to access the curriculum more fully. You may also need to use some of the techniques suggested below.

## Appropriate techniques to support the learning and language development needs of individual learners

You will need to be able to use a variety of appropriate techniques in order to support the language development of individuals. As part of your qualification, you should be able to give examples of how you have used the following examples as much as possible.

### Introducing, explaining and illustrating key vocabulary related to subject content

You should always ensure that bilingual pupils have been given any key vocabulary when they are working on a new subject or topic. You should also be aware that they may not know the word in their own language if it is a new subject that they have not encountered before. It may help them to take home lists to parents, so that they can discuss key vocabulary at home. Always use key vocabulary as much as possible in context so that pupils become used to it.

### Scaffolding writing tasks

This means that you will need to give support to pupils by providing them with help when structuring writing. This might be simply through showing them by modelling correct writing such as letter formation and grammar, but may also be by providing specific activities to support the way in which they put a piece of writing together, such as the use of writing frames.

### Scaffolding oracy

This is giving support to the way in which bilingual pupils structure their spoken language. You might do this by helping them to think about logical progression in the way in which they speak, for example, 'First I am going to talk about x and then the reason that it happened.'

### Modelling oral and written language to support acquisition

This means that you will need to show correct oral and written language to pupils through your example. Although it is likely you will do this in any case, you should always remember to use the correct form of language rather than jargon or slang when you are speaking to bilingual pupils who are first starting to learn the target language.

### Integrating speaking, listening, reading and writing

Although it is important for pupils to hear the spoken word as much as possible, they should also be using language skills for reading and writing. You should ensure that when you are reading and writing with pupils you are also speaking to them, so that they hear the target language and that one reinforces the other.

### Reinforcing language learning through repetition

Repetition is often used with very young children when they are learning their mother tongue and you should also use it with bilingual pupils to help them to remember and consolidate language. You should remind them of vocabulary they have learned and provide opportunities to revisit previous topics and subjects.

### Encouraging learner responses and promoting interaction using different forms of questioning

You should always use different forms of questioning when talking to pupils so that you encourage them to think and respond in different ways.

## Using culturally accessible learning materials

> **Link**
>
> See TDA 2.4 Equality, diversity and inclusion in work with children and young people, for more on this topic.

### Using peer support to promote thinking and talking in first languages

If you have a number of speakers of the same language, or if you are bilingual yourself, you may use pupils' first language in order to promote thinking and talking. This will be useful as it will encourage pupils to speak and formulate ideas about what they want to say.

## Feedback to the teacher on the learner's participation and progress in relation to the learning activities and language development

When you are working with bilingual and multilingual pupils, you will need to provide frequent feedback to teachers on their progress both with the activities undertaken and their language development. This is because teachers will need to know how pupils have managed specific tasks and will also need to know where the pupils experienced difficulties with language. You may also need to report to other professionals such as form tutors, the Special Educational Needs Coordinator (Additional Support for Learning Teacher) and possibly EAL (English as an Additional Language) teachers who visit the school. You should have opportunities to contribute to meetings and/or paperwork such as individual education plans concerning pupils with whom you are working. It is important that there is a joined-up approach from all those who are working with bilingual pupils so that their progress can be measured. You may feed back to teachers verbally following each session or through the use of feedback sheets or other written methods.

> **Functional skills**
>
> **English: Speaking, listening and communicating**
> You could ask the class teacher if they would mind if you recorded the discussion between yourself and the teacher when you are giving feedback about a child (as long as you change their name for confidentiality purposes). Doing this would provide you with a good record of a discussion that you could show your assessor.

## CASE STUDY: Providing feedback to teachers

Hulya works as a bilingual assistant in a secondary school which has a high number of Turkish speakers. She works with the same pupils each week and once a month she has some time set aside with the SENCO in order to give feedback on the progress of different pupils; this is then passed on to teachers. She also speaks regularly to Tamara, the EAL teacher from the local authority, who comes into school to monitor the progress of the pupils. She does not have time to speak to teachers herself as the timetable does not give them time for this. She is therefore unable to feed back on specific learning activities unless this is done informally in the staff room, but this is not always possible.

- What do you think about this situation?
- Would you say anything if you were in Hulya's position?

### DVD activity

Video clip 4 – Supporting EAL pupils
Watch the clip of an assistant working with a bilingual child.

1. Find an example of how the assistant models the correct language (in particular, if the child makes an error). Does she use any other helpful strategies? What do you think of her use of praise and of constructive feedback?

2. Why is this sort of activity useful? What kinds of activities and resources might you use with bilingual and multilingual pupils in school? Give examples of work you have carried out with pupils and show how you work with the teacher to ensure a consistent approach. This should include both planning and feedback.

3. Show how you gather information about the pupils with whom you work. Why is it important to obtain recent and relevant information when you are working with these children?

## Getting ready for assessment

Your assessor should have the opportunity to observe you working with the bilingual or multilingual pupils you support. Be prepared to be able to talk to your assessor about the pupils' backgrounds and language needs as well as demonstrating a range of strategies for supporting their learning. You may also wish to include for your portfolio any resources that you have made for pupils you support and witness testimonies from parents, teachers or outside agencies to say how you have supported bilingual pupils. Check with your assessor that you have covered as much of the assessment criteria as possible.

## Check your knowledge

1. Give three examples of ways in which you can demonstrate respect for the values and cultures of those who speak English as an additional language in school.

2. How can you find out more about the backgrounds and interests of individual pupils? Why is this useful when helping them to develop language skills?

3. What kinds of strategies and techniques can you use to support learners when using their target language?

4. How can you encourage speakers of other languages to interact with others?

5. Name two resources you have used specifically to support bilingual learners and describe any you have made or adapted yourself.

6. Which of the following techniques might you use to support the language needs of bilingual learners?

   a) scaffolding writing tasks

   b) asking them to speak in their own language when carrying out activities

   c) reading aloud in the target language

   d) reinforcing new vocabulary

   e) explaining their learning to others.

---

### Websites

The following websites are regularly updated with articles and information to support the inclusion of speakers of other languages.

**www.britishcouncil.org** – the British Council, which is the UK's international cultural relations body

**www.education.gov.uk** – the Department for Education; the standards site has information under EAL learners

**www.freenglish.com** – has resources for those wishing to learn English

**www.mantralingua.com** – this company produces a range of books in different languages

**www.naldic.org.uk** – the National Association for Language Development in the Curriculum aims to raise attainment of EAL learners; the website contains a number of links and resources

**www.teachernet.gov.uk** – type in 'EAL' under 'search'

# TDA 2.12 Prepare & maintain learning environments

This unit looks at some of the different areas in which you will work within the school environment. You will need to be familiar with all locations within the school and how to work safely within them, as well as how to find equipment and materials for each subject area as it will be part of your role to prepare the environment for use.

Most of the assessment criteria for this unit need to be assessed in the workplace; therefore you will need to plan your assessment visits carefully so that your assessor is able to see you carry out the required activities. For more help with this, see the 'Getting ready for assessment' activity at the end of the unit.

## By the end of this unit you will:

1.  be able to prepare learning environments
2.  be able to prepare learning materials
3.  be able to monitor and maintain learning environments and resources.

191

# Be able to prepare learning environments

## The importance of health, safety and security in learning environments

When preparing any **learning environment**, whether this is indoor or outdoor, and whether you use it all the time or not very often, you should always ensure that you are careful to check it for health, safety and security issues before you use it with pupils. This is because at any time, issues may arise which may make the environment unsafe or unsuitable for use by pupils. You should be aware of your school's health and safety policy with regard to setting out learning environments for pupils. It may be that there is specific guidance for doing this, in particular for individual subjects such as science or food technology, or there may be lists of areas in which you should be particularly vigilant. You should know the identity of the health and safety officer and how to report any safety concerns to them. Schools will also have security measures in place, such as gates and entry phones, and procedures for identifying visitors to school such as signing in books and visitors' badges. If you encounter unfamiliar people on school premises, always challenge them politely by asking if you can help them.

### Portfolio activity

Think about the following scenarios.

1. You are going to work with some Reception children in their outside area.

2. You have been asked to carry out a cooking activity with Year 4 using a portable oven in one of the shared areas in school.

3. You are taking a group of Year 1 pupils over the road to the park with the class teacher.

4. You are working with Year 5 on a design & technology activity using hot glue guns and other materials.

5. You are supporting a Year 9 biology class.

6. You are on duty outside on the playground and notice that the fence is broken.

What kinds of health and safety issues might you need to consider in the case of each learning environment? How might you prepare for each activity?

### Link

For more on this topic, see TDA 2.8 Support children and young people's health and safety.

## Organise learning environments to meet the requirements of the planned learning activities and the age range and any particular needs of learners involved

When organising learning environments, you will need to consider each of the areas above so that you can ensure they are adequately prepared. You will need to think about how pupils should be seated and the space needed to carry out the activity, so that they are able to access any materials or resources. You should also think about their physical needs, which may be dependent on their age and stage of physical development, and their fine and gross motor skills. Some children develop more quickly or slowly than their peers and will reach milestones of development at different ages. The majority of children will develop at a similar rate in their first years of school, but this will change as they mature and become older. You may notice that some pupils need more help than others within the learning environment when practising some physical skills. If individual pupils have specific difficulties, they may need help and advice from outside agencies and may be referred to these through the SENCO. For example, a child with immature fine motor skills may need to be referred to an occupational therapist. Different professionals will give the school ideas and guidelines to help the pupil develop these skills.

---

**CASE STUDY:** Supporting different needs when setting up learning environments

Toby is in Year 4 and is unusually tall for his age. He is finding it increasingly difficult to cope in the classroom as the furniture is slightly small for an 'average' sized 9-year-old. In the same class, Niamh has problems controlling her fine motor skills and needs additional support in the form of exercises and practice each day. Callum has cerebral palsy and limited mobility in the classroom. Both his fine and gross motor skills are affected and he uses a walking frame.

- Consider all of their individual needs. How might you support all three pupils when setting out the learning environment?

---

## Potential hazards in the learning environment and how to take action to minimise risks

Whatever the needs of pupils, they are entitled to a safe and secure learning environment. Always be aware of health and safety issues, in particular when working with young children, as they may not be aware of hazards and the possible consequences. It is the duty of all school employees to keep pupils safe and to bring potential hazards to their attention.

### Link

For more on potential hazards and minimising risk, see TDA 2.8 Support children and young people's health and safety.

### Skills builder

Go for a walk around your school and see how many hazards you can identify. Make sure you record and report any which you are not able to deal with yourself. What kinds of things can you do on a daily basis to prevent accidents from occurring?

### Functional skills

**English: Writing**
You could develop your writing skills through writing for a different purpose, by creating a checklist that you could share with other members of staff to inform them of any dangers or daily checks that they need to be aware of.

### Portfolio activity

Obtain a copy of a plan of the school and mark safety equipment using a key on it to include the items listed above. You will then be aware of the location so that you can show your assessor on your assessment visit.

### Key terms

**Safety equipment** – the equipment required by legislation and/or the organisation for ensuring the safety of children, young people and adults in the learning environment

**Learning resources** – materials, equipment (including ICT), software, books and other written materials (such as handouts, worksheets), DVDs and so on that are required to support teaching and learning

## Check that the necessary safety equipment is available and functional

You will need to be aware of the location of **safety equipment** in your school. Although you may have seen items such as first aid boxes and fire extinguishers in school, you should be able to tell others where they are and know where to find them in an emergency. You should also find out how the school monitors their use and ensures that they are checked regularly – for example, fire extinguishers need to be checked annually. Make sure you know what to do in case of emergency – if you are new and the school has not had a fire drill since you started, make sure you tell your line manager.

Safety equipment includes:

- a fully equipped first aid box

- equipment to protect children, young people and adults from accidents, for example, a circuit breaker, cable guards, landing mats for PE, safety goggles for science activities

- equipment for use in an emergency, for example, fire extinguishers, fire blanket, emergency alarms and emergency exits

## Set out learning resources so that learners are able to participate safely and effectively in the planned activities

When working with teachers, it should be clear to you from their plans which **learning resources** are needed for a particular activity. You should be able to set them out without needing to ask for any further help prior to learning activities taking place. If you are working away from the classroom, you may need to ask pupils to help you to bring any resources or equipment that are needed for the task. You should check that resources are set out so that pupils are able to participate safely in activities.

## Be able to prepare learning materials

### Follow relevant manufacturers' instructions and health and safety requirements when preparing learning materials

When you are asked to prepare the learning environment you will also be responsible for getting out **learning materials**. These include:

● general items such as pencils, rulers and paper

● curriculum-specific materials such as paints, science materials or cooking ingredients

● written materials such as handouts and worksheets.

While most materials will be straightforward to get out and use, if the materials you are using have particular health and safety requirements, you should know what these are. Government guidelines specify that all organisations should observe procedures such as carrying out risk assessments when using materials that may be hazardous. Staff and pupils should be aware of this and read instructions before using these types of materials.

### Knowledge into action

Find out, if you do not already know, where the following are kept in your school:

• science resources

• mathematics equipment

• art resources

• general consumables and stock

• PE equipment for indoors and outdoors

• computer equipment such as software, printer inks, CD-ROMs and paper

• RE resources

• musical instruments

• design & technology equipment.

How do staff and pupils have access to additional materials? Find out who is responsible for each curriculum area and how often they are able to buy new materials.

### Prepare learning materials of the quality and quantity required

**Link**

For more on preparing learning resources and materials, see page 201.

In most cases, learning materials which you are preparing and using will be straightforward and you will use them every day. You will be responsible, perhaps alongside pupils, for making sure that items such as pencils, rulers and paper are accessible and are not running short before starting learning activities with pupils. If you are carrying out curriculum-specific activities with pupils, you may need to plan and prepare in advance to make sure that learning materials are available on the day.

## DVD activity

Video clip 5 – Classroom preparation

1. Part of your role is to prepare the environment in school where learning is to take place. Although it may seem straightforward, teachers and assistants will need to have some kind of opportunity to communicate regularly like those in the clip about what needs to be done so that learning environments are fully prepared. You will also need to use your initiative on a daily basis to keep the environment safe, secure and learner ready. Outline some of the ways in which you do this.

2. Find out who is responsible for different equipment and materials in your school and also for health and safety. Does the health and safety policy include guidelines for the preparation and use of learning materials? Think about some of the different subject areas, for example, PE, art, food technology, ICT and Foundation Stage, and outline some of the safety issues which may occur in these environments and how they may be prevented.

3. For all pupils, the classroom and other areas of the learning environment will need to be accessible and safe at all times. Show how you have adapted the learning environment to accommodate pupils who have special educational needs or physical requirements which may be different from other pupils.

4. At the end of the clip, the assistant mentions a health and safety issue which she has noticed in the classroom. What are the procedures for reporting such issues in your school?

## Functional skills

### English: Reading

The procedures for reporting health and safety issues will be found either in the staff handbook or the school's policies. You will need to read these documents carefully to obtain this information.

## Use materials carefully to minimise waste

When using learning materials you should ensure that you do not waste them and that you use items carefully; you should also encourage pupils to do the same. Exercise books, paper and pens are the types of items which pupils may use wastefully and it should be school policy to ensure that pupils are encouraged to think before starting a new book or using a new piece of paper. In many schools there is a set amount of resources for the year and there will not always be funds available to replace stock if it is not used carefully. You should also think about these kinds of issues yourself, for example, when photocopying – can the paper be double-sided? Do you really need to print out emails?

### CASE STUDY: Using materials carefully

Davina is working in a Year 1 class and it is close to the beginning of the year. She has noticed that even though they have spoken to the class about using materials carefully, tops are often left off felt pens and paper is often cut out badly so that it cannot be used again.

- What should Davina and the class teacher do in this situation?
- Why is it important not to allow this to continue?

## Dispose of waste materials safely and with due regard to recycling opportunities and sustainable development

Schools increasingly have recycling bins on the premises for the disposal of paper and plastics, and composting bins for the disposal of waste. All staff, parents and pupils should know where these are and be encouraged to make use of them. Schools may have rotas so that pupils have responsibility for recycling and composting. First-aid waste will usually be collected and disposed of in separate bins, although in some schools it is placed in sanitary disposal containers. If you come across anything sharp which needs to be removed, you should speak to your site manager after making the area safe for others.

*Do you know the location of recycling bins and composting in your school?*

### Over to you!

If possible, when your assessor is in school, point out any recycling points on the premises to show that you are aware of the kinds of measures that are in place.

# Be able to monitor and maintain learning environments and resources

## How environmental factors may affect the learning process and how they should be adjusted for different types of activities

You will need to be sensitive to the needs of pupils when managing the learning environment. As far as possible, all pupils should be given equal opportunities. Those with special educational needs may need to have particular considerations when planning and setting out materials and resources, and the environment may need to be adapted for them. You will need to ensure that you adjust lighting, heating or ventilation if appropriate to ensure that pupils are comfortable, as it is unlikely that they will be able to concentrate if too hot or too cold. Always ensure that pupils have the opportunity to tell you if they are uncomfortable before they start to carry out activities. Factors that will need to be considered include the following.

- **Light:** The light should be appropriate to the activity and may need to be adjusted if required. Consider the use of blinds and curtains if light is too bright.

- **Ventilation:** You may need to open or close windows or doors to ensure that there is a comfortable level of ventilation.

- **Accessibility:** Furniture and resources may need to be moved to allow a pupil in a wheelchair as much access to classroom facilities as other pupils. Their learning may be affected if they are not able to move around to find the resources they need.

- **Temperature:** If the environment is too hot or too cold, pupils will not be able to concentrate on what they are doing and will lose the ability to learn.

- **Sound:** Some pupils may be sensitive to sounds in the learning environment and unable to concentrate if there is too much noise from the area around them or from outside. Autistic pupils, for example, may be disturbed by loud or unusual noises. Although it is not always possible for these to be avoided, you should be aware of the effect that they can have.

## Monitor and adapt the physical environment as needed to maintain health, safety and comfort, make the best use of the space available and ensure access and ease of movement

While you are working on learning activities with pupils, you will need to monitor the learning environment to ensure that pupils are able to continue to work in the most effective environment. This may mean that you need to adjust the environment in different ways while pupils are working.

Pupils should also be taught to get into the habit and routine of returning equipment and materials to the right place after use and making sure that they take responsibility for the tidiness and organisation of their own classrooms.

### Maintain health, safety and security
You should always continue to check the environment, particularly if you are outdoors or away from the school, as the situation may change rapidly and you may need to move pupils away from a particular location if they are unsafe for any reason. If pupils are unwell and unable to continue for health reasons, you should follow school policy in making sure that they are cared for appropriately.

### Maintain the comfort of learners and adults
Always ensure that all those in the learning environment are able to work effectively by giving them clear guidelines for when they will be able to have comfort breaks or drinks. In most schools now pupils have their own water bottles on tables so that they are able to have drinks when needed. See also above on adjusting environmental factors.

### Make the best use of the space available
You should ensure that the space you are working in is used in the most efficient way and that pupils have enough room to work in. You may have to adapt the space and move furniture around to use the space effectively.

### Ensure access and ease of movement for all
You should check that everyone in the learning environment is able to move around easily when required and that equipment and materials are accessible to all learners, in particular those who may have difficulties with mobility. You may need to improve access to doorways so that pupils who have mobility needs are catered for.

**CASE STUDY:** Environmental factors

Donatella is working with a group of Year 5 pupils in an area of the school grounds on a hot day and notices that some workmen are setting up in the road outside to start drilling. She carries on with what she is doing but is soon unable to continue due to the noise, as nobody is able to hear what is being said. In addition, one of the pupils has bad hay fever and is very uncomfortable.

- What would you do in this situation?
- Would you be able to continue with the learning activity?

## Support learners to select learning resources and materials relevant to their learning tasks, and use resources safely and correctly

Although you will need to prepare the learning environment before use by making sure equipment and resources are available, you will also need to ensure that learners are able to select and use any further resources that they require themselves in order to carry out learning activities. Young children will need very clear direction and will need to know where resources and materials are kept in particular areas of the classroom or learning environment so that they are able to select those which are relevant to what they are doing. Older pupils should be able to select those resources they need, although if these are in different areas of the school, such as a library or another specific resource area, they may need permission before going to get them. If pupils are clear on where to find things, they will develop their independence and self-help skills.

You will also need to show pupils how to use resources safely and correctly in the learning environment. If necessary, you will need to do this before they start the learning activity to ensure that it is not interrupted. If you do see a pupil who is using resources inappropriately or in a manner that is unsafe, you will need to intervene.

**CASE STUDY:** Using resources correctly and safely

Lizo is working with Year 7 during a chemistry lesson and the pupils are looking at some of the different equipment which they will have access to in the subject. Most of them are looking at it carefully, drawing and labelling the different items. However, one of the boys in the class has picked up some equipment and is laughing and playing around with it. Lizo goes over and speaks to him and the boy stops, but later in the lesson Lizo sees that he is doing it again.

- What should Lizo do this time?
- Why is it important not to let this behaviour continue?

## Supporting learners to accept responsibility for the safe use and care of the environment, equipment and materials, and returning equipment and materials after use

When working with pupils on learning activities, you should always encourage them to be responsible for the safe use and care of equipment and materials as well as the general environment. Pupils should take a pride in their surroundings and in their learning environment, and you should have high expectations for this. You can also support pupils in developing their responsibility by giving roles to different individuals – for example, pupils can be responsible for different areas of the room or for particular equipment. It is also a good idea to draw pupils' attention to general safety issues that they can control within their environment, for example, pushing chairs under desks when they get up. In this way they will start to develop their own responsibility for safety. Good habits such as ensuring that the learning environment is always kept tidy and that equipment is stored and put away safely will encourage pupils to do the same.

It is also likely that at some point you will be working with pupils using equipment or materials with which they will need to be particularly careful. Pupils who are working with design & technology tools or using PE equipment, for example, will need to be reminded about safety each time they use them. Approach this by asking rather than telling younger children in particular what they need to remember, so that they can start to initiate these thoughts on their own.

## Follow organisational procedures for reporting deficiencies, damage and shortfalls in stocks of equipment and materials

You should know about school policy for reporting any damaged equipment or materials that you come across in school. Most schools will have a book in which you can record details of broken equipment. The caretaker or site manager will usually be responsible for checking this and for dealing with issues such as replacing general on-site consumables, such as light bulbs or paper towels. You should ensure that any damaged equipment or materials are out of the way and cannot be reached by pupils. Such items should be labelled but if you cannot do this, the member of staff responsible should be informed as soon as possible.

**Reflect**

Consider the different ways in which you demonstrate how to support learners to take care of and store equipment and materials safely. What kinds of strategies do you and teachers use to support them in taking responsibility?

### Portfolio activity

Find a list of staff in your school and annotate it for your portfolio, showing staff responsibilities for different resources and materials.

Other items of stock or consumables such as learning materials may be monitored by different members of staff in school. Subject coordinators may manage equipment and resources for their subject area; the art coordinator, for example, will need to keep up to date on the amount of materials being used at any given time. They may have their own systems in place for doing this and you will need to find out how to report any shortages to them. Different subject coordinators need to make sure that there are enough materials if a particular activity, such as working with clay, has been planned for a whole year group at a particular time. More general consumables which are used on a daily basis such as pens, photocopy paper, printer ink and so on are also likely to be monitored and ordered by a particular person. If you notice that stocks are running low, as these items tend to run out quickly, you should know who this person is and report any shortages when you find them.

### Functional skills

ICT: Developing, presenting and communicating information; Using ICT
You could create a database where you store all the information on staff responsibilities that you have found out. As this file could possibly contain contact details, it should be password protected. Try to use a secure password (a password that contains a mixture of numbers and letters) to protect this file.

---

**BEST PRACTICE CHECKLIST:** Preparing and maintaining learning environments

- Prepare the quantity of materials and resources required for the number of pupils
- Check in good time that there are sufficient materials for the activity.
- Remember safety when using tools and equipment.
- Ensure you are aware how to use any unfamiliar equipment before use.
- Keep wastage of materials to a minimum and dispose of waste appropriately.
- Return materials and store equipment correctly after use.
- Report any shortages in materials or equipment to the appropriate person.

## Getting ready for assessment

This unit is divided into three sections:

- preparing the environment
- preparing materials for use
- monitoring and maintaining the environment and resources.

In order to cover performance, it is useful for your assessor to observe you setting up different environments for pupils and both setting out and putting away resources and equipment for pupils. You should also be observed making any changes during the learning process, such as adjusting lighting and ensuring furniture is appropriate, or removing any damaged equipment. Your assessor may also wish to discuss with you the roles of different members of staff concerning the ordering and preparation of learning resources and materials. You should also show them the location of safety equipment while you are showing them around your school. There are some overlaps in this unit with the assessment criteria for heath and safety (TDA 2.8) and you may be able to show your assessor how you take these issues into account when setting out the environment.

## Check your knowledge

1. Give examples of three things you should do when preparing any learning environment for use by pupils.
2. Why should you consider the age and needs of pupils when setting out the learning environment?
3. What kinds of hazards might you find in the learning environment?
4. What kind of safety equipment might you find in schools?
5. What consideration should you give to waste materials and safety when recycling?
6. How might you need to adapt the learning environment during learning activities?
7. What kinds of environmental factors will make a difference to whether pupils are able to settle to their learning?
8. Show how you might support learners in accepting responsibility for the safe use of equipment and materials and the learning environment.
9. Which of these are considered to be safety equipment?
   - a) fire extinguishers
   - b) safety goggles
   - c) oven gloves
   - d) mats for PE
   - e) fire exits.

**Websites**

**http://inclusion.uwe.ac.uk** – Inclusion UK
**www.diseed.org.uk** – Disability Equality in Education
**www.hse.gov.uk/coshh** – guide to the control of hazardous substances

# TDA 2.13 Provide displays in schools

This unit is about how you set up and design displays in school. You will need to be able to demonstrate that you follow school policy and that you ensure school procedures are also followed for displays. You will also need to show that you are able to design, set up, maintain and dismantle displays.

## By the end of this unit you will:

1. understand the school policy and procedures for displays
2. be able to design displays
3. be able to set up displays
4. be able to maintain displays
5. be able to dismantle displays.

# Understand the school policy and procedures for displays

## The school policy for displays

Your school may have a separate policy for **displays** or it may be within your art policy. It is likely that this guidance will set out what you need to do when putting together a display, for example, whether pupils' work or the information displayed will need to be mounted and/or labelled with each pupil's name. If you have been asked to put together a display for any reason, you should always check with the art coordinator and discuss what you are planning to do, to ensure that you are following school policy. Displays may be wall mounted or free standing. The display must be designed with a specific purpose in mind.

### Key term

**Displays** — the arrangement of material (graphic, text and/ or objects) into an assembly specifically intended to attract people's attention and interest, or to provide information, or to educate, or a combination of these

### Functional skills

**English: Writing**
You could practise writing for a different purpose if you completed this portfolio activity in the form of a set of instructions. Take care with your spelling and grammar, and make sure that you organise your work clearly.

### Portfolio activity

Find out whether your school has a separate policy for displays and if not, whether there is written guidance on what you should do. If not, speak to your art coordinator and write a reflective account about what you should remember when putting together a display.

## The importance and purposes of displays in the school

Displays in school may be for a number of different purposes. You should be very clear on what your particular display is to be used for.

### Presenting information

Displays in school may be there to make sure that important information is displayed to pupils, parents or staff. There may be specific boards in

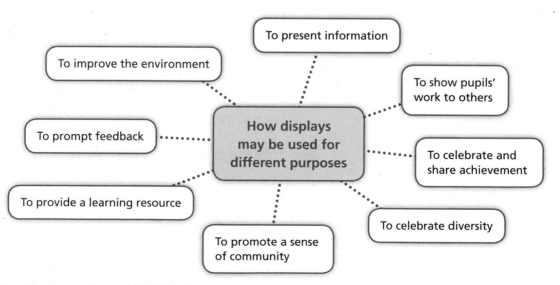

*How displays may be used for different purposes.*

school which are set aside for this purpose, for example, in an entrance hall or lobby, outside staff rooms or in sixth form areas.

### Showing pupils' work to others

It is important for pupils' self-esteem that they see their work displayed around the school; this reinforces their learning and shows others what they have achieved.

### Celebrating and sharing achievement

Displays in shared areas of the school may show pupils who have achieved in a range of areas. These might be related to school systems such as house points or merit marks. They may be shown close to display cases and relate to different subject areas such as sport, music or academic achievement.

### Celebrating diversity

Displays will often celebrate diversity in the school by showing a range of culturally diverse images with a caption. They may also be linked to specific religious or cultural events such as Diwali, Eid or Christmas.

### As a learning resource

These kinds of displays will be designed to enhance pupils' learning experience by showing artefacts or topic-based information for them to use. It is likely that they will be classroom based, but they may also be in subject areas of the school, or in areas which all pupils may use such as the hall. They may include tables which display items to enhance learning and invite pupils to interact and try things out for themselves.

*How do you think seeing displays of their achievements enhances pupils' self-esteem?*

### Promoting a sense of community and belonging

You may find displays which give pupils and staff a sense of belonging by promoting community cohesion. This means through valuing how all staff and pupils work together and also how the school is part of the wider community and how it promotes those links.

### Improving the environment

Displays will always improve the environment as they are stimulating, colourful and informative. They will brighten up different areas of the school and contribute positively to the learning environment. The only exception to this is that they can in some cases over-stimulate pupils who have special educational needs. If you are working with a pupil who finds displays distracting, for example, you may need to address this with your teacher or seek the advice of your SENCO.

### Promoting feedback

These kinds of displays are designed to encourage the viewer to engage with the subject and to fill in or feed back to the creator in some way. They may, for example, remind pupils about putting forward their names for a particular event or include a suggestion box.

### Functional skills

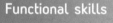

**ICT: Using ICT**

You could use a digital camera and take photographs of the different displays around your school. You could then label them with their different purposes.

### Over to you!

Take a look around your school at the different displays. See whether you can identify their purpose in each case. Do you think they achieve what they set out to do?

### Skills builder

Plan and put up a display which links with pupil learning. Show how it has been used by pupils as part of the learning process.

### Functional skills

**ICT: Developing, presenting and communicating information**

By using the computer to enhance your displays, you will use a number of different layout and editing techniques. Remember to use text boxes and images appropriately.

## How displays are used in the learning process

Displays can be used in the learning process in different ways. Your teacher may use them in the classroom environment to support pupils through reminding them about different aspects of their learning, for example, vocabulary lists in a modern language environment, or different strategies to use when working on mathematics calculations. You may also find that they refer to these kinds of displays while teaching. Displays may also show different items or artefacts relating to a specific topic so that pupils can look more closely at them; for example, washboards and washing dollies, chalk boards, wooden pegs, mangles and so on may be displayed if pupils are studying the Victorians.

It is important to use displays creatively to make a stimulating and welcoming environment for pupils. When displaying their work, you will need to ensure that you display the work of all children and young people and not just the most appealing. All pupils should be able to see their work on display, as it promotes confidence in their own learning. You can add labels and pupils' names to displays, but make sure that these are easy to read and spelled correctly.

## Requirements and procedures for carrying out a risk assessment for displays

Although this may seem obvious, it is important to note and take heed of the requirements and procedures for carrying out a risk assessment for displays. This may involve speaking to the health and safety officer before you start to put up the display, or adapting what you are doing so that you do not put yourself at risk.

Many accidents in schools are caused by staff who do not comply with health and safety requirements, and who stand on tables and chairs or balance on items which are inappropriate. Often rules and regulations are displayed in staff rooms and then ignored by teaching staff who say, 'I'm only standing on it to staple one corner', and who are then hurt by falling off an insecure surface. If you are in any doubt about your safety when putting up a display, you should speak to your site manager and health and safety officer before attempting to put up the display.

# Be able to design displays

## Plan the design and content of the display to meet an agreed purpose

When preparing your display, you will need to make sure that your design is the most appropriate for its use. You will need to think about how you put together different items to display them to the best effect. As already observed, displays may be set up for a range of purposes. However, there are also different ways and places in which they may be set out, for example:

- hanging displays
- wall displays
- table displays
- window displays
- 3D displays.

You should check that your intended design is fit for the purpose of your display – for example, a hanging display may not be the most appropriate way of giving information as it may move around. Also, if you have not done so already, check with the teacher who has asked you to put together the display to ensure that what you are planning to do fits in with their requirements.

## Involve pupils in planning the design and content of the display

Although this may not always be possible, and in particular if you work with very young children, it is a good idea to plan the design and content of the display with the involvement of pupils wherever possible. In this way they will be able to input their own ideas and feel more part of the process. If you work with upper Key Stage 2 or secondary pupils, they will often be able to contribute significantly to the design, although they may need some direction as they work. This is good for pupils who may be more creative and involves them in a different aspect of design. They may also be able to input a range of additional materials.

## Select and create materials relevant to the purpose of the display and encourage the involvement of pupils

As well as displaying pupils' work or the information which you need to share with others, you should try to use additional materials to enhance your display and make it more eye-catching. A display about undersea creatures, for example, may benefit from having green and blue crepe paper plants to make it more 3D and add colour to pupils' work. You should always think about how work can be displayed to best effect. Pupils may also be able to develop materials for the display and work with their peers to do this. You may find that they are able to contribute some materials of their own which may be helpful.

---

**CASE STUDY:** Select and create appropriate materials

Siobhan is working with Year 7 and 8 pupils on a recycling project which is designed to give information to others about how items can be reused. She has selected and put up some information about recycling which the younger pupils have written, as well as including some recycled materials. However, some of the pupils have been making different objects during design & technology with reclaimed materials, for example, bags using different-coloured bottle tops, which she had not known about. They ask Siobhan if they can also display some of these alongside the information.

- Why is it important that the pupils are able to do this?
- How can Siobhan encourage pupils to put forward their ideas in this way?

---

# Be able to set up displays

## Locate the display in an appropriate and accessible place for users

It is important that you consider the purpose of the display and whether it is being put in the most appropriate place for its users. Remember in particular, if you are working with very young children, that they will need to be able to see labels and names clearly, so ensure that these are not too high.

You should make sure that you consider the following.

- What is the display for?
- Who needs to be able to see it or use the information?
- Will they get maximum benefit in its location?
- Are they able to add to the display if this is appropriate?

You may have been told where to put the display and not have any control over its location; sometimes there may be situations in which you need to fill a particular board. If this is the case, you may be able to make it more eye-catching or put up information posters in the school to tell pupils where to find it.

---

**CASE STUDY:** Locate the display in an appropriate and accessible place

Mandy has been asked to put up a display in an upstairs corridor, giving details of the new school council. This includes the identity of different members of the council, including photographs and their class, as well as details of meetings and what the council will be discussing. This is useful information for pupils about issues which concern them, but the place in which Mandy has been asked to put it is not very central for them and is in a dark corner.

- Should Mandy say something?
- What else could she do?

---

## Display all relevant material and use clear labelling and layout to acknowledge and celebrate pupils' work

When you have put up pupils' work, you should ensure that any labelling is clear and that you have followed school policy for displaying pupil names and mounting work. Always use paper strimmers, as they will provide clean straight lines and this will make your display look much clearer. It is important to celebrate what pupils have done by presenting it well and showing them that we value their work. If names are not included or if it is put up badly, this does not give a good impression. Your layout should always be such that spacing and alignment are in proportion and that the display 'flows' easily — beware of positioning work or labels at an angle, as this can make the display look disjointed and harder to read. When using labels, try to make sure that you use the same-sized writing on work and captions — although headings should be larger — so that it can be read easily. If you are going to hand write any captions, always make sure this is very neat and clear.

*How clear do you think this display is?*

If you have planned your display carefully, you should be able to include all relevant material, as you will have allowed for enough space. It is worth asking another individual to check the display when you have finished, ensuring that you have included everything that is needed for it to make sense. You may need to move some items around to ensure that crucial information is included. Always ensure that you have a clear title and subheadings if necessary or if the display is in different sections.

## Check that the display meets relevant health, safety, security and access requirements

When putting together your display, it is important to make sure that it meets health and safety requirements. As well as being careful when putting it up, you will need to check that it does not present a risk to others in any way. If you are unsure, you may wish to check with your premises officer or health and safety representative while you are working.

- Is the display blocking or close to a door or fire exit?
- Will it prevent pupils from moving around safely, in particular any pupils who have special educational needs?
- Is it at the correct level for all pupils to see it clearly?
- Is the display likely to set off any sensors when the school is empty?
- Do window displays let in adequate light?
- Are any artefacts which are being displayed on tables safe for pupils to handle?
- Are there any staples or pins left in the display board which could be harmful?

**CASE STUDY:** Meeting health and safety requirements

Charlie has put up a hanging display in the Reception classroom by attaching some string across the room and fixing the pupils' work to it. Although this is very effective, he has just learned that the premises officer was called during the night because one of the pieces of work had fallen down and set off a sensor which had triggered the burglar alarm.

- How could this have been avoided?
- What could Charlie do in the future to avoid this happening?

**BEST PRACTICE CHECKLIST:** Putting together displays

- Think carefully about your display and location before you start.
- Prepare the background and choose backing paper and borders that will complement the work or theme — or reuse previous backing paper if possible.
- Use a paper strimmer rather than scissors to keep lines straight.
- Position the pupils' work or key information with pins so that it can be moved as you work and then stapled at the end.
- Involve pupils and ask for their ideas if possible.
- Decide where to put any captions and keep labels the same font and size.
- Check that all displays are safe.
- Ensure names are visible.
- Be prepared for pupils to touch and use interactive displays!

# Be able to maintain displays

## The optimum time duration for the display by reference to its theme, purpose and materials used

You should make sure that displays do not 'outlive' their purpose, by leaving them for too long or by letting them become tatty and untidy. They will need to complement the work that pupils are undertaking at a particular time or be relevant to something which is taking place during the current term if possible. If they are left for too long, it gives pupils the message that displays are not valued by the school as they have outlived their usefulness. This can be difficult as displays take time to create, but they can also be recycled if necessary. Christmas displays in particular should always be taken down before the end of the autumn term so that you do not come back to them at the beginning of the new year.

**Functional skills**

**Mathematics: Interpreting**
You could calculate what percentage/fraction of the people you asked appreciate the displays. You could also use your results to create a chart and write a short conclusion on what your results show.

**Over to you!**

Carry out a 'display survey' in your school. Ask pupils and staff to think about a range of issues to do with displays. Do they notice when they are changed? Do they appreciate a display which has been put together well? How often are pupils involved? You may wish to feed back your results to your art coordinator.

## Maintain the display in a tidy, clean and correctly laid-out condition, and monitor the display for stability and safety and take appropriate action if required

You must regularly check all displays in school, not just those which you have put up, to keep them in a safe, tidy and correctly laid-out condition. All staff are responsible for keeping the school safe and tidy, and displays are part of this. Some displays, particularly those which are interactive or which are placed in corridors, can be easily knocked or work can be torn. If you see any display in this condition, you should always repair it as soon as possible or inform the appropriate person if resources have become damaged. You should also check display boards which are free-standing as they can be knocked over easily — make sure there is something to secure them and if you are at all unsure about their safety and stability, check with your health and safety officer.

## Assess the display regularly for its continuing usefulness and attractiveness and add to or amend as required

You should keep an eye out for displays which have become outdated or which may no longer be required (see below). If they are yours, you may wish to speak to the teacher who originally asked you to put them up, and consider changing them for something brighter and more appropriate. If you have not put them up yourself, you should speak to the person responsible for displays and mention it to them. The learning environment needs to be attractive and inviting to pupils, and this should be reviewed constantly.

You may need to amend and/or update the display depending on its purpose. Some displays can be put up and left alone until they are taken down — however, others may need to be updated or checked by the creator to make sure that any additions are noted — for example, if pupils have been invited to vote or put their own ideas forward.

# Be able to dismantle displays

## Dismantle the display as soon as it is no longer required

You should always remove any displays when they are no longer required. Tired and outdated displays (for example, a fireworks display which is still up in March!) can be very disheartening to look at for pupils and staff alike. However, you should try to ensure that there is another display to go in its place, as empty display boards can also be demoralising to look at for any length of time. One strategy used

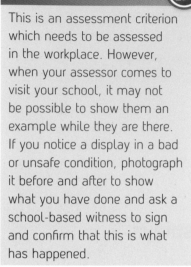

**Portfolio activity**

This is an assessment criterion which needs to be assessed in the workplace. However, when your assessor comes to visit your school, it may not be possible to show them an example while they are there. If you notice a display in a bad or unsafe condition, photograph it before and after to show what you have done and ask a school-based witness to sign and confirm that this is what has happened.

by schools is to move displays around — for example, a display which has been up on a classroom wall and has not been seen by many people could be transferred to a more public area of the school if this is appropriate. In this way, displays which have taken a long time to create can be seen and appreciated by more people.

## Store or return materials and equipment used in the display in accordance with school policy and procedures, and dispose of waste materials safely and with due regard to recycling opportunities and sustainable development

You may need a range of materials and equipment when putting up your display — ensure that you have returned them to the correct place after you have finished. You may also find that you have been asked to dismantle a display which you were not responsible for putting up — in this case you may need to find out where specific equipment or materials have come from in school. The display may also have used other resources or equipment which will need to be returned to the owner or disposed of appropriately.

When dismantling displays, always ensure that you put waste paper into recycling bins where possible and return any materials which can be reused to stock cupboards or art rooms. If there are any other materials which need to be thrown away and are biodegradable, or can be returned to the outdoor environment safely, you should always make sure that you do this.

### Link

See page 197 for more about recycling materials.

### Reflect

When dismantling displays, how much do you consider recycling and sustainable development? Think about items which you could save and the way in which you dispose of or reuse materials.

### CASE STUDY: Disposing of materials

Rick is a support assistant who is not involved with displays at all in his school. However, he has been asked to take down an old display as the board needs to be reused as soon as possible. He takes down the paintings and labels, and then removes all the backing paper and borders as well. When the teacher who had asked him to remove it sees what he has done, she says that it is not school policy to remove backing paper, as it can easily be reused.

- Is Rick in the wrong?
- Could he have done anything differently?

## Getting ready for assessment

In order to provide evidence for this unit, you should keep photographs of any displays which you have put together, particularly those which have involved the input of pupils. You should also give information about their purpose and content and any health and safety issues which you have had to deal with. You should aim to have examples of a good range of displays which you have been involved with and show these to your assessor when they come into the school.

## Check your knowledge

1. Why are displays important in school?

2. What might you look for in a display?

3. What kinds of risks should you be aware of when you are putting together a display?

4. Give three reasons why it is important to plan displays carefully.

5. Why is it a good idea to involve pupils where possible and how can you do this?

6. Who is responsible for making sure that any damaged displays are put right as soon as possible?

7. What should you do if you see a display in an unsafe condition?

8. Why is it important to have read and know the school policy for displays?

9. Where might you go to look for inspiration and/or ideas when putting together a display?

## References and further reading

There is a large number of books available, including the following.

- Andrew-Power, Kirstie and Gormley, Charlotte (2009) *Display for Learning*, Network Continuum Education
- Fitzsimmons, Jim, Wansborough, Martin and Whiteford, Rhona (1996) *Hands on Display*, Belair – A World of Display
- Harrison, Patricia (2003) *An Eye for Display*, Belair – A World of Display
- Taylor, Lynn (2006) *Rules of Display*, Hodder Gibson

Teachers' TV and the Times Educational Supplement also regularly run items on display which can be found on their websites if you type in 'display' as a key word – see **www.teachers.tv** and **www.tes.co.uk**

### Websites

The following sites all provide resources for producing displays.

**www.twinkl.co.uk**
**www.teachingideas.co.uk**
**www.tpet.co.uk**
**www.classdisplays.co.uk**

# TDA 2.14 Support children & young people at meal or snack times

In your role as a teaching or learning support assistant, it is important that you have knowledge of a healthy balanced diet and the benefits for children's health and well being. This will enable you to support children to make healthy food choices. You must demonstrate that you are able to support hygiene practices and procedures and promote positive behaviour during meal and snack times.

## By the end of this unit you will:

1. know the principles of healthy eating for children and young people
2. know the benefits of healthy eating for children and young people
3. know how to encourage children and young people to make healthier food choices
4. be able to support hygiene during meal or snack times
5. be able to support the code of conduct and policies for meal and snack times.

215

# Know the principles of healthy eating for children and young people

## Outline the nutritional requirements of a healthy diet for children and young people

All children need a healthy diet to help them to grow and develop. Their diet must also support their high energy needs. A healthy diet is one which includes plenty of fruit, vegetables and starchy foods.

The Food Standards Agency has produced guidance on what constitutes a healthy diet. The Eatwell plate provides a good illustration of what a healthy balanced diet should comprise.

*The Eatwell plate.*

Starchy foods help to give growing and active children the energy that they need. These foods also contain many of the nutrients needed in children's diets such as calcium, iron and B vitamins. About one-third of their diet should be made up of carbohydrates, which are found in starchy foods. These include foods such as:

- potatoes, yams, plantain
- breads — wholewheat, granary, bagels, chapattis, pitta bread
- beans, peas, lentils
- wholegrain breakfast cereals.

Fruit and vegetables are a good source of vitamins and minerals. It is recommended that children and adults have at least five portions of fruit and vegetables each day. Fruit and vegetables are a good source of vitamin C, in particular citrus fruits, tomatoes and potatoes. Green vegetables also contain iron.

Milk and dairy produce such as milk, cheese, yoghurt and fromage frais are a good source of calcium. These foods also provide protein and vitamins A and B12. They vary in fat content. For instance, butter and some cheeses are high in fat, so should only be eaten in small amounts.

Meat, fish, eggs and pulses are a good source of protein, vitamins and minerals. Some meat has high fat content so it is better to include leaner cuts such as turkey and chicken without skin. Fish is a healthy choice and provides many essential minerals and vitamins. Oily fish such as salmon, mackerel, sardines and herring should also be included in the diet. Oily fish is a good source of vitamin A, vitamin D and Omega 3 fatty acids.

Fats and sugars should only make up a small part of the diet of children and young people. Saturated fats are found in fatty meats, pastries, butter, ghee, chocolate and cream, and should be avoided. These should be replaced, wherever possible, with unsaturated fats. Unsaturated fats are in foods such as oily fish, nuts and seeds, vegetable oils and spreads. Sugar, although giving energy, contains few essential nutrients. Sugar is added to many foods such as fizzy drinks, jams and sweets.

Drinks are also part of a child's balanced diet. Children should drink water regularly throughout the day. Other drinks such as semi-skimmed milk, fruit juices or sugar-free squash will give children variety. Fizzy drinks have little nutritional value so should be discouraged.

## Describe examples of healthy meals and snacks for children and young people

A healthy meal is one that provides balance. Fruit and vegetables are essential but if they are not balanced with other foods, children will not get all the nutrients they require. The Eatwell plate (left) gives guidance on the proportions for each type of food.

When designing a menu, consider the nutritional balance over a whole day. Even when children eat a well-balanced meal, their diet may include unhealthy snacks or drinks. Designing healthy meals and snacks which attract children requires some thought. Children often have fixed ideas on what they do and do not like. For instance, children often refuse vegetables, but including them in a dish such as stir-fry may tempt children to eat them.

### Functional skills

**Mathematics: Analysing**
Once you have completed the portfolio activity, you could do some mathematical calculations to show what percentage of the healthy diet is fat and sugar, protein, carbohydrates and fruit and vegetables. Remember that a balanced diet contains all of these in proportion.

### Portfolio activity

Select one of the following age groups:

- 5 to 7 years
- 7 to 11 years
- 11 to 16 years.

Design a healthy diet for one day. Include breakfast, lunch and dinner and also snacks and drinks. Try to incorporate foods in the right proportions within each main meal. Also consider the overall balance of nutrients throughout the day.

# Describe how culture, religion and health conditions impact on food choices

It is important that there is a selection of foods available which meets the dietary needs of all children. There is a number of factors which can have an impact on the food choices made by children and young people. There may be restrictions because of health, cultural or religious reasons, or personal choice.

## Health conditions

### Food intolerance

Children may have intolerances to certain foods. An intolerance is different from an allergy. Children who are intolerant to foods have an adverse reaction if they eat certain foods. A common food intolerance is cow's milk. Milk contains a type of sugar called lactose. Some children cannot digest milk properly and this can cause stomach pains or diarrhoea. Food intolerance can cause unpleasant and sometimes long-term symptoms.

### Food allergies

When children have food allergies, their immune system is affected. Some common foods which cause an allergic response are eggs, nuts and seafood. When children eat foods to which they have an allergy, their body's immune system overreacts. This can be life-threatening. The signs, symptoms and actions to be taken will be dealt with later on in this unit.

### Coeliac disease

This is a condition where the body cannot absorb gluten, which is found in wheat, barley, rye and oats. Symptoms in children include diarrhoea, tiredness and poor growth. Children with coeliac disease must have a gluten-free diet.

### Diabetes

Children with diabetes do not produce insulin. Sometimes, following activity or when children have not eaten enough carbohydrates, their blood glucose levels can fall. Children with diabetes must have a balanced diet which includes starchy carbohydrates. They must also eat regularly. This may mean that children must eat additional snacks in class, particularly when they have been active.

## Link

Emergency situations such as a 'hypo' and anaphylaxis (an allergic reaction to certain foods) are described in TDA 2.2 Safeguarding the welfare of children and young people.

## Religious and cultural dietary variation

Table 1 gives an outline of the dietary restrictions of cultural and religious groups. There may be variations within different religions, so it is important that individual dietary preferences are known.

| Religion/culture | Dietary restrictions |
|---|---|
| Hindu | Strict Hindus are vegetarians. They do not eat beef or dairy products that contain rennet. Some Hindus do not eat eggs or shellfish. |
| Sikh | Sikhs do not eat **Kosher** or **Halal** meat, as they do not believe in ritual slaughter. There are no strict rules but many Sikhs are vegetarian. |
| Muslim | Muslims do not eat pork or foods which contain the by-product of pork, such as gelatin. Other meats can be eaten if they are Halal (slaughtered in accordance with Islamic law). |
| Jewish | No pork or shellfish is eaten. Jews require Kosher foods (meats that are slaughtered a particular way). Foods must also be prepared correctly, for example, using separate knives/boards for different types of food. Some foods are not eaten together, such as dairy products and meat. |

Table 1: Dietary restrictions of different religions and cultures.

### Key terms

**Kosher** — food which is prepared in accordance with Jewish dietary law

**Halal** — 'permissible' foods allowed under Islamic law

## Vegetarianism and veganism

Children and young people may be vegetarian or vegan because of personal choice or it may be linked to religious or cultural reasons. Vegetarians do not eat meat, fish, seafood or animal by-products such as gelatin. Vegetarians usually eat milk, eggs and cheese if made from vegetarian rennet. Vegans do not eat meat, fish or seafood or any foods of animal origin such as milk or eggs.

It is important that children who do not eat meat and fish have choices which include protein foods such as beans, lentils and tofu, and iron from leafy vegetables, wholemeal breads and fortified breakfast cereals.

### Functional skills

**Mathematics: Interpreting**

You could do a survey of your school, year group or class that shows how many of the children are vegetarian or vegan. You could then convert this information into fractions and percentages, and display your results in a chart. Compare this to a friend's data at another school and see if the figures are similar. Your results might show, for example, that there are more vegetarians at the older end of the school because the children understand more about food sources.

# Know the benefits of healthy eating for children and young people

Children's overall health and well-being is dependent on their dietary choices. You only have to watch children playing to realise that they require large amounts of energy.

A well-balanced diet will provide the nutrients needed for:

● energy — needed to keep children alive, to ensure activity and to keep warm

● maintenance of the body — growth, tissue repair, healthy skin, teeth, hair, red blood cells, immune system.

Children who have a balanced diet will be less susceptible or prone to infections and illnesses and have less time off from school. Many schools now provide a breakfast club as teachers recognise that children concentrate better when they have eaten a nutritious breakfast.

## Describe the benefits of healthy eating for children and young people

When children make healthy food choices in school, they are more likely to do so outside school. Establishing good eating habits at an early age is also likely to stay with them in their adult lives.

The government has set out the proportion of key nutrients which should be included in a school lunch.

**VITAMIN A**
GOOD FOR THE eyesight AND SKIN. IT HELPS OVERALL GROWTH AND TISSUE REPAIR.

**PROTEIN**
HELPS GROWTH AND REPAIR OF THE BODY. IT ALSO GIVES energy.

**VITAMIN C**
HELPS TO PREVENT INFECTION AND DISEASE. IT ALSO HELPS CHILDREN TO absorb IRON.

**ZINC**
HELPS CHILDREN TO GROW AND REPAIR TISSUE. IT ALSO improves THE IMMUNE SYSTEM.

**CARBOHYDRATES**
PROVIDE CHILDREN WITH THE energy THEY NEED.

**IRON**
HELPS TO BUILD THE red blood cells, WHICH TAKE OXYGEN AROUND THE BODY.

**FIBRE**
A TYPE OF CARBOHYDRATE WHICH IS non-digestible- FIBRE IS NEEDED FOR A HEALTHY DIGESTIVE SYSTEM.

**CALCIUM**
IS ESSENTIAL TO HELP TO BUILD STRONG BONES AND TEETH. IT also HELPS TO BUILD MUSCLE AND IMPROVE nerve function.

**FOLATE**
REQUIRED FOR growth AND TO PREVENT ANAEMIA.

*The benefits of essential nutrients for growing children and young people.*

### Functional skills

**ICT: Developing, presenting and communicating information**
You could design a poster on the computer (using either Word or Publisher) that promotes healthy eating. You could also run a competition in school where the children design posters to be displayed around the school building linked to healthy eating.

## Describe the possible consequences of an unhealthy diet

Studies show that at least 16 per cent of 2- to 15-year-olds are obese (source: Department of Health, 2004). Studies show a low consumption of fruit and vegetables and high consumption of foods which are high in fat and sugars. Guidance to schools sets maximum levels for fats, sugar and salt.

Fat provides energy for children but has a far higher calorie content than carbohydrates. Too much fat in the diet will lead to obesity and ill health. Obese children are likely to become obese adults with all the associated health risks, such as heart problems and diabetes.

Sugar can occur naturally in food such as honey and fruit, but foods with added sugar should be avoided as they will lead to tooth decay. Up to one-quarter of the added sugar consumed by children between the ages of two and ten is in their drinks.

Salt is essential in the diet to maintain water balance and for nerve and muscle function, but too much salt can cause tiredness and cramps, and can lead to high blood pressure. It is difficult to know how much salt we eat, as salt is added to most processed foods. Salt levels for children must be less than for adults. Daily recommended levels by the Food Standards Agency are:

- age 4–6 years: less than 3 grams
- age 7–10 years: less than 5 grams
- age 11–14 years: less than 6 grams.

### Dieting

Dieting is becoming common among girls who are influenced by their peers or the media. Girls worry about their weight and often make food choices which affect their health. This may also mean skipping meals, which leads to a poor diet. In some instances the pressure to diet can lead to **bulimia** and **anorexia nervosa**

All children require foods which give energy, but it is particularly important during the growth spurt which happens during puberty. Without these foods the result may be lack of energy and lethargy. Studies show that young people have deficiencies in particular nutrients which can affect health and well-being. Some of the common deficiencies in teenagers are:

- iron deficiency — at least 25 per cent of girls and 12 per cent boys do not have sufficient iron in their diet. This can lead to anaemia
- calcium deficiency — it is thought that 25 per cent of teenagers have calcium deficiency. This can lead to problems with teeth and bones, and possibly osteoporosis in later life.

### Over to you!

Research packaging to find out where there are hidden sugars — for example, cereals, canned foods.

### Key terms

**Bulimia** — this eating disorder involves binge eating then vomiting or the use of laxatives. It may not involve weight loss but will cause ill health

**Anorexia nervosa** — an eating disorder which involves self-induced weight loss. It is more common among girls

## Describe how to recognise and deal with allergenic reactions to food

Unlike food intolerances, allergenic reactions can have immediate and life-threatening effects. Children only need tiny amounts of foods they are allergic to in order to have a reaction.

If children experience an allergenic reaction, you may notice that they:

● complain of tingling or burning sensation of the lips or face

● have swelling of their lips and face

● are wheezing

● complain of feeling sick or vomiting and/or stomach pains

● have diarrhoea

● complain of itchy skin or have a blotchy skin rash.

In severe cases, anaphylactic shock occurs. The reaction can happen within a few moments. Anaphylaxis may include the symptoms above and may also cause:

● changes in heart rate

● breathing difficulties

● confusion

● loss of consciousness.

If children at the school are known to have food allergies, it is essential that all the staff know this. Children who are at risk of anaphylaxis may carry or have available in school an adrenaline injection kit known as an EpiPen® or Anapen®. All staff should know if these are carried or where they are kept within the school. Even if the symptoms are not severe, or a child has injected adrenaline, emergency medical help must be sought by phoning 999.

## Describe where to get advice on dietary concerns

You can seek advice from health professionals, such as specialist nurses and dieticians. You can also find out information through charities, books or websites. It is important when researching information in books or on the web to ensure that the information is both up to date and reliable.

### General information on diet and nutrition

The Food Standards Agency is a government department. It was set up to provide a wide range of information relating to food, for example, nutrition, safe food handling and labelling. The Food Standards Agency can provide information on a range of issues and concerns in relation to food (www.food.gov.uk).

### Guidance for schools

The healthy schools initiative is a joint initiative between the Department for Education (formerly DCSF) and the Department of Health. There is a range of advice available through this programme in relation to healthy eating (www.healthyschools.gov.uk). The School Food Trust is another organisation which works to promote health through providing education and advice on food (www.schoolfoodtrust.org.uk).

### Advice for children with particular dietary needs

It is important that staff can access advice on particular dietary needs or conditions of children and young people in the school. Specialist health professionals will work closely with schools. The National Health Service website (www.nhs.uk) provides details of health conditions, symptoms and dietary advice. Third-sector organisations (charities) also provide reliable advice on specific dietary problems.

**Functional skills**

**ICT: Finding and selecting information**
When searching on the Internet, it is important that you take account of bias and copyright restrictions on information.

**Portfolio activity**

Research organisations or individuals, useful reading materials and websites where you can obtain information for at least three dietary concerns which you may come across.

## Know how to encourage children and young people to make healthier food choices

### Describe the food policy of the setting

The policy of the setting must promote and monitor the whole experience of children and young people in relation to the food. The following information refers to schools but includes settings such as breakfast clubs, after-school clubs and foods provided on educational visits. Since 2006 all meals and snacks provided by schools must be balanced and nutritious. These national standards cover:

- meals provided by the school
- snacks provided by the school including vending
- packed lunches
- foods purchased off site and brought into the school
- the availability of water to drink.

The school's policy must include ways it will ensure that all food provided and eaten in school is healthy. It should also provide information on ways that the school will ensure that children are given the skills and knowledge to make healthy choices. Effective food policies will involve the whole school including governors, staff, catering staff, children and parents. This will ensure that the policy is relevant and benefits all those it will affect.

**Functional skills**

**English: Writing**
**ICT: Developing, presenting and communicating information**
You could produce an information leaflet for parents about healthy eating that promotes them sending their child with a healthy packed lunch to school. It is important to include some information from the school policy if it is relevant.

The National Healthy Schools Programme was introduced to improve the overall health and well-being of children and young people. It also provides guidance for schools when developing policies. The programme has four themes. The theme relevant for this unit is Healthy Eating. Although the programme is voluntary, the majority of schools have worked towards the guidelines to achieve Healthy Schools Status.

### Over to you!

Find out if your school has Healthy Schools Status or is working towards it.

### Skills builder

Obtain the school's food policy and find out how the policy was developed. It may have been through meetings, questionnaires, surveys, involving children through school councils and so on. This task will develop your research skills.

## Describe ways of encouraging children and young people to make healthier food choices and to eat the food provided for them

The whole food experience is important to encourage children to make healthy choices, whether they opt for school meals or bring their own packed lunch. The choices which children make when they are young are likely to stay with them as they grow. Consider the experience of children in your school regarding the following questions.

### Do children have the opportunity to contribute to menus or the range of food on offer?

Involving children and young people in school policy making is a good start to encourage children's interest in eating healthy food. This could involve helping to design menus or tasting sessions with opportunities to give feedback on food on offer.

### Is the food appetising – displayed well and at the correct temperature?

Look at how the food is displayed in the school dining hall. Does it look appetising? Food which is displayed well and is kept at the right temperature is more likely to encourage children to choose food provided by the school.

### Is the whole dining experience pleasant for children and young people?

How easy is it for children to access food? A dining hall which is easy to access and has comfortable dining areas and a sociable atmosphere will encourage more young people to opt for healthy school meals rather than going out of school, and maybe choosing an unhealthy alternative.

*How healthy is the food on offer at your school?*

### Does the food on offer meet the dietary requirements of all the children?

The menu should offer interesting and real alternatives for children with special dietary needs because of health, culture or religious reasons. Some children may choose to be vegetarian. If children's choices of healthy foods are restricted, they may choose unhealthy options.

### Do children know about foods and their own nutritional requirements?

If children are to make healthy choices, they must have an understanding of nutritional values in foods and the potential effects on their health. Children can explore these across the curriculum, for instance, through science, food technology and in Personal, Social, Health and Economic education (PSHE) lessons. From a very young age children should be involved in food tasting and cooking activities to increase their interest in what they eat. Some schools have their own gardens where children can grow fresh vegetables and fruit.

### Are parents and carers involved in developing school policy?

It is difficult to encourage children to change their eating habits unless parents are also on board. This can be achieved by involving parents in policy and menu development. They can contribute their ideas through questionnaires, in meetings or attending taster sessions. Parents are often surprised by changes in the menu on offer, as they have memories of their own school days.

*How can you involve children in thinking about healthy alternatives in a lunchbox?*

## Lunchboxes

Research by the Food Standards Agency shows that the majority of children's lunchboxes contain foods which are high in saturated fats, salt and sugar. It was found that less than one-quarter of lunchboxes met the government's recommended standards, meaning it may be difficult to make changes to healthy alternatives overnight.

---

**CASE STUDY:** Leon's lunch

Rosie works as a teaching assistant in Year 1 of the local primary school. She supports children at lunchtime. Rosie has noticed that Leon's lunchbox contains a high proportion of foods which are high in saturated fats and sugar. He always brings a white bread sandwich with butter and often cheese, a packet of crisps and cake or chocolate biscuits.

In support of the National Healthy Schools Programme, Rosie has been asked to work with children in class to help them to understand the importance of healthy foods. She will also liaise with parents to encourage them to provide healthier foods for their children.

- Suggest an activity which Rosie could carry out in class with a group of children which will develop their knowledge about food.
- Produce an information sheet for parents on healthy alternatives for Leon's lunchbox.

---

## Buying food off site

The school's healthy food policy will extend to food sold in the school tuck shop, vending machines and foods brought into school. In secondary schools there is evidence that many children continue to purchase unhealthy foods from local shops and takeaways. Research has shown that children make choices based on problems of queuing in the school canteen and cost – rather than not liking the food. Policies are difficult for schools to enforce so educating children about healthy eating and improving the school meal experience is central to developing good eating habits.

## Supporting and encouraging children and young people to eat the food provided

Healthy eating is about children making the choices, so you need to consider ways that you can do this. Children should never be forced to eat the food provided. You must never show annoyance or get angry. Children can vary in their appetites, so knowing individual children and their dietary needs is important. Children who have smaller appetites may be daunted by large portions.

## Functional skills

### English: Writing
You could write a diary of a time when you have supported a child at a mealtime or helped to make a mealtime more enjoyable for children. Consider the following.

- What did the children learn at the mealtime?
- What did you promote at the mealtime?
- What would you do differently in the future?

## BEST PRACTICE CHECKLIST: Meal and snack times

- Make mealtimes fun — meal and snack times should be social occasions. Children will associate good feelings with eating their food.
- Be positive about foods — never show your dislike of particular foods.
- Be a good role model — eat healthily yourself.
- Give choice — if a child is reluctant to eat vegetables, ask, 'Would you like carrots or broccoli?' rather than, 'Would you like vegetables?'
- Point out foods that are new to children. Giving food names and providing information on ways it promotes health, where the food comes from or how it grows will spark interest.
- Suggest new foods are tried alongside favourite foods — a small portion at first.
- Make sure that children can eat easily and have suitable cutlery — spoons the right size or special utensils for children with disabilities.
- If children are reluctant to eat particular foods, suggest alternatives which give the same nutrients. For instance, dried fruit counts as one of the five a day for children reluctant to eat fresh fruit.

# Be able to support hygiene during meal or snack times

## Explain the importance of personal hygiene at meal and snack times

When supporting children at meal and snack times, it is important that you follow school procedures in respect of personal hygiene. One of the most effective ways to prevent contamination is hand washing. **Microbes** can stay on hands for as long as three hours, so it is essential that you wash your hands frequently when working with children and young people. You must always wash hands:

- before preparing foods
- before eating or supporting children with meals or snacks
- after going to the toilet.

Hands should always be washed thoroughly in warm water. Areas between fingers and thumbs need to be washed carefully. Also remember the area under rings which can harbour germs. Hands should then be rinsed and dried using a clean towel or paper towel, or by air drying.

## Key term

Microbes — germs, including viruses and bacteria

Remember:

● keep cuts or sores always covered with a dressing
● do not cough or sneeze near foods
● keep hair tied back and do not brush hair near food
● keep nails clean.

If you have any gastrointestinal problems, you must report this and not handle foods or support children at mealtimes.

## Demonstrate good hygiene practice in relation to own role in food handling and waste disposal

Food poisoning is caused by microbes which can easily be spread through hands, knives and other utensils or chopping boards. Tea towels can also be a source of contamination. When serving meals or preparing snacks, you must always follow hygiene procedures.

● Clean surfaces, utensils and boards after preparing foods with hot water and washing-up liquid.
● Keep clean all areas where food is stored.
● Use clean towels, or preferably paper towels or disposable cloths.

Particular care must be taken when disposing of foods.

● Dispose of waste food immediately.
● Bins should have a lid and liner.
● Bins must be emptied and cleaned regularly.

## Demonstrate ways of encouraging children and young people's personal hygiene at meal and/or snack times

It is important that children follow good hygiene practice. By the time children start school, they should be able to take care of their personal hygiene. You should explain the reasons for good personal hygiene particularly at snack and mealtimes. Teaching activities relating to personal hygiene should form part of the curriculum.

It is important that you give children sufficient time for hand washing before snack and mealtimes. Young children may require guidance and support to ensure that they wash their hands properly. Older children may need gentle reminders. Other ways to encourage children's personal hygiene include:

● modelling hygienic practice
● demonstrating the correct way to wash hands, or for older children, putting up notices about it
● giving children information about the way that germs spread
● reminding children to cover their mouth/nose when sneezing and coughing
● praising children when they demonstrate hygienic practice.

# Be able to support the code of conduct and policies for meal and snack times

## Describe the setting's code of conduct and policies for meal and snack times

The layout and organisation of the dining and snack areas can have a direct impact on behaviour and noise levels. Children's experience can also affect whether they choose a meal provided by the school or bring their own packed lunch.

### Entering and exiting the dining area

If there are large numbers of pupils, there are likely to be staggered times for pupils to eat, to prevent long queues. Queuing can cause frustration; children become bored and get annoyed if they think their favourite foods will run out. Food service can be speeded up if children know what the menu is before they enter the dining room. Does your school advertise the menu or even have procedures for older children to order their food? Find out about the school's timetable. Schools may end lessons for some groups earlier and have a later start time for others.

When exploring the policy and code of conduct, also consider:

● ways that children exit the dining area. Younger children may need to wait until the whole group have finished their lunch, but older children may be allowed to leave when they have finished

● the grouping of the children. Can they choose where to sit or do they always have to sit at the same table? Are children with school meals and children with packed lunches allowed to sit together? Children may make choices because they want to sit with friends.

### Collecting and serving foods

Primary schools may choose to have small eating areas with family groups where meals are served at the table. There may even be family groupings where an adult or older child serves the lunch or food may be served to children at a counter. In secondary schools there will be a cafeteria system where children choose their own foods and then pay at a till or use tokens.

### Clearing away

The code or policy must include clear guidance on how crockery, leftover foods and packaging will be cleared away. There are usually lunchtime supervisors appointed to clear away crockery for younger children, although some smaller schools may encourage children to take away their own plates. There is likely to be a system in place for older pupils to clear away when they have finished.

**Over to you!**

Before you start to look in depth at the policy of the setting, spend some time observing what happens at lunch and/ or snack times. The policy will depend upon:

- the number of children
- the ages of the children
- space available and layout
- the timetable.

*How do children tend to be grouped at mealtimes in your school?*

### Noise levels

Noise levels can affect the dining experience of children. There will be some noise but consider whether this is social interaction or if it is at a level which is not acceptable. It would be inappropriate to expect children to eat in silence but if children begin to shout across to friends the noise level gradually rises. The layout of the dining hall can help to reduce noise levels. Circular tables where children can face each other are preferable to long dining tables. Some schools play music which can have a calming effect.

### Conduct at the table and in the dining area

The policy on conduct at the table and in the dining area must be known and understood by staff, children and parents. The policy should set out the boundaries of behaviour, including the responsibilities of children to keep the eating area clean and tidy. Lunch and snack times should be enjoyable and social occasions.

### Sustainable food policy

Many schools have taken a new look at food policies in schools and have introduced initiatives which encourage both children and staff to choose food provided by the school. Some enterprising schools have introduced a range of initiatives including:

● using local producers to supply ingredients

● improving and extending menus

● offering breakfast and food after school

● growing own produce

● supplying local shops — for example, with sandwiches.

## Apply skills and techniques for supporting and encouraging children and young people's positive behaviour in the dining area including table manners

Children may need to learn table manners if they are unused to sitting and eating formally at a table. It is important that you know and consistently follow the code of behaviour of the setting. Try concentrating on the wanted behaviour by:

- eating with the children and young people
- role-modelling table manners and general behaviour in the dining area — using cutlery, passing foods, saying please and thank you, moving calmly and so on
- giving children choice
- giving children responsibility
- praising children when they are using good manners
- applying the school's reward system which is in place, for example, stars, house points.

## Apply skills and techniques for dealing with inappropriate behaviour in the dining area

The school will have a policy on the sanctions available to staff when children and young people display inappropriate behaviour. These are likely to be set out in the school's behaviour policy. There will be guidance on the sanctions that you can make and when you must report the behaviour to the child's teacher.

Strategies that you could use in the first instance include:

- reminding children and young people of the policy of the setting
- explaining why rules are in place in a positive way, for example, 'Please walk in the dining area as you may bump into someone carrying food' rather than 'Stop running'
- speaking calmly but firmly to children — never shout across the room.

When children do not respond to reminders about behaviour or display unacceptable behaviour, you should report this. Always report concerns:

- when children are repeatedly displaying unwanted behaviour and not responding to reminders
- when children are putting their own or others' health and safety at risk
- if children's behaviour is concerning and out of character.

Always seek advice when you are unsure about the action to take.

## Getting ready for assessment

Learning outcomes 1, 2 and 3 of this unit provide the knowledge that you need to enable you to support children. To achieve learning outcomes 4 and 5, you will need to demonstrate your own skills.

- Find out about the nutritional standards to which schools must adhere.
- Find out who is the person responsible for food within the school.
- Read the school's policy and ask questions about any parts of this you are not sure about.
- Talk to the children and young people about the food choices they make and the reasons why.
- Collect ideas for menus and snacks.
- Observe snack and mealtimes.
- Ask permission to plan and carry out an activity with a group of children relating to food.
- Keep a logbook with reflections from your observations and evidence of how you have supported children during meal and snack times.

## Check your knowledge

1. Name the five food types identified on the Eatwell plate.
2. Name three health conditions which impact on a child's diet.
3. What is the key nutrient which helps to build healthy teeth and bones?
4. Which vitamin is important for healthy eyesight and skin?
5. What are the recommended salt levels for children aged 7 to 10 years?
6. What is the first action to take if a child shows signs of an allergic reaction to food?

   a) Call the child's parent to check if they have an allergy to food.

   b) Seek immediate medical help.

   c) Wait for a few minutes to see if the child recovers.

7. Which agency provides advice on healthy diets?
8. Suggest three ways to prevent cross-contamination when preparing snacks for children.

### Websites

**www.dh.gov.uk** – Department of Health
**www.food.gov.uk** – Food Standards Agency
**www.nhs.uk** – information on children's health conditions which impact on diet
**www.schoolfoodtrust.org.uk** – School Food Trust

# TDA 2.15 Support children & young people with disabilities & special educational needs

This unit is for those who work in mainstream or special schools with pupils who have special educational needs or disabilities. You will need to be able to relate well to a variety of people including parents, carers and other professionals in order to provide the best possible care and support to pupils with these needs.

## By the end of this unit you will:

1. know the rights of disabled children and young people and those with special educational needs

2. understand the disabilities and/or special educational needs of children and young people in own care

3. be able to contribute to the inclusion of children and young people with disabilities and special educational needs

4. be able to support disabled children and those with special educational needs to participate in the full range of activities and experiences.

## Key terms

**Special educational needs (SEN)** — children who have learning difficulties or disabilities that make it harder for them to learn or access education than most children of the same age

**Disabled** — the Disability Discrimination Act (DDA) defines a disabled person as someone who has a physical or mental impairment that has a substantial and long-term adverse effect on their ability to carry out normal day-to-day activities

# Know the rights of disabled children and young people and those with special educational needs

## The legal entitlements of disabled children and young people and those with special educational needs

As a teaching assistant it is likely that you will be asked to support children and young people who have **special educational needs (SEN)**. You will need to have some idea about the kinds of laws which may affect the provision which your school makes for pupils who are **disabled** and have special educational needs.

There have been many changes to legislation in the UK over recent years which have affected this and a gradual increase in entitlements for these pupils. Table 1 gives a brief list in date order.

| Law | Details |
|---|---|
| Education (Handicapped Children) Act 1970 | Until this time, children with special educational needs were looked after by the health service. This Act transferred the responsibility of their education to the local authority, and as a result many special schools were built. |
| The Warnock Report (1978) | This was a report rather than an act of legislation but it had an impact on subsequent Acts of Parliament as it was a study of the needs of pupils who have special educational needs. It introduced a number of suggestions as to how children with these needs should be supported – through access to the curriculum, changes to the curriculum and changes to the environment. It influenced the Special Educational Needs (SEN) Code of Practice 2001 through its focus on inclusion. |
| Education Act (1981) | This was based on the findings of the Warnock Report and gave additional legal responsibilities to local authorities as well as power to parents. |
| Education Reform Act (1988) | This Act introduced the National Curriculum into all schools in England and Wales. Although this meant that all schools had to teach the same basic curriculum, it allowed schools to change or modify what was taught for SEN pupils if the basic curriculum was not appropriate for them. |
| Children Act (1989) | This states that the welfare of the child must at all times be considered and their rights and wishes should be taken into consideration. |
| Education Act (1993) | This Act required that a code of practice be introduced for guidance on identification and provision of special educational needs. The role of the SENCO was introduced in schools and parents were able to challenge local authorities about providing for pupils with SEN. |
| Disability Discrimination Act (1995) | This law made it illegal for services such as shops and employers to discriminate against people with disabilities. It was extended in 2005 to education, which has meant that people with disabilities must have better access to buildings and facilities through the construction of ramps, lifts, disabled toilets, better signage and so on. |

| Law | Details |
| --- | --- |
| SENDA/Special Educational Needs Code of Practice (2001) | The Special Educational Needs and Disability Act strengthens the rights of parents and children who have special educational needs to a mainstream education. For more on this, see below. |
| Every Child Matters (2004) | This was put into place to ensure that all organisations and agencies involved with children between the ages of birth and 19 years should work together to ensure that children have the support needed to: <br>• stay safe <br>• be healthy <br>• enjoy and achieve <br>• make a positive contribution <br>• achieve economic well-being |

Table 1: Legislation affecting children with disabilities and SEN.

## The assessment and intervention frameworks for disabled children and young people and those with special educational needs

### SEN Code of Practice 2001

The Code of Practice, in place since 2001, changed the way in which assessment and intervention for children and young people was carried out in schools. Most importantly, the following came into effect.

● A child with SEN should have their needs identified which will normally be met in mainstream schools or early education settings.

● Those responsible for SEN provision must take into account the views and wishes of the child.

● Professionals and parents should work in partnership.

● Provision and progress should be monitored and reviewed regularly.

● Local education authorities (LEAs) should make assessments in accordance with prescribed time limits.

The Code of Practice also outlines the way in which assessments should be carried out in early years, primary and secondary settings, and gives a clear structure to the way in which assessments are carried out.

### Over to you!

Find a copy of the SEN Code of Practice 2001. There should be one in your staff room, or your SENCO will have a copy. If you look through the contents, you will see the key areas of parent partnerships and pupil participation. What do you think about these headings? Why do you think the code has to provide so much information and guidance?

### Early Years Action/School Action

At this stage, the school or early years setting will put additional strategies in place if the pupil is finding it hard to keep up with their peers. This will usually take the form of additional targets on an individual education plan (IEP).

### Early Years Action Plus/School Action Plus

If the pupil has been on Early Years or School Action for some time and is still behind their peers, they may be moved on to Early Years or School Action Plus. This means that the school will consult outside agencies for further assessments, advice or strategies for supporting the pupil's needs.

### Statement of Special Educational Need

This means that the pupil will be assessed as to whether they need a statement of SEN and additional support in school. The school will need to gather all the paperwork from professionals who have worked with the pupil, in addition to providing evidence of the strategies they have used. If the pupil has serious SEN or disabilities, they may have been assessed before entering school or nursery and issued with a statement then.

### Common Assessment Framework (CAF)

The Common Assessment Framework was introduced in 2009 and is designed to be used across all children's services. Its purpose is to identify additional needs at an early stage through a holistic approach to children's needs and to encourage the working together of different agencies. It is not designed purely for those who have special educational needs and may be used where pupils are at risk from harm or you are concerned about an aspect of their behaviour. If you have concerns about a child, you should always speak to your school's SENCO.

For more information, see www.ecm.gov.uk/caf or see references at the end of the unit.

## The benefits of early recognition and intervention for disabled children and young people and those with special educational needs

The Special Educational Needs Code of Practice in 2001 introduced the identification and early intervention for young children before they start full-time primary education. The reason for this was that the sooner intervention can be put in place for pupils with these needs, the greater the benefits for their learning. Many early years workers had been able to identify children who would need extra support, but there was no mechanism for starting to put provision in place before the child started school. This meant that the process was delayed when provision could have been put in place. Following the introduction of the Code of Practice, more children have entered school with a **statement of special educational need**. The benefits of this are:

**Key term**

Statement of special educational need – process to gather additional funding for the support of pupils who are deemed to need extra support

- maximum information will be available to all professionals to enable them to support the pupil

- pupils will start to receive support sooner which means that they start to benefit straight away

- the sooner support is put in place, the better for the child's learning and development

- professionals in school are prepared for the arrival of children with specific needs and are able to put in provision sooner, for example, through additional resources such as equipment, staffing and training

- any adaptations can be made to the environment before the child starts to attend school.

---

**CASE STUDY:** The benefits of early recognition

Tom is 4 years old and is about to enter school in Reception. He is partially sighted and has very specific needs, and already has a statement of special educational need, although he will only have ten hours' support through this. The sensory support team are able to come to the school during the term prior to his starting and speak to the SENCO about the kinds of adaptations and equipment that Tom will need. They are also able to tell her that Tom is very self-sufficient and has adapted very well to his visual impairment.

- Why is this information helpful?
- What else might it be possible to do to support Tom during his first few weeks in school?

---

## The purpose of individual plans for disabled children and young people and those with special educational needs

**Knowledge into action**

Ask your SENCO if you can look at an individual support plan and pick out the details which you think are of most benefit for pupils. You may be able to keep a copy if you remove all personal details and highlight it for your portfolio.

Pupils who have special educational needs may need to have individual education plans to ensure that they have access to the curriculum. Although lesson plans should always include differentiated activities for pupils who have additional educational needs, these may need to be individualised further and individual education plans will give pupils specific targets to work on. If you plan alongside the teacher, you may be able to make suggestions at this stage for the pupils you support. You may also have had input from other professionals as to the kinds of strategies or equipment which you are able to use. Any additional training you may have had around the needs of the individual may also give you ideas about the kinds of activities and resources which will be beneficial.

You may still need to adapt work, however, if the pupil is finding it challenging. You will need to monitor pupil participation and intervene if necessary, so that they are able to achieve the learning intention.

# INDIVIDUAL EDUCATION PLAN

Name of pupil: Peter Lim

Date of birth: 31 Aug 02          TA  Ken Lavey

| Refer to Diagnostic summary sheet for background and assessment data |
| --- |

This IEP current from Jul 2009          to Oct 2009

Goals to be reviewed after three          months

| Summary of current level of performance | Peter demonstrates fairly good on-seat and on-task behaviour. He is a visual and experiential learner. However, he lacks focus and has a short attention span. |
| --- | --- |
| | He has no knowledge of alphabets and numbers and is unable to discriminate the alphabets and numeric digits (from 1 to 5). He does not discriminate or name objects when asked and does not attend to pictures or photographs. He also echoes the label of an object that is being said for the previous one. |
| | He works better when given a work system and is able to carry out simple Take-Do-Finish (left to right) tasks. |
| Present educational needs | To introduce the numeral 1 and 2 by allowing him to feel and trace the numerals that are made from different materials and of different sizes. Encourage him to imitate the sound from teacher and say aloud the number when pointing to the numerals. |
| | Teach him the recognition of the numerals through activities such as singing songs, matching games, reading of numerals in objects (e.g. numerals found in boxes, clock, books). |
| | Teach him the concept of sequencing and associating the numerals to actual number objects. |

| Long-term goals | Goal 1 | Goal 2 | Goal 3 |
| --- | --- | --- | --- |
| | Recognition of numerals 1 and 2 | Sequencing numerals 1 and 2 | Associating numerals 1 and 2 to quantity |

*Part of an Individual Education Plan.*

## The principles of working inclusively with disabled children and young people and those with special educational needs

**Inclusion** is a process by which schools, local education authorities and others develop their cultures, policies and practices to include all pupils. It does not just refer to pupils with special educational needs, but all pupils through the benefits of equal opportunities in schools. However, inclusion has come to be associated more closely with special educational needs, as the term has been used widely since the introduction of the SEN Code of Practice in 2001. The theory is that with the right training, strategies and support, nearly all pupils with special educational needs can be included in mainstream education successfully. The benefits of inclusion should be clear — that all pupils are entitled to be educated together and are able to access the same education without any form of discrimination or barriers to participation.

When you are working with pupils who have special educational needs, you will find that many professionals and parents speak about the danger of 'labelling' children and young people. This is because it is important that we look at the needs of the individual first, rather than focusing on the pupil's disability or impairment. In the past, the medical model of disability has been used more frequently than the social model (see Table 2) and this kind of language has promoted the attitude that people with disabilities are individuals who in some way need to be corrected or brought into line with everybody else. This has sometimes led to unhelpful labelling of individuals in terms of their disabilities rather than their potential.

You should be realistic about the expectations you have of the pupils you support and consider their learning needs. For some, although not all, the curriculum will need to be modified and pupils may need additional support. However, it should not be assumed that all SEN pupils will always need additional support and you should encourage them to be as independent as possible.

## BEST PRACTICE CHECKLIST:
### Working inclusively with children with disabilities and SEN

- Have high expectations of all pupils.
- Celebrate and value diversity, rather than fear it.
- Be aware that all pupils have more in common than is different.
- Encourage the participation of all pupils in the curriculum and social life of the school.
- Work to include pupils in the main activities of the class wherever possible.
- Develop 'can do' attitudes in pupils through appropriate degrees of challenge and support.

| Medical model | Social model |
|---|---|
| Pupil is faulty | Pupil is valued |
| Diagnosis | Strengths and needs defined by self and others |
| Labelling | Identify barriers/develop solutions |
| Impairment is focus of attention | Outcome-based programme designed |
| Segregation or alternative services | Training for parents and professionals |
| Ordinary needs put on hold | Relationships nurtured |
| Re-entry if 'normal' or permanent exclusion | Diversity is welcomed and pupil is included |
| Society remains unchanged | Society evolves |

Table 2: Medical and social models of disability (source: Disability Discrimination in Education Course Book: Training for Inclusion and Disability Equality).

# Understand the disabilities and/or special educational needs of children and young people in own care

## The relationship between disability and special educational needs

Pupils with special educational needs are defined on page 6 of the 2001 Code of Practice as having a learning difficulty if they have 'a significantly greater difficulty in learning than the majority of children of the same age', or 'a disability which prevents or hinders them from making use of educational facilities of a kind generally provided for children of the same age'. Disability is therefore considered a special educational need only if it hinders the pupil from participating in the day-to-day activities which are enjoyed by others. Having a disability may mean that a pupil has additional needs and therefore needs support. However, not all pupils who have a disability will have a statement of special educational needs, as many are independent and able to participate without support.

## The nature of the particular disabilities and/ or needs of the children and young people with whom you work, and the special provision required by them

For these assessment criteria you will need to identify specifically the details of particular disabilities or special educational needs of pupils with whom you work and discuss how you have managed them with the support available to you. You will need to show how you have worked with others in the school and local authority to provide a high-quality service and offer **special provision** for these pupils. For example, you should have information from within your school through teachers and the SENCO about the pupil's needs. You may also work with professionals such as occupational or physiotherapists who may advise you on the kind of provision and additional equipment or specialist aids which should be provided by the school and give suggestions as to how you can best support them.

### Key term

**Special provision** – provision which is additional to, or otherwise different from, the provision made generally for children of their age in mainstream schools in the area

### Skills builder

Talk to your assessor or write a reflective account to provide details of the pupil or pupils with whom you work and how you support them. Always remember to change names.

# Be able to contribute to the inclusion of children and young people with disabilities and special educational needs

## Information about the individual needs, capabilities and interests of the children and young people and those with special educational needs with whom you work

You will need to obtain information from:

- children and young people themselves
- family members
- colleagues within the setting
- external support agencies
- individual plans.

It is important that you get to know pupils and find out about their capabilities and interests as soon as you can. In this way you will be able to support them best in school both through the curriculum and in additional ways. If you are working with a pupil who is new to the school, it is likely that the SENCO will set up a meeting so that the school can discuss with parents or carers and the child themselves how they plan to work together. Many parents who have children with disabilities or special educational needs will have become experts on the need or condition. They may have researched in detail what is available and have access to support groups or other sources of help. They will also be in a good position to offer support to others, as they will be sympathetic to their situation and will have experienced the kinds of difficulties faced by other families. Partnerships with parents and families is crucial to the process of working with pupils who have special educational needs. Schools will need to ensure that they are as supportive as possible through clear communication and discussion with parents.

In addition, schools may wish to meet or talk to any other agencies or professionals who have worked with the pupil in the past. If these professionals are not available, they will be invited to send reports and recommendations in order to assist the school in making provision. If the pupil is not new to the school, you should have the opportunity of meeting with colleagues to discuss their progress alongside the pupil where possible. On a less formal level, it is very important that you get to know that pupil's interests so that you can support them through a greater awareness of their personality.

### Portfolio activity

Show how you have sought additional information about a pupil with specific needs and where you found it. Explain how parents and carers of pupils have been involved, as well as the pupils themselves, and outline the involvement of additional agencies.

### Functional skills

**ICT: Developing, presenting and communicating information**
You could create a leaflet containing the contact details of the additional agencies that your setting works alongside. You could save this document and email it to other members of staff so that they could use it for future reference.

241

# Barriers to participation for disabled children and young people and those with special educational needs with whom you work

All pupils, whatever their needs and abilities, have an equal right to education and learning. Equal opportunities should include not only access to provision but also to facilities within and outside the school setting. Schools and other organisations which offer educational provision must by law ensure that all pupils have access to a broad and balanced curriculum, and remove **barriers to participation**.

**Key term**

Barriers to participation — anything that prevents the child or young person participating fully in activities and experiences offered by the setting or service

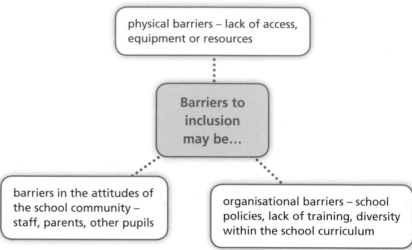

physical barriers – lack of access, equipment or resources

Barriers to inclusion may be...

barriers in the attitudes of the school community – staff, parents, other pupils

organisational barriers – school policies, lack of training, diversity within the school curriculum

*Barriers to inclusion.*

## Physical barriers

Since the Disability Discrimination Act was amended in 2005, there should be no reason that a child or young person who has a disability or special educational need should not be able to gain access to an educational institution or to its facilities. If you are supporting a pupil who has additional needs, make sure that all staff are aware of the provision which needs to be made to ensure that they are able to participate. This may mean adaptations to the environment or the purchase of additional resources or equipment.

## Organisational barriers

Your school should have an up-to-date equal opportunities or inclusion policy which sets out its priorities for developing inclusion. It should also ensure that all staff who are working with pupils who have additional needs are fully trained and able to do so with the full support of the school.

## Barriers in the attitudes of the school community – staff, parents and other pupils

This barrier can be one of the more challenging to overcome as it may be hard to change opinions and attitudes of others. You should always remember that the needs of the child or young person come first and should stand up for the rights of the pupils you support.

**Functional skills**

**ICT: Finding and selecting information**
You could use a search engine to look on the Internet for different resources that you could use to support the children in your care. Make a list of the resources that you find; you could then share it with the SENCO.

**Link**

For more on this topic, see ways of supporting participation and equality of access on page 245.

## Work with children, young people and others to remove barriers to participation

You will need to be able to show that in your work with children and young people, you actively remove any barriers to participation which exist as they arise. These may be straightforward, such as improved training opportunities or meetings set up to ensure that all staff are aware of the needs of the pupil. The most important aspect of this is continued communication between the school, home and outside agencies on a regular basis to ensure that the pupils' needs are being met in the most effective way. However, barriers may also be to do with attitudes of others, which may be more difficult to challenge. While you should always remain professional, you may find it appropriate to refer those who hold particular views to your SENCO or Head Teacher.

---

**CASE STUDY:** Removing barriers to participation

You have just started to work with Kayleigh in Year 5 who uses a wheelchair. One of the parents in the class comes to see you and says that Kayleigh will not be able to go on a week-long residential trip which is due to take place early in Year 6, as there are no facilities for 'children like that'. You are concerned both by the attitude of the parent and by the possibility that Kayleigh may not be able to go on the trip.

- What would you do?
- How can schools go about removing social barriers such as these which may exist?

---

## Ways of supporting inclusion and inclusive practices in own work with disabled children and young people and those with special educational needs

It is important to remember that the child or young person should be at the very heart of your practice. Your role is to empower them to be able to achieve to the best of their ability. This will involve getting to know them, finding out about their strengths, dreams and needs, so that you can ensure that they are valued and given as much support as they need.

As well as your support for individuals, you can also show that you support whole-school inclusion and inclusive practices in a number of ways. You will need to speak to your assessor about your school's inclusion or equal opportunities policies and identify the way in which pupils who have special educational needs and disabilities are included in all school activities. You should also be able to identify the measures which are taken in your school to promote inclusion and the kinds of attitudes and expectations which staff and parents may have towards pupils who have special educational needs. You should as part of your practice always ensure that you include all children and young people both in curricular activities and through the wider work of the school — for example, in school councils, sports days, and support for one another and the school.

*Have you seen inclusion being demonstrated during events at school?*

---

**CASE STUDY:** Supporting inclusion and inclusive practices

Julia works in a mainstream secondary school with John, who has Asperger Syndrome, a form of autism. Although John manages quite well in school, he can find some situations difficult and is taking some time to get used to the differences in his secondary school from those in his small primary. At breaktime today, John has come to find Julia as he has been bullied by some older boys in the school, who have been calling him names. He is very upset.

- What can Julia do in this situation?
- How can she support John and the school through making sure that inclusive practice is part of the whole-school ethos?

# Be able to support disabled children and young people and those with special educational needs to participate in the full range of activities and experiences

## Adaptations that can be made to support disabled children and young people and those with special educational needs to participate in the full range of activities and experiences provided by the setting

Adaptions should be made to support participation of disabled children and young people and those with special educational needs in relation to:

● the environment
● activities
● working practice
● resources.

You will need to know how the pupil or pupils you are supporting differs from their peers in their expected pattern of development. If you routinely work with pupils of a particular age range, it will be easier for you to identify whether they are fitting the normal pattern of development for their age. (See TDA 2.1 Child and young person development, for stages of physical and cognitive development.) You will also get to know what they are capable of doing, or if tiredness or medication is affecting whether or not they can continue.

### DVD activity

Video clip 6 – SEN (physical impairment)

1. In this clip, the teaching assistant is supporting a child with special educational needs to participate in a PE lesson. List some of the ways in which the teaching assistant supports the child throughout the lesson. How does she remove any barriers which exist to the child's learning?

2. This lesson was filmed in a mainstream school where the child has been included fully with the rest of the class. Think about the kinds of benefits this will have for all of the children. Give examples of inclusion in your own setting and how this works.

3. Sara, the teaching assistant in this clip, works closely both with parents and with the class teacher to ensure that the child she supports is able to participate in whole-class activities as much as possible. Which other professionals might be involved in supporting special needs provision in schools, and how might this help teaching assistants?

If you are supporting pupils with special educational needs, both you and the teacher will need to make sure that planned activities are appropriate for the needs of the pupil. If tasks are too difficult or unsuitable, they may become frustrated or anxious which will make them reluctant to attempt further activities. If you are unsure of the kinds of activities which may be suitable, always make sure that you find out exactly what pupils are able to do by finding out more about their specific needs, through asking parents or professionals who work with them, or others who have supported them in the past.

## Support children and young people to use specialist aids and equipment as necessary to enable them to participate in activities and experiences

If you work with specialist equipment, you will need to be able to show this to your assessor and explain how it is used. For example, you may work with a pupil who needs to use mobility equipment such as a walking frame in order to access the curriculum fully. In this instance you should talk through its use and your role in setting it up and using it safely for the pupil. The increased use of technology in schools has meant that pupils will often have aids which require you to have specific training. If you are unable to show your assessor, you will need to have a professional discussion or write about what is involved.

---

**CASE STUDY:** Supporting children using specialist aids and equipment

Sid has been asked to work with Kim, a pupil in Year 8 who communicates using specialist equipment through the computer. Although Sid is trained in the use of the software, it has recently been updated and now has several functions with which he is not familiar. Kim has shown him what she can but is unable to give too many details, due to her communication difficulties. He has asked to go on additional training but none is available for several months.

- What should Sid do in this situation?
- How can he best help Kim so that she gets the support she needs?

---

## Ways of supporting participation and equality of access and how to work in partnership with children, young people and others to review and improve activities and experiences

Provision in schools may be affected by any of the barriers to **participation** (as shown earlier), if the school does not take active steps to make sure that they do not occur, to ensure **equality of access**. It is important that schools:

- have high expectations of pupils and develop their attitudes of self-belief through appropriate challenges

- celebrate and value diversity, rather than fear it

- are aware that all pupils have more in common than is different

- encourage the participation of all pupils in the curriculum and social life of the school

- work to include all pupils in the main activities of the class wherever possible.

You will need to support participation for children and young people who have special educational needs through the way in which you encourage and involve them in their teaching and learning. This should mean that you encourage their participation in thinking about the kinds of strategies which have worked well for them and what they may have found more challenging. They should also be able to make their own suggestions and put their ideas forward, whether this is through parents and carers, external professionals, or through discussion with school staff.

**Key terms**

**Participation** — asking children and young people what works, what does not work and what could work better, and involving them in the design, delivery and evaluation of services on an ongoing basis

**Equality of access** — ensuring that discriminatory barriers to access are removed and allowing for children and young people's individual needs

## Getting ready for assessment

The most useful way of gathering knowledge base evidence for this unit is to have a professional discussion with your assessor. You should decide beforehand what you would like to cover so that you are ready to answer, but should be able to talk about the particular needs of the pupil or pupils you support and your role in relation to this. An example of a plan for discussion might be:

- look through and talk about the pupil's individual education plan (IEP) and discuss their needs

- describe the relationship between the school and the child's parents, and specific support which is needed

- explain how you plan to support the pupil's individual needs and the use of any specialist terminology or equipment.

## Check your knowledge

1. What is meant by special educational needs?
2. Does having a disability mean that a pupil has special educational needs?
3. Name two pieces of legislation which affect the provision for pupils with special educational needs.
4. Why is it important for pupils who have a statement of educational needs to have an individual education plan?
5. What are the principles of inclusion?
6. Name the three barriers to inclusion.
7. What kinds of adaptations may need to be made to support pupils to participate in educational activities and experiences?
8. How can you support equality of access for children and young people who have additional needs?

## References and further reading

There are a number of magazines and periodicals which are available for school staff who support pupils with special educational needs. You should also keep up to date by reading the *Times Educational Supplement* and checking websites such as those listed here.

- *Special Children* magazine
- *Special!* magazine
- Common Assessment Framework (CAF) – DFES publications. You can download this at **www.teachernet.gov.uk/publications** (ref: IW91/0709)
- SEN Code of Practice (2001) – DFES publications. As above, ref: DfES 0581/2001

### Websites

**www.bbc.co.uk/health** – this website has advice for a range of conditions and illnesses
**www.cafamily.org.uk** – this is a national charity for families of disabled children
**www.direct.gov.uk** – go to 'Disabled people' for advice and support
**www.ncb.org.uk** – National Children's Bureau, a national organisation supporting parents and children
**www.specialfamilies.org** – this is another national charity for families of disabled children

# TDA 2.16 Support children & young people's play & leisure

This unit is for those who support or supervise children or young people's play and leisure activities. You will need to be competent in supporting play and leisure, and in helping children and young people to manage risk and challenge. You will also need to be able to reflect and improve on your own practice.

Learning outcome 2 and assessment criteria 3.4 should be assessed in the workplace.

## By the end of this unit you will:

1. understand the nature and importance of play and leisure
2. be able to support children and young people's play and leisure
3. be able to support children and young people in balancing risk and challenge
4. be able to reflect on and improve own practice.

249

# Understand the nature and importance of play and leisure

## The importance of play and leisure for young people and how play and leisure contribute to their development

Play and leisure are an important part of pupils' learning. Children and young people of all ages, needs, backgrounds and cultures will benefit from having the opportunity to be creative and make choices about their play and relaxation.

*Benefits of play and leisure.*

### Promotes creativity and imagination
Children and young people need to use their imaginations and have different opportunities to do so. If left to their own devices, for example, on playgrounds or in role-play situations, they will usually make up games and play with one another.

### Develops social skills and builds friendships
Play is an important part of developing children and young people's social skills, and learning about taking turns and sharing. They will also be making and developing friendships and cooperating with one another, as well as learning about one another's different backgrounds.

### Encourages independence
Play encourages pupils to experiment with their ideas and to have control over their environment in different situations.

### Builds communication skills
Through play, children and young people will develop their skills of communication and language, as well as their vocabulary.

### Promotes decision making
Play enables children and young people to be responsible and have control of different activities in the setting.

## The requirements of the UN Convention on the Rights of the Child in relation to relaxation and play

The UN Convention on the Rights of the Child, which the UK signed in 1990 and ratified in 1991, is an international human rights treaty which acknowledges the rights and freedoms of all children under the age of 18. There are 54 articles in the Convention which cover a range of rights including primary education, healthcare and the right to a good standard of living. The articles set out how children should be entitled to:

● equal opportunities
● develop to their fullest potential
● education
● be with their parents
● be heard.

In addition, children are entitled to a range of play and leisure activities according to Article 31.

> 'States Parties recognise the right of the child to rest and leisure, to engage in play and recreational activities appropriate to the age of the child and to participate freely in cultural life and the arts.
>
> 'States Parties shall respect and promote the right of the child to participate fully in cultural and artistic life and shall encourage the provision of appropriate and equal opportunities for cultural, artistic, recreational and leisure activity.'
>
> *UN Convention on the Rights of the Child*

The Convention is aimed at protecting children and enabling them to grow up in a safe, secure and healthy environment. The UK has taken on board many aspects of its thinking in legislation that has been devised since 1989.

## The characteristics of freely chosen, self-directed play and leisure

The characteristics of freely chosen play and leisure are that children and young people should be given exactly that — opportunities to self-direct and motivate their own activities. Children and young people's play should be self-directed as much as possible, because this encourages them to have ownership of their environment. In many school and home situations, children are told what they have to do; play gives them an outlet for their creativity and also to have some control of their experiences. Play opportunities will also need to be appropriate for the age and needs of the pupils. Your setting should provide a range of different activities and resources which give pupils the chance to explore their environment in a spontaneous way through opportunities which are suitable for their different needs.

# Be able to support children and young people's play and leisure

## Own role in supporting children and young people's play and leisure activities

Adults will have a number of responsibilities when supporting children and young people's play and leisure activities. You will need to ensure that you do not intervene unless it is necessary; however, the activities will need to be set up so that you are able to observe whether support is needed. Your own role should be to:

● promote variety and choice and be flexible

● involve pupils in decisions about their play environments

● follow the requirements of your setting

● respect pupils' rights to explore and adapt play opportunities

● identify when pupils may need support.

### Promote variety and choice and be flexible

In order for play to stimulate pupils, they will need to have a choice of activities which will give them the chance to select those which appeal the most. If they are routinely given a limited number of activities, or if play opportunities are regularly repeated with no consideration given to the needs of the pupils, they will be less likely to be excited and motivated to use them. They should also have play opportunities which are flexible enough for changes to be made by pupils as they see fit. This gives them further opportunities to have control over their environment and decide on how they are going to be used. An example of this might be an environment with a dressing-up box containing a variety of fabrics, clothes and hats for children to use as they want.

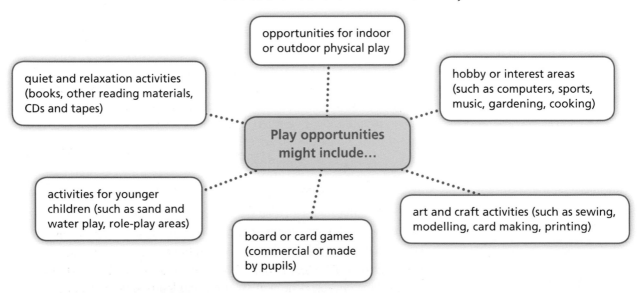

opportunities for indoor or outdoor physical play

quiet and relaxation activities (books, other reading materials, CDs and tapes)

hobby or interest areas (such as computers, sports, music, gardening, cooking)

**Play opportunities might include...**

activities for younger children (such as sand and water play, role-play areas)

board or card games (commercial or made by pupils)

art and craft activities (such as sewing, modelling, card making, printing)

*Can you find an opportunity to exploit all the benefits of play?*

You should also monitor the use of different activities, because some may be more popular than others. If you notice that some areas or activities are hardly used, you may wish to change or remove these.

## Involve pupils in decisions about their play environments

Children and young people are more likely to feel that they are part of the learning experience when they have opportunities to contribute and put forward their ideas in different ways. It will help to harness their enthusiasm and further their learning opportunities. When you are planning play environments for pupils, it therefore makes sense to give them the chance to suggest the kinds of activities they would like to explore. You can do this through discussion with pupils, where you should make sure that they all have the opportunity to contribute. In this situation, make sure that those who are more confident or appear to have more ideas are not taking over the group or intimidating others.

You may also wish to encourage pupils' input through other means, for example, by having an open ideas box or a policy of encouraging them to speak to adults about their ideas whenever they occur. It is important that if pupils are to be encouraged to do this, that adults always respond to them appropriately, as pupils will be reluctant to make suggestions if these are not acted upon or discussed.

## Follow the requirements of your setting

You should ensure that when you are creating environments for children and young people, you are aware of the particular requirements of your school. This means being mindful of issues such as timetabling, space, safety and resources available. It is not sensible, for example, to plan to spend large amounts of money on resources or play opportunities if you have not checked whether this is available. You will also need to ensure, if pupils need to be supervised or supported while carrying out a particular activity, that staffing levels are adequate.

## Respect pupils' rights to explore and adapt play opportunities

You will need to be able to provide support sensitively so that pupils do not feel that their play is being undermined by an adult. This means that you should deal with the issue which needs addressing and then withdraw if possible so that play can continue. The support you give may be:

● verbal — pupils may need to know something such as the rules for a particular game

● practical — through your showing them how to use a piece of equipment.

You should also be careful that you do not intervene in such a way that any individual's **credibility** is damaged in front of others, especially when working with older pupils. If you are asked by pupils to help them to adapt the environment, you should invite them to help you and then check that they are able to continue without further support.

**CASE STUDY:** Supporting children and young people's play and leisure

As part of the plan for school development this year, St Saviour's Primary are rethinking the layout and facilities in the playground areas. At a whole-staff meeting, the head teacher has asked the staff to think about how the budget could be used and the kinds of equipment, games and shelters they may be able to put on both the infant and junior playgrounds.

- What might you suggest to the rest of the staff?
- What would be the benefit of pupil involvement at this early stage?

**CASE STUDY:** Recognising how and when to get involved

Ramira is supervising a group of 11- to 15-year-olds during a wet breaktime. There is a range of facilities for the children to choose from. Ramira notices a group of pupils around the table football and she observes that one of them who is about to have a turn is looking anxious. Ramira goes to the table and says, 'Come on Chris, let's get them!' She then starts to take over what is happening in order to encourage him to participate.

- Has Ramira done the right thing?
- Do you think that this action might encourage Chris or dissuade him from joining in?

## Identify when pupils may need support

Pupils may seek your help or you may notice that it is needed. It is therefore important that you are able to see what is happening during play sessions so that you can intervene if required. Older pupils will need less support, but you should still be on hand in case you are required.

Pupils may actively seek your help during play sessions for a number of reasons, for example, because they have had some kind of disagreement and need a mediator to discuss what they should do. Pupils may also need support with the use of resources or equipment, or there may be safety issues which mean that you need to give assistance.

## Give attention to children and young people's play and leisure activities while being sensitive to own impact on activities

You will need to look out for situations in which children or young people need support in order to increase their involvement in play activities. As someone who works regularly with these pupils, you will be in the best position to judge whether they are engaged in their activities or whether it may be a good idea to intervene. The kinds of things you should look out for may include:

- pupils who are not joining in with an activity
- pupils whose body language indicates that they do not want to participate
- pupils who are using equipment inappropriately or who are overexcited
- young children who are not making the most of play opportunities available
- pupils who are putting themselves or others in danger.

You will need to be sensitive about how you respond, if you judge that it is necessary to become involved. If you are unsure, it may be a good idea to observe the situation for a little longer before doing so. It is important to intervene, however, if a child or young person does not appear to be enjoying the activity or if there is any danger to children's safety.

Pupils may also seek your help during play sessions for a number of reasons. Sometimes this may be because they have had some kind of disagreement and they need to have a mediator to discuss what they should do. They may seek your help or you might notice that it is needed. In some cases, children and young people will need support with the use of resources or equipment, or there may be safety issues which mean that you need to go to their assistance. For these reasons, it is important that you are able to see what is happening so that you can intervene if required. Older children may need less support, but you should still be on hand in case you are needed.

It is likely that pupils will make it clear to you if they no longer need your help and you will be able to tell if they are playing happily without you. In this situation you should not continue, as there is a chance that you

**BEST PRACTICE CHECKLIST:**
Supporting play

- Ensure that any intervention is offered for a reason.
- Ask the pupils what they would like you to do.
- Remember that you are there to support the children's independence.
- Give support in such a way that pupils will be encouraged to think for themselves.
- Do not 'take over' activities or overexcite pupils.
- Leave pupils when they are ready for you to do so.

could inhibit what they are doing. It is important that you do not try to take over their activity, as this would mean that it was no longer being directed by them. You may need to leave pupils gradually, particularly if they have sought your help — for example, if they have needed to show you how to play a game. You should tell them that they are managing well and ask them if they still need you to stay with them.

## Routine safety checks on areas used for children and young people's play and leisure before, during and after play and leisure activities

You should have systems in place in your school for routine safety checks on play and leisure areas before, during and after children and young people go to use them. These may be carried out by your site manager or health and safety officer, and may include a tick list of prompts in order to ensure that all areas have been covered (see below). You will need to think specifically about outdoor areas if they are to be used because even if they have been left safe on the previous day, they are more likely to change due to environmental factors.

---

### Garden check form
(to be kept by the outside door)

☐ General check of garden for litter/sharp objects/animal mess

☐ Sandpit – cover at end of day

☐ Water tray – ensure empty

☐ Writing area  check writing equipment out/put away

☐ Shed – ensure unlocked/locked at start/end of day

☐ Side gate and garden gate – check bolts top and bottom and padlock at end of day

☐ All tables clear and chairs piled up

---

*An example of a safety check form for an outdoor area.*

## Supervise children and young people's play and leisure ensuring their safety

**Link**

For more on this topic, see TDA 2.7, Maintain and support relationships with children and young people.

Children and young people may need to have supervision in different areas while they are engaged in play activities. Although due to the nature of the activity you should not be standing over them or giving them unsolicited help, you should make sure that you tell them where you will be if you are needed and give them any support which they ask for during their play. You will also need to be able to monitor their safety at all times.

## Prior to play activities

You will need to ask pupils to think about the environment, discuss safety, equipment and resources they might need, how to work cooperatively with others, what to do if they need help and how long they have to carry out the play activities.

## During play activities

If you are supervising the play environment, ensure that you can see what different groups of children and young people are doing. For example, if working with younger children in an outside area, you will need to be able to see them so that you can intervene if required. Pupils may also ask you to take part in play activities with them. If this is the case, you should be prepared to do so! You may also need to extend activities for children or young people who are cautious about trying out new activities.

## Following play activities

You will need to ensure that the pupils know when they need to stop and how to finish the session. This is sometimes difficult if they are engaged in their activities, so it is a good idea particularly with older children to tell them how much time they have at the start. At the end of the session you will need to work with the group to ensure that the setting has been tidied up.

# Interact with children and young people in a way that demonstrates interest, respect, encouragement and praise

You will need to be mindful that you should demonstrate these skills whenever you are interacting with children and young people, and not just when supporting play and leisure. It is important for children and young people that you show them that you mean what you say and respect their privacy and decision making.

# Be able to support children and young people in balancing risk and challenge

## The value of risk and challenge in children and young people's play and leisure

Risk and challenge are valuable in play and leisure situations because it is likely that they will spontaneously arise during the course of the activities. As a result, children and young people will need to be able to learn to deal with them for themselves as they are playing. This should teach them to develop their confidence and independence in being able to manage their own decisions and awareness of safety and in coping with challenges.

## What is meant by unacceptable risk and challenge in children and young people's play and leisure

Unacceptable risk and challenge would be play and leisure activities in which children and young people are placed in situations which are not safe or which pose a threat to their security. While it is good for pupils to have some element of risk in their play, adults in a position of responsibility should at no point place children and young people in danger. Examples of this danger might be:

- giving children and young people resources to use in their play which may be dangerous
- allowing children and young people to use a larger area for their play than adults can reasonably supervise, or where exits are not secure
- giving children and young people challenges as part of their play which could pose a danger to them
- giving children and young people a completely free rein in their choice of play activities without checking first.

*What risks or hazards are present here?*

## Why it is important for children and young people to manage risk and challenge for themselves and ways of encouraging them to do so in play and leisure activities

Children and young people will need to learn how to assess circumstances which may pose a risk to themselves or others. This is particularly important in play situations where pupils may not have focused adult supervision. At a young age, children will need adults to discuss with them regularly why we need to have rules and what kinds of risks may arise in different situations. A way of demonstrating this may be involving pupils in discussing and agreeing **ground rules** when starting a new play opportunity. This gives them further ownership of the activity and also encourages them to think about safety and consider the needs of others in addition to their own. In addition, the fact that they have discussed and agreed the ground rules means that if they are broken, you will be able to point out to them that these were agreed before they started the activity. As pupils become older, they will need to start to think about this for themselves and in new environments, adults should ask them to think about rules and safety. While pupils are in school, there should always be some adult supervision so that pupils can access support quickly if needed.

### Key term

Ground rules – agreed rules for a play opportunity; covering issues such as behaviour, health and safety, cooperation, respect or other issues

### Portfolio activity

Consider the ways in which you and your colleagues in school encourage children and young people to manage risk and challenge.

> **BEST PRACTICE CHECKLIST:** Managing risk and challenge
>
> - Carry out risk assessments on all new learning environments.
> - Ensure pupils have opportunities to think about safety and discuss ground rules when starting new activities.
> - Ensure there is adequate supervision if activities pose a higher risk.
> - As pupils get older, give them more responsibilities so that they gradually get used to thinking about risk for themselves.

# Be able to reflect on and improve own practice

## Reflect on all aspects of own practice in supporting children and young people's play and leisure

While you are supporting pupils with play activities, you should be able to reflect on your own practice and on the kinds of things which have worked and those which have not, so that you can adjust your practice accordingly.

It may be useful to consider how you have supported pupil learning under the headings on page 252. Following this, you may ask pupils about their enjoyment of play and leisure activities. After play activities are finished, you may also be required to complete administrative tasks to comply with the requirements of your setting. These may be for a variety of purposes and may include the following, which may also help you to evaluate your practice.

- **To record how pupils have managed different tasks:** You may need to fill in records if pupils have used play opportunities particularly well or if they have had difficulties.

- **Accident books or incident reports:** These will need to be filled in following any incidents which have taken place during the day.

- **Attendance registers:** You must ensure that attendance for the session has been recorded correctly.

- **Planning and evaluation sheets:** You should make note of activities which have been popular or unpopular with children or young people so that you have a record and can pass information on to teachers.

- **Notes or memos to others:** The end of the session may be the only time you have available to write and inform other staff about what has happened during the day if you will not be present the following day, or if they need to be notified about something which has happened.

## Identify own strengths and areas where practice could improve and how own practice has been improved following reflection

As in any situation when supporting pupils, you should be able to identify your own strengths and areas where your practice could be improved following learning activities. This may be straightforward, for example, if something happened during the play activity which could have been avoided, or if the activity has gone particularly well. However, you may need to ask for support from your line manager, assessor, or tutor for additional ideas about where your particular strengths lie, or where you may need extra support. You may wish to do this as part of your performance management cycle.

After reflecting on different activities you have carried out with pupils, you will need to think about whether and how your practice has improved. Make sure that you take all areas of the activities into consideration including:

- how much you involved pupils in decision making before the activity
- whether the pupils devised ground rules
- how much attention you needed to give them during the activity
- how much risk and challenge were involved
- whether you had to intervene for safety reasons.

**Functional skills**

English: Writing
Each of the administrative tasks outlined (right) require you to write in different ways. Your handwriting and spelling are essential so that documents are legible for others. Also, you need to consider the level of detail that you include in each of these tasks.

**Link**

For more on this topic, see TDA 2.6 Help improve own and team practice in schools.

**Skills builder**

This part of the unit is about your own practice and how you should consider your work in play and leisure with children and young people through reflection. Show how you have done this by including evaluation forms or reflective accounts which highlight how you have used your experience to improve your practice.

## Getting ready for assessment

For this unit, you should be able to show how you have set up and managed play experiences for pupils, while encouraging them to maximise their ownership of different situations and allowing them to face risks and challenges. You should write about or show your assessor at least two environments that you have set up in school, showing how you have included pupils' views in decisions about the selected activities.

## Check your knowledge

1. Give four reasons why play and leisure is important to the development of children and young people.

2. Underline the sentences below which are part of your role when supporting children and young people's play and leisure:

   a) to promote pupils' rights

   b) to ensure pupils are able to play when they want

   c) to keep pupils safe

   d) to make sure play areas have new equipment whenever possible

   e) to identify when pupils might need support.

3. What impact might you have as an adult on children and young people's play, and why is it important that you are sensitive to this?

4. What kinds of safety checks should you carry out before, during and after play and leisure activities in school?

5. Give three examples of the value and importance of risk and challenge to pupil learning and development.

6. Why is it a good idea to discuss and implement ground rules with pupils when supervising play?

7. Why is it important to be able to reflect and improve on your own practice when supporting play and leisure activities?

### Websites

**www.4children.org.uk** – support with children's centres, extended schools and play provision
**www.playworks.org.uk** – information and resources about playwork
**www.unicef.org.uk** – information on the UN Convention on the Rights of the Child

# TDA 2.17 Support children & young people's travel outside of the setting

On occasions it will be necessary for all children to travel outside of the school setting. This may take place daily for children who need to be dropped off and picked up at the school. For others, travel is necessary when they participate in educational visits. Strict legislation guidelines and policy are in place to minimise the risks to children when they travel.

All adults have a responsibility to ensure children's safety so it is important for you to know about the relevant policies and procedures. To achieve learning outcomes 2 and 3, you must demonstrate your skills to support children when they travel.

## By the end of this unit you will:

1. know the policy and procedures for children and young people's travel outside of the setting

2. be able to support the arrival and departure of children and young people

3. be able to support children and young people during travel.

# Know the policy and procedures for children and young people's travel outside of the setting

## Organisational and legal requirements for children and young people's travel outside of the setting including adult/child ratio requirements

It is important that you know about the school's policy for children's travel and the legislation which underpins it.

Employers have specific responsibilities when providing travel for children and young people under the Health and Safety at Work etc. Act 1974. Those supporting children during travel also have a duty to ensure their safety. The Management of Health and Safety at Work Regulations 1999 set out the statutory requirements of employers. These include their responsibility to carry out a risk assessment on all travel arrangements within the school. Employers must also demonstrate that they are taking care of their employees, children and any voluntary helpers. The local education authority are the employers in maintained schools, for example, community schools. The governing body are employers in non-maintained and voluntary-aided schools.

The law gives responsibilities to others in relation to travel.

- Head teachers have responsibility to implement the policy of the employer and to ensure that arrangements comply with regulations.

- Teachers must ensure that they have detailed planning in place; they have a duty to safeguard the pupils during travel and visits and to maintain discipline.

- Non-teaching staff along with teachers share the 'common law' duty to act as a responsible parent or **in loco parentis** during visits, including when travelling.

Regulations for children's and young peoples travel are in relation to the transport, the driver and the journey.

### The transport
The Road Traffic Act 1991 places a duty on local authorities, governors and providers of transport to ensure that vehicles are safe and unlikely to cause injury. There have been many changes in the law regarding seatbelts and restraints. Children travelling in coaches and minibuses must sit in a front-facing seat and use a seatbelt. Some minibuses also have side-facing seats, but children cannot use these. The only exemption is where public service vehicles are used by local authorities to transport pupils to and from school. These vehicles are not required to have seatbelts.

**Key term**

In loco parentis – in place of the parent

### The driver

Professional drivers must be qualified and hold a public service vehicle (PSV) licence. They must follow regulations on the number of hours they may drive without a rest. Non-professional drivers such as teachers or teaching assistants may drive school minibuses. Training should be provided and drivers must be over 21 years old. Many schools expect staff to undertake the MiDAS minibus driver awareness scheme. Information can be found at www.road-safety.co.uk. There are certain restrictions on the number of pupils who can be transported, depending on the length of time the licence has been held. On longer journeys it may be necessary to have two drivers. Although there is no specific legislation in place, a school's policy may require there to be two adults on school minibuses who are able to drive.

### The journey

The length and type of journey will have a bearing on the number of supervisors or escorts. On educational visits the adult–child ratio will be observed. For longer journeys, or when using public transport, additional supervisors will be required. Older children travelling to and from school, even when arranged by the local authority, may travel without supervision but children under 8 years and those with additional needs will require an escort.

Schools must develop their own policy and procedures but these will vary depending upon the type of school, ages of the children and young people and any special requirements. Policies must, however, meet the legislative requirements. Policies should include each of the features below.

**Over to you!**

Find out about the type of school where you work and who are the employers.

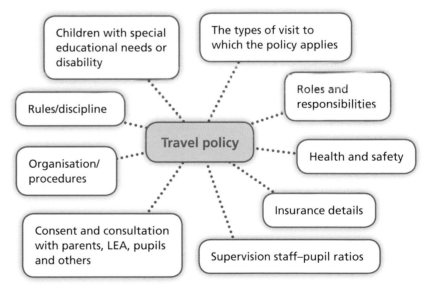

*Travel policy.*

### Sustainable travel plan

In 2003 the government announced that all schools, working in partnership with their local education authorities and transport authorities, should produce a sustainable travel plan by 2020. Over a number of years there has been an increase in children travelling to and from school by car, even for short journeys. This has increased congestion and dangers to children around the school gate. The aim of the scheme is to promote greener ways of travel and so protect the environment. Another positive outcome is that children become fitter. Many schools now have travel plans in place which include:

- walking buses — children walk to school accompanied by adults

- cycle initiatives — depending on age and ability, children cycle independently, with escorts or parents

- park and stride — providing a safer place to park and then walk the final part of the journey to school

- shared cars — using schemes for reducing the number of cars at the school gate.

*Are walking buses used at your school?*

## Supervision

For any type of travel arrangement, a risk assessment will be carried out. This will take into account the type and length of journey, mode of transport, age of children and activities to be undertaken if it is an educational visit. This will determine the ratio of adults to children.

The following guidance for visits was provided by the Department for Education and Skills (now the Department for Education) for visits which are not high risk:

- 1 adult to 6 children in Key Stage 1 (Years 1–3)

- 1 adult to every 10–15 pupils in Key Stage 2 (Years 4–6)

- 1 adult for every 15–20 pupils in secondary schools.

There should be a higher ratio for children in the Reception class or for a group which includes any children with special educational needs or a disability.

It is the responsibility of the group leader to assess the risk of the type of travel and/or visit when making a decision about the number of adults who will accompany the children. When assessing ratios, the group leader should also ensure that there is an adequate number of adults in the event of an emergency. Ideally there should be supervisors of both sexes travelling with mixed groups, but this is always required when travel involves an overnight stay.

Educational visits are now an important aspect of a child's education, so children often travel outside of the setting. Educational visits may take place regularly or occasionally.

Regular visits may include:

● weekly visits to the swimming pool
● transfers to another educational setting, for example, to a local college
● after-school sports events.

Occasional visits may include:

● visits to places of interest to support the curriculum, for example, field trips, visits to the theatre, museums or art galleries
● adventure activities, such as abseiling
● residential trips – within the UK or abroad.

# Different travel arrangements which are appropriate to the individual needs of children and young people and the range of journeys which are being undertaken

## Arrangements for travel to and from school

The 1944 Education Act established the right of children to free transport to school. The 1996 Education Act extended these duties, which are set out in the statutory guidance document, *Home to School Travel and Transport Guidance*. This Act identifies children who are eligible for transport to and from school each day.

Local authorities have a duty to provide transport for children who have to travel more than two miles, for children aged under 8, and three miles for children over 8 to their school. Children who have special educational needs or a disability and who cannot reasonably be expected to walk a short distance will qualify for free to-and-from school travel whatever the distance. They may also require an escort.

Statistics show that 18 per cent of children who are killed or seriously injured on the roads are travelling to and from school (Royal Society for the Prevention of Accidents (RoSPA), 2001). Although this number appears high, it is a lower percentage than for pupils who travel to and from school independently.

## Mode of transport

The purpose, frequency, numbers and age and any particular needs of the children will have a bearing on the mode of transport used. Transport arrangements may include walking, school minibus, private cars, taxis and coaches. It may involve using public transport such as trains or local bus services. For older children making residential trips, their transport may involve ferries or aircraft.

When making decisions about which mode of transport to use a number of factors must be taken into account by the organiser. The method of transport will depend upon the type of visit and route to be taken, as well as departure and arrival times. For example, walking may be appropriate for pupils going to the local park but for a team travelling to another school – via a route on busy main roads at the end of the school day – a minibus will be more appropriate to ensure that they arrive on time. Another factor to be considered is the length of the journey. For longer or more difficult journeys, travelling by public transport could be difficult. It may mean a number of stages and a long wait between services. The organiser will also need to consider the need for:

- **Food and drink** – will there be a requirement for refreshments on the journey?
- **Comfort and hygiene** – will there need to be comfort breaks, is the transport suitable for the age and individual needs of pupils?
- **Overnight accommodation** – does the length of the journey mean that pupils will need to sleep during the journey or make a stop en route?
- **Supervision and support** – do risk assessments highlight that there is a need for increased supervision on some modes of travel, for example on public transport or when walking?
- **Equipment and belonging** – does the organiser have to consider ways of transporting equipment or belongings which would mean that public transport or walking would be difficult?

## Describe the importance of children, young people and adults involved having complete and accurate information about travel arrangements in good time

Those involved must be informed of travel details, mode of transport and responsibilities. This includes:

- adults who are accompanying the children
- children and young people
- parents or carers.

Information for parents and pupils may be incorporated with a parental consent form. This must be provided early to ensure that there is time to complete and return the consent forms and information regarding any medical or particular needs. If complete and accurate information is not provided, it may result in a delay of the start of a visit, worry or confusion, or may even put children at risk. The information should include:

- where children should meet before they travel
- the mode of transport
- the time the transport is due to leave and when children are expected to meet
- contact details if a child is unable to travel on the day or is delayed
- when the transport is due to return and if necessary the responsibilities of parents or carers to be there on time to collect children
- how parents or carers will be contacted in an emergency or if there is a delay.
- the expectations of children's behaviour
- dress for travel, for example, school uniform or casual clothes.

It is important that children and parents are kept up to date with any changes or delays to travel arrangements. For children who have school-to-home travel via taxi or minibus and are picked up from home, additional information must be provided. For instance, parents may need to contact the transport company directly if their child is unable to attend school.

---

**PARENTAL CONSENT FORM**

**Educational visit to:** Warwick Castle          **Year:** 5

**Date of visit:** Thursday 19th May 2011

**Name of child:** _____ **Date of birth:** _____

**Class:** _____

I wish my son/daughter to take part in the educational visit to Warwick Castle.

I have read the accompanying letter and agree that he/she can take part in all the activities described. I have been informed of the departure and return times.

I have completed and returned the medical consent form.

**Parent/guardian name:** _____
(Please use block capitals.)

**Parent/guardian signature:** _____

**Contact:** Home telephone number: _____

Mobile telephone number: _____

Emergency contact number: _____

*Please return this form with the medical consent form to the school office by Friday 29th April 2011.*

*An example of a consent form.*

## Typical preparations which children and young people and those accompanying them on journeys would have to make for the range of journeys undertaken

Preparations for journeys must be made some time before the event to ensure that any potential risks are reduced and the journey can take place without any problem or delay. Preparations will vary depending upon mode of transport and length of journey.

Immediately before the visit, the lead teacher must check:

● transport arrangements with the company or times if using public transport

● that parental consent is available for each child travelling

● supervisors' availability and that they are Criminal Records Bureau (CRB) checked

● contact details, medical and other information about any additional needs for each child travelling

● essential equipment for the journey, for example, first-aid kit

● the agreed route, timings and scheduled stops with the transport company

● contingency plans including emergency contact numbers.

Adults accompanying children must be prepared for the journey and anticipate any problems which may occur en route. Adults accompanying the children will have a list of children for whom they have responsibility during travel, with details of any medical or additional need. If you have been asked to support children with a particular need, having information well before travelling will give you the opportunity to ask questions about their requirements. Children should also be informed of the group they are assigned to.

It is important that very young children or those with special educational needs and disabilities are well prepared for travel, including regular travel to and from the setting. Young children could be shown photographs of transport, or what they will see on the route. They should be given time to discuss how they are travelling and who is travelling with them. A buddy system could be used, pairing a child with a more confident friend. Children with autistic spectrum disorders can be severely affected by change when taking part in a school visit, or changes in escort or transport to or from school.

### CASE STUDY: Working with parent supervisors on visits

Aberfield School has arranged a visit to a farm for children from Reception and Year 1. A coach has been booked for 9.30. Information had been sent to parents and consent has been given. Angie works at the school as a teaching assistant. That morning she arrived early to support the teacher to prepare for the visit. Angie helped to check that they had everything to take on the coach. When the coach arrived, Angie and a parent helper got on the coach first to guide children to their seats. Three children (one of whom was the daughter of the parent helper) started to get upset when they were guided to separate seats. The parent told them that as it was a short journey, they could sit together.

- How should Angie respond to the parent?
- What might she say and how can she support the child who is upset?

## Issues that might occur when supporting children and young people's travel and the contingency arrangements appropriate when children and young people are travelling

The vast majority of journeys happen with no issues or problems, but when planning a journey, a risk assessment will take account of any possible hazards or problems. Risk assessment should be ongoing throughout the journey and take account of changing circumstances. For example, the weather may change, or there may be traffic problems.

| Possible issues | Contingencies to minimise the impact |
|---|---|
| Children being taken ill | • Have at least one first aider accompanying the group<br>• Have sufficient staff to ensure that one member of staff can stay with a child who requires medical treatment<br>• Have medical history and emergency contact details for all those travelling |
| Children being injured | • Ensure that there are safe pick-up and drop-off points for buses, coaches or taxis that do not require children to cross roads<br>• Observe safety rules when travelling by foot. Plan walking routes, cross at pedestrian crossings, foot bridges, adequate supervision<br>• Maintain adequate supervision when travelling on trains/ferries and clear rules on where pupils are allowed to go unaccompanied |
| Transport problems such as breakdowns, hold ups, accidents | • Check routes/road conditions before leaving, including alternative routes<br>• Allow sufficient time including time for stops<br>• Ensure adult supervisors and children know how the position of the emergency door<br>• Carry out a practice evacuation<br>• Carry phones and have emergency contact details<br>• Carry water and snacks<br>• Have contingency money available |
| Children displaying inappropriate behaviour | • Ensure that children, supervisors and their parents understand rules of behaviour<br>• Have sufficient supervisors accompanying children<br>• Identify children with particular behaviour problems, for example, Attention Deficit Hyperactivity Disorder (ADHD) or children on the autistic spectrum, and ensure an adequate level of supervision<br>• Know procedures to return children whose behaviour is unacceptable or a health and safety risk when on school journeys |

*Table 1: Travel issues and contingency plans.*

*How easy do you find it to work with parent helpers on educational visits?*

# Be able to support the arrival and departure of children and young people

Part of your role and responsibility may be to support children as they arrive and depart. This may be children who travel to and from school each day or when travelling on educational visits. Support for children arriving and leaving school each day will depend upon their age and ability. Older children may arrive at school by public or specially commissioned transport. Children over 8 years are likely to travel to and from school independently.

## Obtain information about the children and young people to be dropped off/picked up

The school will have registers of children who are to be dropped off and picked up from school. You must ensure that you have these details which will include:

● the number of children and young people

● the names of the children and young people

● the age of the children and young people

● where the children and young people are coming from or going to

● the travel arrangements for individuals and/or groups of children and young people

● any additional needs the children or young people involved may have.

## Communicate arrangements to colleagues when relevant

It is important that information is checked each day and any amendments to the arrangements communicated with colleagues. These should be communicated verbally, but it is also important to keep a written record. Changes to arrangements may be for a number of reasons such as a change of escort or information which needs to be sent home with the child.

## Remind children and young people about health and safety issues relating to arriving at and leaving the setting

The school will have a responsibility to ensure that the transport drops pupils off at a safe place. This will usually be a designated pull-in area, where children can alight safely and enter the school without crossing a road. You may be required to supervise pupils to ensure that behaviour is maintained and they go directly into the school or school grounds. Waiting for transport is a particular risk for children as they will soon become bored. It is essential that children know where they must wait and the importance of waiting their turn to get onto the transport. If behaviour is inappropriate, you may need to speak to the child or young person. Where behaviour continues or impacts on safety of the child, young person or others, you should remind them of the rules and report concerns immediately.

## Follow the organisational procedures

Younger children, or children with special educational needs or a disability, will need support as they arrive and depart the school. Children may arrive at the school by:

- coach
- minibus
- taxi
- walking bus.

**Supervising the arrival**

It is important to remember that you will be the first person that children meet as they arrive at school. A smile and cheerful greeting can make a difference to each child's day. Where possible, stagger arrivals to avoid congestion and behaviour problems.

In most instances, the pupils will have an escort. The escort has the responsibility to ensure that children are handed over to an adult with the authority to receive them. It is likely that you will be known to the escort, but you should always carry ID. The escort will pass on any information from the parents and report if a child has not travelled. You should keep a record of any messages and pass them to the child's teacher as soon as possible. On occasions the escort may pass on medicines for a child. These should be taken to person responsible for administering medication. Where possible, you should support children's independence and encourage them to carry their own belongings into the school.

## Supervising the departure

You must ensure that children are supervised at all times while waiting for the transport. For children in Key Stage 1 or those with additional learning needs or a disability, this will be inside the building until the transport arrives. As with arrivals, a register must be kept to check that each child or young person is safely on the bus, minibus or taxi, or has left with the walking bus. You need to check that the child has everything in their bag to be taken home. Most settings will have a home/school diary which is important, as it allows messages including concerns to be sent from home to the teacher and vice versa. Essential messages or medicines should always be passed directly to the escort.

## Checking that all children and young children have been accounted for

Whatever method of transport is used, it is essential that each child is accounted for and escorted into the building. You should have a register of children, the expected arrival times and the mode of transport. It is critical that you know the time of arrival so that you are ready to receive children as they arrive. Children should never be left waiting on the transport. If a child is listed on your register but does not arrive on the transport, you should check if any messages have been received and report to the manager or teacher responsible immediately. There will be procedures for contacting parents, so you must check whose responsibility this is.

## Dealing with any issues arising when children and young people are arriving at or leaving the setting

You may have to deal with a range of issues in your role of supporting the arrival and departure of children. Knowing and understanding the policy and procedures of the settings will help you to take the correct action.

**Non-arrival of transport** — Check out procedures for arranging alternative transport and informing parents in the event of non-arrival of transport or breakdowns.

**Changes in transport arrangements** — Drivers and escorts may be known to you, but at times there may be changes. It is essential that you check if there is a change of personnel and never pass children to drivers or escorts you do not know.

### Knowledge into action

Find out and record information about:

- which children are eligible for school transport
- the reason for their eligibility
- the type of transport used
- the role of escorts.

Provide support during the arrival and departure of children using different modes of transport and write a reflective account which includes:

- ways that you recorded the arrival of each child
- how you greeted each child
- types of messages passed on and how you communicated these
- any issues or concerns (or possible issues or concerns) identified and how you dealt (or would deal) with them.

### Functional skills

**English: Speaking, listening and communication**
You could collect some of the information that you need to write your reflective account through holding a discussion with the person at your school who coordinates travel arrangements. Plan your questions through before your discussion and then you will be able to contribute effectively.

**Non-compliance with policy and procedures** — Issues may relate to ways that others follow policy and procedures, for example the driver of the school bus is not using the designated drop-off area or children are not using the seatbelts or restraints correctly. It is important that where safety procedures are not followed you challenge this and report to a senior manager immediately. If in doubt, you should not allow children to travel until the issue is resolved.

> **BEST PRACTICE CHECKLIST:** Supporting the arrival and departure of children
>
> - Always be there on time to receive children.
>
> - Have an up-to-date list of children who are expected and the transport they use.
>
> - Younger children and children with additional needs should wait inside until the transport has arrived.
>
> - Know where each child is travelling to.
>
> - Know any additional needs of the children who are travelling.
>
> - Pass on any messages which are sent from home immediately.
>
> - Greet children with a smile!

# Be able to support children and young people during travel

It is essential that you have details of travel plans well before the scheduled visit. This will include the travel schedule, and details of children and adults who are travelling, including those you will be responsible for. You should not underestimate how long it will take to get children ready and on to the transport. Young children, for example, will need to be taken to the toilet just before they travel, to avoid an unscheduled stop!

## Remind children and young people of agreed ways to keep safe during travel

**Link**

For more on this topic, see TDA 2.8 Support children and young people's health and safety.

Children should be prepared for what will happen, how they are expected to wait, and how to get on and then behave when they are on the transport. Before travelling, these safety procedures and the reasons why they exist should be explained to children so that they understand why they must be followed. Reminders should be given during the journey using language appropriate for the children's age and stage of development.

## Respond to the needs of individual children and young people and offer help when required

If children have health needs, you should know what to do if they are taken ill — for example, what to do if a child with diabetes has a hypo or a child with asthma is wheezing and needs help with an inhaler. You may need to carry medication for children or if they require an inhaler, they may carry their own. It is vital that this is checked before departure and readily available during travel. It should never be stowed away in a luggage compartment or left on the transport during breaks.

Some children may be travel sick, so it is important that they are identified and are sitting near an adult. Suitable equipment, such as bags, gloves and paper towels must be readily available, even during short journeys. If children are travel sick they must never be given travel sickness tablets unless consent has been received from the parent or carer. As with other medication, the policy and procedures for the administration of medicines must always be followed. You should also be aware of health problems that can affect any children, particularly on longer journeys. Children can be affected by lack of sleep, food or drink or in very warm weather, so it is important that you are vigilant to the needs of all children.

## Follow organisational procedures for travel

### On foot

For local journeys children may walk, for example, to carry out research on local shops or to do a traffic survey. Many schools provide high-visibility jackets for children when they are travelling, and particularly when walking. You must check that children wear these. The route, including safe crossing places, should be worked out before travelling.

An adult must always lead the group with another adult at the rear and adults spread evenly through the group. Where possible, groups must always cross at pedestrian crossings, or footbridges. Where children must cross roads, the class may need to be split into smaller groups. Children should have received training on road safety but you must always remind them of the rules.

### Public transport

Children may use public transport for educational visits. There are additional hazards for children when waiting for transport. They should wait in safe areas well away from roads or rail tracks. When on public transport there should be clear rules on how much freedom children are allowed, for example, if children must be accompanied at all times on trains or ferries. Older children may not be under your direct supervision but you should give clear rules on where they are allowed to go at all times. You should also give them information on meeting places and times. Children should always know where to go in an emergency.

> **Link**
>
> You will find more information on supporting children's health needs in TDA 2.2 Safeguarding the welfare of children and young people.

## Private transport

For educational visits which are not local, children are often transported via coach or minibus. Children may be assigned to seats so will need to line up in a particular order so that those getting off first can get on first. An adult should be first on the coach or bus so that they can guide children to the seating, ensuring that there are seats left available for supervisors. Children's and adults' belongings should be safely stored and not left in an aisle of coaches or minibuses. This could prevent children from getting off or others reaching them in an emergency. Heavy items should not be stored in overhead compartments.

Before the transport leaves, you must ensure that children for whom you are responsible are seated correctly. Children must be allocated a seat each, and even smaller children should not be allowed to sit three to a seat. Children should always wear the seatbelts provided. The driver has responsibility to remind children under 12 years old, but you should also check that they have put these on correctly. Lap belts must be worn over the pelvis and not the stomach. School minibuses, which are used to transport children with a disability, have special restraints which help the child to sit upright and keep them secure. You must check that these are fitted correctly. If minibuses have side-facing seats, these should not be used for the children. You should be positioned so that you can observe the group of children assigned to your care. If a double-decker coach or bus is used, there should always be at least one adult on the top deck.

Children may be wheelchair users. You may wish to be helpful but you should not operate lifts, ramps and wheelchair restraints in vehicles. Drivers have specialist training and you are not insured to do so.

## Rest breaks

Regular stops should be made on long journeys. These should be planned ahead wherever possible and should be at suitable areas where children are not put at risk by passing traffic. An adult should always leave the coach or minibus first so that children can be guided along a safe route to toilet and/or eating facilities. Children must stay under supervision. For unscheduled stops such as a breakdown or accident, extra care must be taken as the transport may be close to other traffic. Children should be under direct supervision at all times and guided to a safe area to wait.

If pupils are travelling abroad, there will be additional risks when travelling, particularly if the coach or minibus is a right-hand drive. Additional care must be taken when pupils get on and off or during an emergency evacuation.

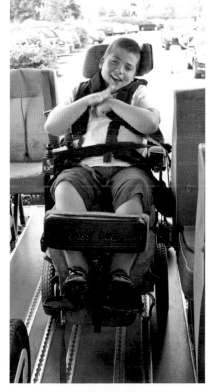

*Do you know how a seat restraint should be correctly fitted?*

> **CASE STUDY:** Working with a supply teacher on a visit
>
> Pria has worked at her local primary school as a teaching assistant for five years. On Tuesday a visit was arranged for children to look at the local shops to support their topic work on the local area. At the last minute the teacher was ill. The visit had been arranged for some time and as a supply teacher had been arranged, it was decided that the visit would still go ahead. The supply teacher was not from the local area, but Pria knew the route well and had accompanied another class on the visit recently.
>
> Pria gave the route map and class list to the supply teacher before they set off. When they got closer to the shops, the supply teacher stopped at the kerb ready to cross, rather than going on to the crossing, which would have meant walking further. Pria was aware that, although the road seemed fairly quiet, there were often large lorries and speeding cars using the route.
>
> - What should Pria have done and said at this point?
> - Could the problem have been prevented?

## Respond to children and young people's feelings and behaviour as they move from one environment to another

When supporting children during travel, it is essential to know the needs of each individual child. You may know the children well, but on the day you should take into account that children are out of routine, often excited and may not behave in their usual way. For younger children, it may be the first time they have used the particular type of transport, so they may be unfamiliar with what is expected of them and what will happen. They may require reassurance at different stages of the journey.

## Encourage children and young people to look after themselves and their belongings during travel

Even young children should be aware that they have a responsibility to keep themselves and their belongings safe, and not take any unnecessary risk which could harm themselves or others. Before the visit it is important that you explain how you expect them to behave. Children need to know for example how they should dress for travel and what they are allowed to take with them. Do they need to take their own snacks or lunch, can they take belongings such as electronic games and what are the rules on mobile phones for older children? It is essential that you understand the school policy and advice for individual school visits so that you can discuss these expectations with the children before departure.

Although school travel is usually provided for children who are eligible until 16 years, Young people with a learning disability or blind or partially sighted children may require transport until they are 18 years old. Where possible, these young people should be encouraged to travel independently. Support may be given initially and then gradually reduced as the young person becomes more confident in travelling alone. There are a number of training schemes available for children and those who support their travel.

### The role of an escort

Escorts may be provided for children who need to travel to and from school each day. This will depend upon a child's:

● age – children under 8 years will usually be escorted

● disability

● particular needs.

The ratio of escorts to children will vary depending upon their age and need. You may be required to escort young children or those with a disability to and from school. An escort may accompany a group of children or only one child if they have a severe learning or physical disability.

The role of the escort is to support children with any difficulty or health problem during the journey, and to liaise between parents and the school. Where there are health and safety risks – for example, long journeys or high numbers of pupils – an escort will accompany children on the transport. During travel, escorts are there to:

● supervise children to ensure that they behave appropriately

● make sure that children do not distract the driver

● support children in the event of a breakdown or accident

● ensure that children alight safely and are met by a parent or carer.

**BEST PRACTICE CHECKLIST:** Travelling with children

• Remind and check that pupils are using seatbelts.

• Allow pupils to sit in front-facing seats only.

• Ensure that there is adequate supervision and that supervisors are positioned so that they are able to observe pupils.

• Ensure that there is adequate supervision of pupils when they are getting on and off transport.

• Complete a head count every time a pupil gets on and off transport.

• Ensure that luggage is stored safely and will not slow down pupils if they need to evacuate.

• Ensure that rules/codes of behaviour are understood and maintained during the journey.

• Ensure that you and other supervisors and pupils know what to do in an emergency situation, for example, where to find escape routes, where to go after leaving the transport.

### Getting ready for assessment

In order to be assessed for this unit, you should have information and other evidence about the kinds of travel you have supported pupils on so that you can show this to your assessor. This unit requires competence in supporting the arrival and departure of children and young people and supporting them on journeys outside of the setting.

### Check your knowledge

1. Name two laws which underpin the health and safety policies for children's travel

2. What does the term 'in loco parentis' mean?

3. What are the recommended adult—child ratios for low-risk educational visits?

4. Suggest two ideas that schools could introduce to improve their sustainable travel plan.

5. Which Act of Parliament first introduced the right of children to free school travel?

6. Give two reasons why children would be eligible for school transport.

### Useful resources and websites

- *Health and Safety of Pupils on Educational Visits* (1998) DfES Publications
- *A Handbook for Group Leaders* (supplement to Health and Safety of Pupils on Educational Visits)
- **www.hse.gov.uk** – Health and Safety Executive
- **www.teachernet.gov.uk/visits** – advice on organising educational visits, and tips on sustainable school travel

# TDA 2.18 Support extra-curricular activities

This unit is about supporting a range of activities which are held outside normal school hours. These may consist of setting up, checking health and safety aspects, and ensuring that children and young people are motivated to carry out the activity. You will also need to make sure that you start and finish sessions correctly.

## By the end of this unit you will:

1. be able to prepare for extra-curricular activities
2. be able to deliver extra-curricular activities
3. be able to bring extra-curricular activities to an end
4. be able to reflect on own contribution to extra-curricular activities.

# Be able to prepare for extra-curricular activities

## The aims and content of the extra-curricular activity

You may be supporting or carrying out **extra-curricular activities** in a range of different situations and contexts. Extra-curricular activities are of benefit to pupils as they enable them to try out or practise activities which they wish to work on in more depth or in which they have an additional interest. They provide enrichment to pupils' school experience through giving them a wider range of activities. You will need to be able to supervise a group of pupils and be clear on the aims and content of what you are doing.

The aims of the activity are the purpose of what you will be doing, or why you are doing it. The content of the activity is exactly what you are going to be doing for that session and for those which come next. For example, the aims of a fitness class are to encourage the participants to get fit, while the content is the kinds of exercise you will do to help them achieve it.

You may have been given lesson plans or outlines to help you, or you may have devised these yourself. Either way, you should be able to report back to others on what you are doing with the pupils and how you will be going about it.

### Portfolio activity

Write a reflective account about the extra-curricular activity which you supervise in school. If you have more information, use this and highlight the aims and content of what you will be doing.

## Equipment and resources for the activity

You will need to obtain equipment and resources for the activity in advance, so that the learning environment is ready for pupils when they arrive. Occasionally when running after-school or lunchtime clubs, you may be limited in the amount of time you have to set up, as the location or room you need is in use until the end of the previous session. In this situation you may also need to rely on pupils to help you (see also below). If you are going to be off site you will need to carry out a risk assessment (see page 129 for more information on this) and should have the correct staff–pupil ratio. This is dependent on the age of pupils and your school will have its own policy on how many adults will be needed.

You should also ensure that you are prepared well before the activity takes place, so that you are not trying to find resources at the last minute. You must make sure that you have enough equipment for the needs of pupils — in particular if any have special educational needs — and that it is in working order. Not only does late preparation make the activity more stressful, it is also much harder to do!

## Prepare the environment for the safe conduct of the activity

You should check the environment you will be working in as you are setting up, to ensure that it is safe for children and young people to work in. You should check the needs of pupils to ensure that you are aware of any who may have special educational needs or issues with mobility. If you are getting out large apparatus or equipment, you will need to remember health and safety regulations, and also make sure you leave enough time for safety checks. Take a look around the environment and complete the following checks.

● Look at floor surfaces to ensure they are not wet or slippery.

● Check any wires are not likely to be tripped over during the activity.

● Check that that equipment is not damaged or broken.

● Make sure fire exits are clear.

● Ensure pupils will have access to any equipment they need and will be able to move around safely.

● Always check with your health and safety officer that the environment is safe if this is the first time you have run the activity.

## Support children and young people to prepare for the activity

You should involve children and young people wherever possible and when time allows in setting up the activity. Pupils may have responsibilities such as putting out specific equipment or going to collect attendance registers. This means that you will have less to do yourself (although they may need a reminder!) but it is also good for developing pupils' responsibilities. You will need to check that they have brought any items or equipment for which they are responsible themselves, such as kit or costumes. It is also often helpful to set out ground rules and expected behaviour with pupils during the first session so that you are prepared for any issues before they arise.

When any equipment or resources have been prepared, you will need to support children and young people in getting ready for the activity. Depending on its nature, this may involve preparation such as:

● warming up if the activity is physical, such as football, gymnastics or fitness clubs

● ensuring pupils have everything they need to carry out the activity — for example, in an art or other special interest club — getting together their pieces of work — or scripts and sets or props for drama activities

● making sure pupils are in the correct position and ready to work, and that instruments are tuned — for example, in musical activities.

> **CASE STUDY:** Preparing for extra-curricular activities
>
> Carolyn is running a new drama club for Key Stage 2. She has not done an extra-curricular activity with pupils before, although she is an active member of her local drama group and saw this as a good opportunity to develop her professional skills in school. On the day of the second session, Carolyn has come straight to the hall from her own day's work in Year 3, although she was held up by a parent at the end of the day. When she arrives in the hall, she finds a number of pupils running around and making a lot of noise. There are 15 children in the club.
>
> - Could Carolyn have prevented this from happening?
> - What should be the first thing she does now?

# Be able to deliver extra-curricular activities

All of these assessment criteria will need to be assessed in the workplace.

## Interact with children and young people in a way that makes them feel welcome and at ease

**Link**

For more on this topic, see TDA 2.7 Maintain and support relationships with children and young people.

This may sound obvious but if pupils are coming for an extra-curricular activity, you will need to make them feel welcome. They may not have been involved in these kinds of activities before, or may be anxious about taking part, particularly if they are very young or have recently started at the school. You should always try to encourage pupils as much as possible through the way in which you communicate with them — body language, positive praise and showing that you are enjoying the activity yourself will all help with this.

> **CASE STUDY:** Making pupils feel welcome
>
> Marcia runs a lunchtime pottery club for Key Stage 3 pupils. She has always done this and the pupils have been coming for some time. She does not really enjoy it but has the expertise and feels there is an expectation that she should do it. However, lately the club has attracted much less interest — there are fewer pupils, the ones who arrive are coming late, and Marcia is losing the little enthusiasm she had. When she asks them why they are coming to the club late, the pupils tell her that it is boring.
>
> - How should Marcia react to this?
> - Do you think it is worth saving the club? If so, how should she go about it?
> - Is there anything else she could do?

## Organisational procedures for checking the children and young people are present, and making sure their dress and equipment are safe and appropriate

You should always ensure that you comply with the school's regulations for checking attendance. You should have been provided with a list or register of names so that you know who is present and can sign pupils in at the start and out at the end. Even if you think that you know exactly who has arrived, it is very easy for one person to be missed, and you will be accountable for each pupil who is present.

You will also need to make sure that pupils have brought the correct dress and/or equipment to carry out the activity as soon as you can, so that you know if there are any problems — it is important to ensure that everyone is able to work safely on activities. If they do not have the correct equipment, they should be aware at the start of the activity that this will not be possible.

## Skills and techniques for ensuring the children and young people understand the activity, and use skills and techniques to engage and motivate them to actively participate in extra-curricular activities

In a similar way to your work when supporting learning activities, you will need to ensure that children and young people have a clear understanding of the activity and what they need to do. Before you start, and depending on the activity, you may need to discuss with them the importance of safety or check that they understand the nature of the activity.

If the extra-curricular activity requires you to teach the whole group something completely new that they have not done before, you will need to take them through step by step, allowing them to ask questions as you go. This may include learning new vocabulary, repeating instructions, and allowing plenty of time. If the activity requires them to use specific equipment which is new to them, you will again need to allow them time to explore it and become familiar with using it before you start. Although they may be keen to learn the skill, you should ensure that you take them through instructions slowly to ensure they carry out the activity safely.

While carrying out the activity you should continue to engage and motivate pupils through giving them opportunities to develop their skills and giving praise where appropriate. Always be aware that they have joined the group because they have an interest in the activity or subject, and so will want to learn or practise the activity, which may not always be the case when you are supporting pupils with school work. You should be able to use their enthusiasm to encourage them to participate actively in the activity.

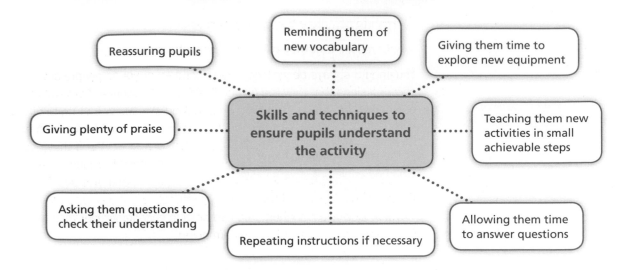

*Skills and techniques to ensure pupils understand the activity.*

---

**CASE STUDY:** Ensuring pupils understand the activity and what they will be doing

Chris is taking a group of pupils for a trampoline club. The activity is new to them and they are all keen to start. They all go over to the trampoline but after welcoming them all, Chris calls them all over to sit on the floor and goes through some ground rules before starting to talk about what they will be doing today. He says that they will all get a turn but that first he needs to make sure they all understand the need for safety and how to use the equipment.

- Why is it important that Chris should talk to the group before doing any work on the trampoline?
- What has he said to them which is encouraging and will keep their enthusiasm?
- Is there anything else which you think he could have done during this starter session?

---

## Recognise when children and young people need encouragement and/or help with activities, and provide them with additional explanations and demonstrations where necessary

However interested and engaged pupils are in the activity, there may be times when they need encouragement or help to continue. They may approach you and seek additional support, but it is possible that they will not always ask for it for a variety of reasons. They may:

- not want their peers to see that they need help

- not realise that they are approaching an activity incorrectly

- wish to complete the activity themselves
- not realise that they are losing concentration.

You should always be vigilant in case children or young people are showing signs that they are finding it difficult to continue. Look out for pupils who are lacking concentration, looking anxious or looking to others in the group to see what they should be doing. If a pupil looks as though they need help, you should ask them if they are all right or if they need you to explain something further. You may also need to model what to do for pupils who are finding the activity difficult and give additional explanations. If you find that a pupil is struggling but wants to complete the activity without support, you can provide encouragement through praise and recognising what they are doing.

---

**CASE STUDY:** Recognise when children and young people need encouragement or help

Yosef has been leading a science club in school for a few weeks. He has started to carry out some detailed investigations which the pupils have chosen to do and they are all working on them. One pair of pupils seem to have been looking at what they need to do for some time and are talking to one another quietly, but have not made a start at all.

- What should Yosef do first?
- How else might he provide support without doing it directly himself?

---

# Be able to bring extra-curricular activities to an end

## Prepare children and young people to finish their activities

You should always make sure that you give children and young people adequate warning when it is nearly time for them to finish their activities. This is because they will then have preparation time to finish what they are doing and bring it to an end. Very young children may not understand the timescale if you tell them that they have five minutes to go, for example, but most pupils will find it helpful to be told how long they have left to complete what they are doing. With older pupils, you may just need to remind them to look at the clock every so often, as some activities will require you to keep a close eye on the time. If you prepare pupils to finish their activities, they may be able to use up any resources or materials, or if they are carrying out a physical activity, they may be able to start to cool down, or have some recreation time.

*How does being aware of time remaining help pupils when they're finishing activities?*

## Give the children and young people clear and supportive feedback on their participation and progress

As the activity draws to an end, you should be able to give pupils clear feedback on their participation and progress, especially if you have not done so during the session. It is important for children and young people to have some idea how they have managed the activity. If you end the activity on a positive note, pupils will feel more encouraged about returning for the next session and will be enthusiastic about what they have done.

> **CASE STUDY:** Giving clear feedback on pupil participation and progress
>
> Jeff has been working with some Year 10 pupils who have just started to do some voluntary work for a local charity. They have been helping to sort out harvest contributions and to log where the different foods will be sent. The pupils have spent some of their Saturday morning moving the provisions and checking them off so that they can be sent out on the Monday morning. Before sending the young people home, Jeff speaks to the whole group and passes on the charity's thanks that they have worked so hard and given up some of their weekend to help.
>
> - Why will this be of benefit to the pupils?
> - Could he have given any other feedback to them?

## Encourage children and young people to say how they feel about activities and respond to their feelings appropriately

As they are carrying out extra-curricular activities in their own time, you should encourage pupils to talk about how they feel about them. It is worthwhile to ask pupils what aspects of the activity they enjoy or what they find less appealing (see also below on feedback). This will give you valuable feedback and help you in planning future sessions.

## Follow organisational procedures for the safe and orderly departure of children and young people from the activity session, and clearing and storing equipment and resources

**Functional skills**

**English: Reading**
You could develop your reading skills by highlighting all the relevant policies in your setting that link specifically to your extra-curricular activity.

As with starting activities, you will need to follow the correct procedures for ensuring that pupils finish and leave the premises safely. In many cases, pupils will already have helped you to clear away and store resources and equipment. If they have done this, you will need to have factored in some tidying-up time at the end of the activity. However, it may be the case that pupils are not able to help you to do this, for example, if it is not appropriate or if equipment is too large to be moved. You should make sure that pupils put any materials and equipment away neatly and without rushing, so that it is stored in the right place for the next person.

Depending on the time of day when you are running the activity, you may be sending pupils to their next lesson, to morning or afternoon registration, or off site. If you are sending them to another location in school, you should always ensure that they leave in an orderly manner and you should remind them about their behaviour when moving around the school. When seeing children and young people off the premises, depending on their age you will need to check that you have seen parents or that you know how they will be getting home safely. With younger pupils, you should make sure that you are aware of the school policy for their departure and at what age pupils are able to leave the premises unaccompanied. Always see pupils off site slowly and carefully, and ensure that you are able to account for each of them in case you are asked about a specific pupil later.

---

**CASE STUDY:** Safe and orderly departure of pupils from the session

Eve has just finished an after-school cross-country club with Years 3 and 4. She has taken the pupils back to the school to meet the parents. As she is walking back into school, some of the parents take their children and wave to Eve to show her that they are going. However, when she gets back to school, two of the pupils are missing and she is unable to remember if she has seen the parents.

- What do you think the organisational procedure should have been in this instance?
- How could Eve have avoided this happening?

---

**BEST PRACTICE CHECKLIST:** Delivering extra-curricular activities

- Always prepare equipment and resources well in advance.
- Make sure pupils have brought the correct clothes or equipment with them.
- Check health and safety issues before, during and after the activity.
- Make sure pupils know what to do in case of evacuation of the premises.
- Encourage pupils to take responsibilities during sessions.
- Develop positive relationships with children and young people.
- Keep an eye on pupils to see whether they may need additional help.
- Give them time after completing sessions to talk about the activity.
- Use a variety of feedback following the activities to inform and improve your practice.

# Be able to reflect on own contribution to extra-curricular activities

## Use feedback from children, young people and colleagues to reflect on and improve own contribution to extra-curricular activities

You should always think about your own contribution to any extra-curricular activities which you have carried out with pupils, so that you can evaluate it and consider any changes. It is worth giving pupils a feedback sheet when you have completed a series of lessons to see whether pupils have reacted to it as you might have expected. You should also seek feedback from colleagues to see whether you can gather any additional useful information about the activity. For example, sometimes pupils may talk in class about activities they have carried out before or after school, and whether they have enjoyed them or not.

### Functional skills

**ICT: Developing, presenting and communicating information**
You could produce an information leaflet for the parents in your setting, informing them of the extra-curricular activities available to their children. Try to include a range of different layout styles and images to make your leaflet more appealing.

### CASE STUDY: Using feedback to reflect on and improve activities

Ellie has been running an ICT club at the school for two terms. She has enjoyed carrying out a variety of activities with pupils in Key Stage 2. She decides to give the group an evaluation sheet to ask them about what they have enjoyed and whether there are other things they would like to do in the club. Ellie is surprised to discover that several of the pupils have asked for more help and guidance with Internet safety, which she covered briefly in the first session. Many of the group have also said that they would like to do some more work on developing their keyboard skills, and two pupils think that the group is too big.

- How should Ellie proceed with this information?
- Why is it useful for her to have given out the evaluation form?
- What might she say to the group the following week?

### Skills builder

Devise and trial a feedback sheet for the children and young people who have carried out extra-curricular activities with you. You may wish to ask them questions such as the following.

- What is the best thing about the activity?
- What do you like the least?
- Is there anything you can think of which would improve the activity?
- Would you recommend the activity to your friends?

## Getting ready for assessment

In order to be assessed for this unit, you should have information and other evidence about the kinds of extra-curricular activities you have carried out with pupils so that you can show them to your assessor. In addition, they will need to be able to observe you carry out an extra-curricular activity with a group of pupils — incorporating as many of the assessment criteria as you can, starting with the preparation of the environment and resources.

## Check your knowledge

1. Give three reasons why extra-curricular activities are important.

2. What will you need to do when preparing for an extra-curricular activity?

3. How can you support pupils to prepare for an activity?

4. What kinds of procedures might your school have which you should be aware of when carrying out extra-curricular activities?

5. Why might the kinds of skills and techniques you use be slightly different from those when supporting teaching and learning in class?

6. Give three reasons why you might need to intervene when pupils are carrying out an extra-curricular activity.

7. Why is it important to follow organisational procedures when ending sessions?

# TDA 2.19 Support the use of information & communication technology for teaching & learning

You may use ICT in different ways as part of your day-to-day practice in the classroom across a range of subjects, or be responsible for ICT as a technician or for curriculum support along with teachers. You must show that you use ICT in a way that is stimulating for pupils while ensuring that it is the most appropriate method for their needs and abilities.

## By the end of this unit you will:

1. know the policy and procedures for the use of ICT for teaching and learning
2. be able to prepare ICT resources for use in teaching and learning
3. be able to support the use of ICT for teaching and learning.

# Know the policy and procedures for the use of ICT for teaching and learning

## The setting's policy for the use of ICT for teaching and learning

The school should have an ICT policy which will give you guidelines for using and working with ICT in the classroom. There may be set routines and guidance for the use of equipment which all individuals should follow; for example, pupils or adults to sign a checklist to say when they have borrowed equipment such as digital cameras. The school policy should give the aims and objectives of the school with regard to pupils' experiences and opportunities in ICT.

There will also be school requirements for safety, and for storage and security of ICT equipment. There may be a borough or school policy on use of the Internet and the availability of websites which are suitable for schools.

## The ICT resources used for teaching and learning within the setting

ICT can be used in many ways to benefit pupil learning since it is cross-curricular, as well as being an individual subject area. By its very nature, problem solving and finding things out is at the heart of using ICT, as ICT can support sustained thinking and group work. If planned effectively, ICT may be used for whole-class, group and individual activities. You should remember that ICT does not just mean the use of computers and that it is an area which is constantly changing, so you will need to keep up to date.

Most pupils will enjoy learning through ICT and will benefit from new and innovative technologies as they come into schools. Below are some examples of how **ICT resources** can be used in a number of different ways to support learning and pupil development.

### Whole-class sessions

The use of interactive whiteboards (IWB) in recent years has transformed whole-class teaching. Both pupils and adults are able to use this technology and many of the programmes available encourage participation. The use of IWB technology also enables teachers to display files downloaded from the Internet as well as CD-ROMs, and builds interactivity to encourage active learning.

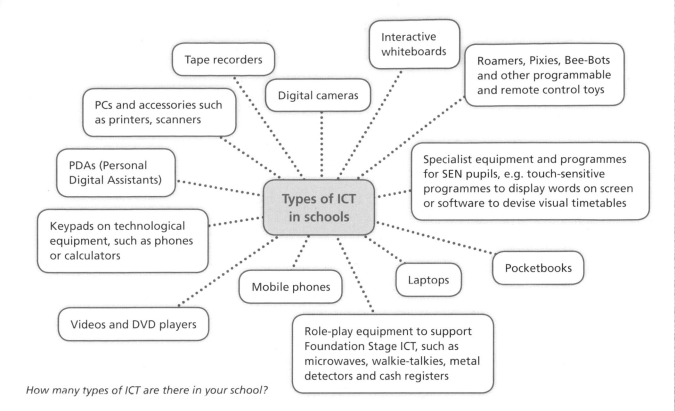

**Types of ICT in schools**

- Interactive whiteboards
- Tape recorders
- Digital cameras
- Roamers, Pixies, Bee-Bots and other programmable and remote control toys
- PCs and accessories such as printers, scanners
- PDAs (Personal Digital Assistants)
- Specialist equipment and programmes for SEN pupils, e.g. touch-sensitive programmes to display words on screen or software to devise visual timetables
- Keypads on technological equipment, such as phones or calculators
- Pocketbooks
- Mobile phones
- Laptops
- Videos and DVD players
- Role-play equipment to support Foundation Stage ICT, such as microwaves, walkie-talkies, metal detectors and cash registers

*How many types of ICT are there in your school?*

*How much support do you have to give pupils when using ICT equipment?*

### Group work

ICT is effective during group work as it can be used to enhance teaching and also encourage pupils to develop their technological skills. For example, programmable toys such as a pixie, bee-bot or roamer can be used in small groups to develop pupils' understanding of programming and also directional vocabulary and spatial development in mathematics.

### Individual work

Individual children can be given opportunities to experiment with different technologies, for example, digital cameras during project work, or specific resources can be used with pupils who have special educational needs.

### Reflect

Consider different ways in which you have used ICT as part of your role in school to support teaching and learning. How often do you work with different technologies with classes, groups and individuals?

### Functional skills

**ICT: Developing, presenting and communicating information**
You could create a spreadsheet containing all the different ICT equipment that you have in your setting. You could also include information on your spreadsheet such as when the equipment was last tested and where it is stored.

## Relevant legislation, regulations and guidance in relation to the use of ICT, for example, software licensing

Legislation and guidance in relation to the use of ICT is regularly updated, and in particular around the area of Internet safety and safeguarding children. There have been a number of recent high-profile cases which have highlighted the importance of awareness of privacy and of the importance of caution when putting information online. Legislation relevant to the protection of children will be relevant in the light of this and can be accessed through the Every Child Matters website at www.education.gov.uk/everychildmatters It is linked to the Children Act 2004 and has sections on safeguarding which include the importance of minimising risk when online.

You should also be aware of the copyright and licensing agreements held by the school in relation to different ICT programmes and materials. There are different kinds of licence depending on the intended use of the software; for example, single use or across a network. Licensing agreements vary, which can cause confusion, so the safest option is to check on individual programmes. If the school has CD-ROMs and other software, these must be used only by the school and not by other parties, and multiple copies of programs should not be made.

For more information, go to the British Educational Suppliers Association website (www.besa.org.uk) and type in licensing under 'search'.

Schools need to comply with the Data Protection Act 1998, which has implications for the use of data which is held on school computers. Individuals have the right to know what information is held about them, and any information about pupils in the school should only be used for the purpose for which it was gathered. Make sure if you are working on pupil information that this is password protected and that you do not leave it on the screen for others to read.

### Functional skills

**ICT: Using ICT**
It is important to understand fully about secure passwords, copyright and viruses prior to completing your functional skills in ICT.

## The setting's procedures for dealing with faulty ICT equipment

As with all other equipment and materials, you should be aware of the school's policy for dealing with faulty ICT equipment. In most cases, schools will have a book so that the ICT technician can check this regularly and fix any faulty equipment as soon as possible. If you wait until technicians are in school or tell them yourself, it is still best to log the problem as well. In the case of smaller equipment, these items should be clearly marked faulty in storage cupboards or placed with other faulty equipment. Computers will need to be labelled faulty with the date and nature of the fault, so that it is clear to others that they should not be used. Any computers or other fixed equipment should be unplugged.

### Over to you!

What is your school's policy? Have you ever had to deal with any faulty ICT equipment? If you have logged anything, you may be able to copy this to put in your portfolio as evidence.

## Requirements and procedures for storage and security of ICT resources in the setting

You should know where ICT resources are kept so that you are able to access them when needed and follow the correct procedures. It is likely that they will be kept locked up, and in some cases equipment such as cameras or laptops may need to be signed out. As many schools now have more portable equipment such as laptops due to increased use of wireless technology, security is even more important. Schools may now have laptop secure storage devices or digitally locked cupboards to ensure that equipment is stored safely. They will usually be in a central location although in some schools, classes may be issued with their own equipment such as a LapSafe®, so that it is more accessible when needed. If you know that you will be needing equipment in advance which is not often used, such as programmable toys, you may need to check that others in the school are not planning to use them.

# Be able to prepare ICT resources for use in teaching and learning

## Manufacturers' and safety instructions for setting up ICT resources and the risks associated with them

When working with ICT, you should be aware of the risks associated with setting up and using equipment, and how these can be minimised. Equipment should be safe as long as it is used properly and checked regularly; however, pupils will need to be reminded regularly of the correct procedures. Younger children should always be taught to switch on and log on correctly and to shut down computers correctly after use as these can be damaged and work can be lost if they are turned off incorrectly. Work which pupils save on school networks or an intranet will usually be password protected and in a named folder for their own class or year group.

If you are setting up and using ICT equipment, always check that you are doing so according to manufacturers' instructions and have run through these or the school guidelines. General instructions for the use of computers, for example, might include:

● good ventilation in and around equipment

● blinds at the windows

● no overcrowded plug sockets

● time limit for use of computers

● chairs at the correct level for screens.

You may also need to remind pupils about how to operate and use smaller pieces of equipment and go through instructions slowly and carefully with small groups.

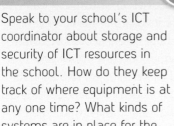

**Knowledge into action**

Speak to your school's ICT coordinator about storage and security of ICT resources in the school. How do they keep track of where equipment is at any one time? What kinds of systems are in place for the security of these resources?

**Functional skills**

**ICT: Using ICT**
You could create a named folder for each of the children in your class so that they can easily save their work once they have completed it. Alternatively, if the children are older, you could write the instructions for them to create their own folder to save their work in.

## Functional skills

**English: Writing**
You could produce an information leaflet for parents on the dangers of cyber-bullying and give tips on how they could monitor this at home. Think carefully about the language you use in your leaflet and remember it is for the purpose of giving information.

Your school policy should give guidelines with specific requirements which you should follow when supporting ICT. It is important that you are aware of what kinds of risks pupils may face and what to do if you discover any hazards or faults. (See also page 294 — dealing with faulty ICT equipment.)

As pupils become more likely to use the Internet, chatrooms, email and mobile phones, there are also dangers involved in the misuse of these technologies. Pupils and their parents or carers should be aware of what the dangers are and what they should do if they have any concerns. Cyber-bullying affects more and more children, and schools are increasingly offering information and guidelines to parents on the use of ICT. For information and support on safe use of the Internet, see the references section at the end of this unit.

### CASE STUDY: Safety when setting up and using resources

Dan has been asked to prepare a number of laptops for use with a group of Year 8 pupils. They will be working in a small room away from others in the school which has a limited number of power points. He has not worked in the room before. Dan removes the laptops from the safe and sets them up in the room ready for use and opens the window to give the room some ventilation, although it is raining heavily outside. He then goes down to the class to get the pupils. The pupils are just coming in from lunch and there are a number of issues which need sorting out in the form room before they are able to start their work, so this takes a while. When they arrive back in the room, some of them have cold drinks with them as it is a hot and muggy day. They start to discuss their work and then move on to using the computers. The behaviour of two of the pupils is not good and they start to mess around near the equipment.

- How many potential safety issues can you find while reading the above paragraph?
- What could Dan have done to make the situation safer?

### Portfolio activity

Use the questions below to help you to evaluate the effectiveness of specific resources you have used to promote pupil learning.

1. Did the ICT resources help pupils to achieve the learning objectives?
2. In what ways was the task successful/unsuccessful?
3. How was ICT used to support learning in other areas of the curriculum?
4. Were you confident about using the resources or do you need additional training in how to use them?
5. Were there sufficient resources/software available for all pupils to use?
6. What might you do differently if you were to use the resource again?
7. Would you recommend use of the resource to others?

**BEST PRACTICE CHECKLIST:** Maintaining health and safety when using ICT

- Check the equipment regularly and report any faults.
- Ensure you know how to operate equipment before the lesson.
- Go through instructions for use slowly and carefully with pupils, especially if they have not used the equipment before.
- Use only the correct accessories with each item of equipment.
- Ensure that pupils are sitting correctly on height-adjustable chairs.
- Ensure that computer screens are at the correct height (eye level).
- Limit the amount of time pupils spend seated at computers.
- Never overload sockets.
- Ensure that the equipment is being used safely.
- Store equipment safely and securely when it is not in use.

**Functional skills**

**ICT: Using ICT**
It is important that you know how to adjust the system settings in order to meet the individual needs of the children in your care.

## Accessories, consumables and information needed to use ICT resources

You may not need to go further than the ICT cupboard to identify and obtain accessories and consumables which you need to use ICT resources. These may be straightforward items such as memory sticks, headphones, copier paper, printer inks and so on. However, if you are working in the ICT department and have been asked to find out about additional resources, you may need to research the kinds of items which are available. The range of ICT materials which are obtainable is increasing all the time and you may not always be aware of what is available or in school. You may use existing suppliers which are known to the school if you need to find specific software or equipment for use. There is also a number of websites which give advice for tried and tested resources which are educationally worthwhile and which encourage pupils to use their own ideas (see the end of this unit). You may find that even in the space of time in which you are completing your qualification, different equipment and materials become accessible. The kinds of materials may include:

- materials from the Internet
- commercial software for computers
- updated or new technical devices such as digital cameras or personal digital assistants which can be used to enhance learning
- equipment which is available to support special educational needs such as switches, voice recognition devices, touch screens or voice synthesisers.

You might also ask pupils and other adults to evaluate resources and activities to help with this.

## Screening devices to prevent access to unsuitable material via the Internet

### Portfolio activity

Find out what screening devices your school has in place to prevent children from finding unsuitable material when using the Internet. You may need to look in your school's ICT policy or speak to the coordinator or technician.

Your school will have screening devices and filters to prevent pupils from accessing unsuitable material via the Internet. These are usually automatically put in place by all schools and local authorities. You should also be on the lookout when pupils are using the Internet in case they inadvertently find inappropriate websites when using search engines. In most schools, pupils are not permitted access to the Internet unless there is an adult present to monitor what they are doing. Pupils may also have their own personal devices such as memory sticks, so the school will need to have a policy on the use of these. If you have any cause for concern, you should report it immediately to your school's ICT coordinator so that this can be resolved.

## Common problems with ICT resources

As you are preparing resources for use, you may find that you need to resolve issues before you have started your work with pupils. These will often be straightforward, for example replacing or charging batteries, making sure equipment is plugged in, or even basic operational issues. You may be able to deal with most of these yourself, but should always refer to others if you are unable to do so, or follow the school's procedure for reporting faulty equipment if appropriate.

# Be able to support the use of ICT for teaching and learning

## Operate ICT resources correctly and safely when asked to do so

You will need to be able to operate ICT resources yourself in order to set them up yourself or be able to pass on these skills correctly and safely to pupils. Make sure that you are familiar with all the relevant resources prior to using them with pupils if at all possible. You should also check that any safety matters have been resolved before pupils start to work with the resources.

---

**CASE STUDY:** Operating ICT resources correctly and safely

Vicky has been sent to work with Year 3 for the afternoon, as the assistant who usually covers during part of the time is off sick. She knows that the class will be doing music but at lunchtime the teacher asks her to set up the visualiser for them so that they will be able to read some music together from a book. Vicky has not used the visualiser before and although she can see how to switch it on, she is unable to get it working through the computer so that the image comes up on the interactive whiteboard at the front of the class. She is unable to find any manual or instructions for the equipment.

- Could Vicky have been any better prepared?
- What should she have done?
- How can she resolve the situation?

---

# Give clear guidance and instructions on the use of ICT resources

You may be asked to give guidance and instructions in different situations when supporting ICT. If you work with other support staff or teachers in the ICT department, it is possible that you will need to carry out training or offer advice on specific resources or equipment for other staff. When working with adults, you will need to plan any training sessions carefully and ensure that you allow them time to explore the resources so that you can then clarify any issues.

When working with pupils, as in other subject areas, it is important that they have a chance to become familiar with activities and equipment when they are first asked to use them. They will need some time for this so that they can concentrate on what they have been asked to do rather than how they are going to do it. By giving them time to explore and become familiar with ICT resources and equipment, you will be saving time in the long run, as pupils are less likely to be distracted by the novelty factor.

# Provide an appropriate level of assistance to enable learners to experience a sense of achievement, maintain self-confidence and encourage self-help skills in the use of ICT

When working with pupils, you need to be able to show that you are providing them with the correct level of assistance. You will need to consider a number of different teaching and learning methods when working with ICT, as these activities may be more appealing to a particular type of learner. Some will be particularly capable when using ICT equipment and resources, and you will want to encourage them while also supporting those who are less confident. Depending on the task you are working on and the abilities of the pupils, you will need to give them different levels of support. It can be challenging to strike a balance between allowing them to work equipment themselves and intervening when they need support. However, it is likely that pupils will be enthusiastic during ICT activities and keen to participate.

You may be supporting pupils who are less familiar with different programs or ICT equipment. In this situation, it will be difficult to get around a large group or the whole class, even if you are working alongside a teacher. It may be useful to pair up a more confident or able pupil with one who is less confident or able, so that they need your assistance less often. You might also have a checklist for pupils to use if they are unable to continue with an activity for any reason, as this will encourage them to develop self-help skills and they may be able to resolve it themselves. In order to monitor pupil learning, make sure that you move around the group, as individuals may appear to be fully absorbed in the task but actually be reliant on the input of others. It may be useful to have a list of the learners' names so that you can make a note of who has met the learning objectives, and add your own comments. If your school has resources such as PDAs (Personal Digital Assistants), you may be able to work with the teacher to track pupil learning during the lesson. With this technology, you will be able to look at how pupils are progressing as they work.

## DVD activity

### Video clip 8 – Supporting ICT

The assistant in this clip is working with a group of Year 6 pupils to take photographs of each other to support their work in literacy, another area of the curriculum. They are working with digital cameras.

1. How does the assistant prepare the ICT suite for use and what does she do to ensure that it is safe?

2. This clip was filmed in 2007 and the technology used here has already moved on. These children may not have used this particular equipment before. How does the assistant ensure that the pupils have time to familiarise themselves with different features? Does she give clear guidance and instructions for their use so that pupils are able to use the cameras effectively?

3. ICT can often be one of the more challenging subject areas to support as there is usually a wide range of ability in any group of pupils, and there are potentially a number of difficulties which may occur. In the clip, the assistant differentiates abilities by putting a less and more able pupil together. Outline some of the ways in which you have overcome difficulties when supporting pupils using different technologies.

4. How does your school find out about and obtain ICT programs and equipment for use in school? How does it evaluate the effectiveness of these materials?

## Monitor the safe use of ICT resources, including Internet access, and intervene promptly where actions may be dangerous

While you are working with pupils using ICT resources, you will need to show that you are monitoring their use at all times to ensure that safety concerns are dealt with straight away, in particular if pupils' actions may be dangerous. You should be aware of the kinds of things which may be unsafe, such as electrical issues. Equipment should be safe as long as it is used properly and checked regularly. However, pupils will need to be reminded regularly of the correct procedures. They should always be taught to switch equipment on and off correctly, and to unplug it if required, or put batteries on to charge. They should also be taught to use ICT equipment carefully and safely as it may be easily damaged, and younger pupils may not be able to work with more fragile equipment. You will also need to monitor any websites if pupils are using them for research, although school screening devices should filter out unsuitable sites.

## CASE STUDY: Monitoring the safe use of ICT resources

Rania is observing a small group of Reception pupils using the two class-based computers. They are working in pairs and she is observing their mouse and keyboard skills as well as their confidence in using the equipment. As she is carrying out the observation, one of the children becomes impatient with her partner and starts interfering, saying it is her turn. She removes her headphones as she wants to swap seats with him in order to use the mouse herself and as a result knocks them to the floor and runs over them with her stool, which is on wheels. The headphones are then damaged and she is unable to use them.

- What should Rania do?
- Could anything have been done to avoid this happening?

### Link

See TDA 2.12, Prepare and maintain learning environments.

### Portfolio activity

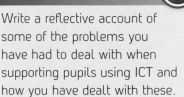

Write a reflective account of some of the problems you have had to deal with when supporting pupils using ICT and how you have dealt with these.

# Problems that might occur when supporting learners using ICT and how to deal with these

Problems may relate to the:

- learning activities
- learning environment
- learning resources
- learners.

Unfortunately, when working with ICT, problems often arise when you are working with learners and you need to have a list of strategies available to deal with these problems.

## Learning activities

The activity may be too challenging or too easy for pupils, which will mean that they will quickly lose interest. Make sure that you are able to modify activities where necessary so that pupils stay on task, or have extension activities available for them to do when the initial activity has been completed.

## Learning resources

There may be a number of problems with the learning resources — for example, you may have difficulty loading or using programs, be unfamiliar with them yourself, or equipment may be faulty. There may also be technical problems which arise as you are working. This can be difficult, as you will not always be able to resolve them, especially if you are working with large groups of pupils and trying to focus on the main activity. You may also find that you do not have enough equipment for the number of pupils. Be prepared to move pupils or put them with others if necessary.

## Learning environment

You may also find that you have problems with the learning environment, perhaps with noise, temperature or ventilation. You will need to ensure that these are adjusted before you continue, to enable pupils to concentrate.

## Learners

There may be a discrepancy between pupils' abilities within a group or class, which means that it is difficult to support their learning. As well as pairing a more and less able pupil together, you need to have a list of other activities for pupils to do in case you need to provide an alternative. You may also have problems with pupil behaviour, in which case you may need to refer to school policy regarding sanctions or send them back to work with the teacher.

In order to minimise problems, always be clear before the lesson what you will be doing and ensure that the equipment you need is available and not booked by others in the school. Make sure you have worked on any new programs and checked the ICT suite or equipment beforehand to make sure that you will be able to operate it when pupils are present.

## Getting ready for assessment

For this unit, the best way to gather evidence is through observation. All of the learning outcomes except assessment criterion 3.5, dealing with problems, must be assessed in the workplace. Your assessor should be able to observe you setting up for and working with pupils on ICT activities, as well as being shown where and how equipment is stored and procedures for recording or reporting faults.

## Check your knowledge

1. Why is it important that ICT is used alongside all subjects as well as being taught as a subject in its own right?
2. What kinds of ICT resources do you have in your school apart from computers?
3. What kind of regulation and guidance should you be aware of when working with ICT?
4. What kinds of measures might your school take in order to comply with legal requirements?
5. Identify how you might resolve common problems when working with ICT.
6. How do you find out about additional resources and support which may be available?
7. What kinds of risks might you need to be aware of when working with ICT resources?
8. How can you encourage learners to work independently as much as possible when using ICT resources?

---

### Websites

**www.bbc.co.uk/schools/teachers** – this site has a number of ideas and links for teaching curriculum subjects across all four key stages

**www.bullying.co.uk** – online help and advice service for combating all forms of bullying

**www.bullyonline.org/schoolbully/mobile.htm** – provides information on bullying by mobile phone, specifically aimed at children

**www.cyberbullying.info** – website raising awareness of cyber-bullying

**www.inclusive.co.uk** – this site gives a guide to some of the ICT equipment which is available to pupils who have special educational needs

**www.kidscape.org.uk** – general bullying resource with specific information on cyber-bullying

# Glossary

## A

**Adolescence** — the name given to the interval between childhood and adulthood

**Anorexia nervosa** — an eating disorder which involves self-induced weight loss. It is more common among girls

**At risk register** — children who are identified as being at particular risk of being harmed or abused

## B

**Barriers to participation** — anything that prevents the child or young person participating fully in activities and experiences offered by the setting or service

**Bilingual learners** — those who have been exposed to two or more languages

**Bulimia** — this eating disorder involves binge eating then vomiting or the use of laxatives. It may not involve weight loss but will cause ill health

## C

**Child Protection Conference** — the conference discusses the risk of harm to the child and decides whether a child needs a child protection plan. Where a plan is required, the role of different agencies to support the plan will be discussed

**Code of conduct** — an agreed set of rules by which all children are expected to behave

**Communicate** — to pass knowledge of or information about something. This can be done:

- verbally
- non verbally
- informally
- formally

**Community cohesion** — the togetherness and bonding shown by members of a community, the 'glue' that holds a community together

**Confidential information** — information that should only be shared with people who have a right to have it, for example, the teacher, your line manager or an external agency

**Continuing professional development (CPD)** — the cycle of training and evaluation of learning which takes place as part of your own practice

**Credibility** — the quality of being believable or trustworthy

**Culture** — shared way of life, including aspects such as beliefs, language, arts and music

## D

**Differentiation** — describes how teachers adjust the learning activities or expected outcomes according to pupils' individual learning needs

**Disabled** — the Disability Discrimination Act (DDA) defines a disabled person as someone who has a physical or mental impairment that has a substantial and long-term adverse effect on their ability to carry out normal day-to-day activities

**Disclose** — share information, often of a personal nature

**Discrimination** — treating an individual or group less favourably because of a personal characteristic such as race, religion or special educational need

**Disempowerment** — when individuals or groups are deprived of influence or power

**Displays** — the arrangement of material (graphic, text and/or objects) into an assembly specifically intended to attract people's attention and interest, or to provide information, or to educate, or a combination of these

## E

**Empower** — enabling the child or young person to make own choices — the opposite of dependency

**Equality of access** — ensuring that discriminatory barriers to access are removed and allowing for children and young people's individual needs

**Ethos** — the atmosphere within the school — a positive ethos gives a sense of shared purpose, values and beliefs

**Evaluation** — an assessment of how well the teaching and learning activities achieved their objectives

**Extended school provision** — extra out-of-school activities, such as breakfast and after-school clubs

**Extra-curricular activities** — activities that are held outside of normal school hours that can benefit the development of children and young people, for example, study support, play and recreation, Duke of Edinburgh award, drama, sport or music

## F

**Format** — the way in which results of observations are recorded and presented

**Feedback** — information you provide the teacher with about the pupils' responses to the learning activities, the materials involved and your contribution to supporting the activity

## G

**Ground rules** — agreed rules for a play opportunity; covering issues such as behaviour, health and safety, cooperation, respect or other issues

## H

**Halal** — 'permissible' foods which are allowed under Islamic law

**Hazard** — anything that has the potential to cause harm

**Health and Safety Executive** — an independent watchdog for work-related health and safety

**Holistic** — involves all the aspects of something rather than just parts

## I

**ICT** — information and communication technology; this covers a range of different activities, equipment and technological devices, such as programmable toys, telephones, videos, timers, keyboards, keypads, computers, software, digital cameras, interactive whiteboards as well as new technologies as they become available

**ICT resources** — includes a range of different equipment and technological devices, such as programmable toys, telephones, videos, timers, keyboards, keypads, computers, software, digital cameras, interactive whiteboards as well as new technologies as they become available

**In loco parentis** — in place of the parent

**In need** — children who are unlikely to maintain, or be given the opportunity to maintain, a reasonable standard of health or development, or whose health could be impaired without the support of local authority services. It also includes children with disabilities

**Inclusion** — a process of identifying, understanding and breaking down barriers to participation and belonging

**Individual education plan (IEP)** — targets and planned implementation strategies for pupils with special educational needs

**Issue** — situation or circumstance that hinders or prevents effective team performance, such as poor co-operation between members of the team or interpersonal conflicts between members of the team

## K

**Kosher** — food which is prepared in accordance with Jewish dietary law

**Significant harm** — the seriousness or impact of harm through a single action or over a period of time

## L

**Learning environment** — an area inside or outside the setting used for learning activities — for example, classrooms, science laboratories, art rooms, the playground, games field or nature areas or areas used for field studies, cultural visits or other off-site activities

**Learning materials** — written materials and consumables needed for the learning activity

**Learning resources** — materials, equipment (including ICT), software, books and other written materials (such as handouts, worksheets), DVDs and so on that are required to support teaching and learning

## M

**Microbes** — germs, including viruses and bacteria

## P

**Participation** — asking children and young people what works, what does not work and what could work better, and involving them in the design, delivery and evaluation of services on an ongoing basis

**Planning** — deciding with the teacher what you will do, when, how and with which pupils, to ensure that planned teaching and learning activities are implemented effectively

**Prejudice** — forming an opinion of an individual or group which is not based on knowledge or facts

**Pro formas** — standard documents or forms

**Puberty** — the stage of physical development at which children and young people's bodies reach sexual maturation. It can begin as early as eight in girls and around two years later in boys. It can go on past the age of 20

## R

**Reflective practice** — the process of thinking about and critically analysing your actions with the goal of changing and improving occupational practice

**Resources** — furniture and equipment needed to support the learning activity, including classroom furniture and curriculum specific equipment such as computers or PE, science or mathematics equipment or, teaching and learning resources to provide effective access to the curriculum, including written materials, videos or DVDs, bilingual and pictorial dictionaries, and bilingual software

**Risks** — the likelihood of a hazard's potential being realised

## S

**Safeguarding** — this term has replaced the term child protection. It includes promoting children's safety and welfare as well as protecting children when abuse happens

**Safety equipment** — the equipment required by legislation and/or the organisation for ensuring the safety of children, young people and adults in the learning environment

**School improvement plan** — document which sets out priorities for the school over a four- or five-year period

**School self-evaluation** — document which looks at and evaluates the school's progress

**SEN Code of Practice** — document which sets out the requirements for the identification and monitoring of pupils with special educational needs

**Significant harm** — the seriousness or impact of harm through a single action or over a period of time

**Special educational needs (SEN)** — children who have learning difficulties or disabilities that make it harder for them to learn or access education than most children of the same age

**Special provision** — provision which is additional to, or otherwise different from, the provision made generally for children of their age in mainstream schools in the area

**Statement of special educational need** — process to gather additional funding for the support of pupils who are deemed to need extra support

**Statutory** — power given in law

**Stereotyping** — making assumptions about an individual, for example, because of their race or a disability

## T

**Target language** — the additional or second language needed by bilingual learners to access the curriculum, such as English as an additional language (EAL) or Welsh as a second language

**Team** — people with whom you work on a long-, medium-, or short-term basis, relating to the support provided for a specific pupil or group of pupils

**Tokenism** — giving the appearance of an inclusive environment

**Transitions** — any significant stage or experience in the life of a child or young person that can affect behaviour and/or development

# Index